WEEKEND GETAWAYS
IN PENNSYLVANIA

WEEKEND GETAWAYS
IN PENNSYLVANIA

BILL SIMPSON

PELICAN PUBLISHING COMPANY
Gretna 2000

The word "Pelican" and the depiction of a pelican are trademarks
of Pelican Publishing Company, Inc., and are registered in
the U.S. Patent and Trademark Office.

Library of Congress Cataloging-in-Publication Data

Simpson, Bill, 1950-
  Weekend getaways in Pennsylvania / Bill Simpson.
    p. cm.
  Includes index.
  ISBN 1-56554-397-1 (alk. paper)
  1. Pennsylvania Guidebooks. I. Title.
F147.3.S46 1999
917.4804'43—dc21   99-41076
                                                            CIP

Information in this guidebook is based on authoritative data available
at the time of printing. Prices and hours of operation of businesses listed are subject to change without notice. Readers are asked to take this
into account when consulting this guide.

Photo on p. 2: *Gettysburg National Battlefield*

Printed in the United States of America

Published by Pelican Publishing Company, Inc.
1000 Burmaster Street, Gretna, Louisiana 70053

CONTENTS

A PENNSYLVANIA PROFILE

Pennsylvania means **"Penn's Woods,"** and the name came from King Charles II of England in honor of Admiral William Penn, father of William Penn, the founder of the colony. When the first Europeans arrived in Pennsylvania, it was almost unbroken forest. Millions of trees have since fallen, but millions more remain, and approximately half of Pennsylvania is still forest. Take a drive across Route 80, and you'll rarely have a view that doesn't include a wooded hill or mountain. Philadelphia and Pittsburgh are the areas of Pennsylvania that get the most publicity, but most of the state is a land of farms, small towns, lakes, and forests.

Pennsylvania is a diverse place, and a place where a great many events of **American history** took place. The signing of the Declaration of Independence, the nation's first turnpike, the nation's first covered bridge, the nation's first trip by steam-powered locomotive, the world's first oil well, and the country's most famous battle all took place in Pennsylvania. Celebrating that history has always been an important part of Pennsylvania tourism, and a new program has identified eight heritage areas throughout the state. They are:

Oil Heritage Region, (800) 483-6264

Delaware and Lehigh National Canal Heritage Corridor, (610) 861-9345

Lackawanna Heritage Valley, (800) 229-3526

Rivers of Steel Heritage Area, (412) 464-4020

National Road Heritage Park, (724) 329-1560

Lincoln Highway Heritage Corridor, (724) 668-8330

Allegheny Ridge State Heritage Park, (814) 942-8288

Schuylkill Heritage Corridor, (800) 443-6610

It's not unrealistic to say that an event that took place in Pennsylvania in 1859 made our entire modern way of life possible. In **Titusville,** Colonel Edwin Drake sank the world's first successful oil well, and northwestern Pennsylvania quickly became the world's first oil-boom region. The oil in the region didn't last, but the world's love for oil did. Today, the **Drake Well Museum** in Titusville remembers the events that led to cars and airplanes and plastic bags, as well as thousands of other items that everyone uses every day.

Despite the abundance of history to be found in Pennsylvania, history isn't Pennsylvania's only attraction. Shoppers flock to **Reading,** where the concept of outlet shopping began, and to **Adamstown,** the self-proclaimed "Antiques Capital of the World." **Hershey** has a sweet history, and the candy and the roller coasters are still big attractions. Small towns such as **Wellsboro** and **Bedford** offer history, shopping, and great bases for outdoor adventures.

In many places, the great outdoors are the main attraction. **Ricketts Glen** has woods, water, and waterfalls. You can enjoy them without having to rough it because the park offers modern cabins for rental. Pennsylvania has its own version of the **Grand Canyon—Pine Creek Gorge** is beautiful and quiet, and a rail trail has made it accessible to everyone. **Presque Isle,** in Erie, draws millions to enjoy its beaches and trails, and the **Allegheny National Forest** is 500,000 acres of wilderness and recreational opportunities.

Pennsylvania has an interesting past and an interesting present. It's a good place to get away from the frequently frantic pace of modern life.

What Is A Getaway?

Americans lead hectic lives, and we often take that pace with us on vacation. Instead of relaxing, we rush around so much that when we get home, we need a vacation to recover from our vacation.

This book won't make any value judgments on what an appropriate pace for a weekend getaway is, but the book will take you to places where you can't possibly get everything done in one weekend and to places where you'll feel comfortable just watching the trees grow.

Hershey, Adamstown, and **Gettysburg** will keep you moving, while **Ricketts Glen, Mount Gretna,** and **Eagles Mere** will invite you to take a stroll and just slow down. Pennsylvania is a diverse place, and these getaway spots reflect that diversity. Whether you like to go, go, go or to take life slowly, you'll find plenty of opportunities to do what you like in Pennsylvania.

What is a Weekend?

By definition, a weekend is Saturday and Sunday, but for *two* good reasons it makes sense to take weekend getaways in the middle of the week. The first reason is crowds. They're smaller during the week. The second reason is cost. Many places, especially hotels and motels, have higher prices on weekends than during the week because demand is highest on Friday and Saturday nights.

Here's an example: During the summer of 1998, a Best Western in Erie offered a $39.95 price on rooms from Sunday through Thursday. On Fridays and Saturdays, the rooms cost $89.95. That's an extreme example of the discounts available during the week, but smaller discounts are more common.

Equally important is that the crowds are smaller during the week, and if you're looking to get away from crowds, you'll have better success on weekdays. Many hotel and motel managers say that Sundays are their slowest nights, so an excellent "weekend" extends from Sunday afternoon through Tuesday.

The one drawback to such scheduling, of course, is that many events take place on Saturday and Sunday. Football and festivals happen on weekends, so it's hard to enjoy them during the week. But if you're looking for quiet and relaxation, consider a weekend getaway in the middle of the week.

Pennsylvania's Weather and Geography

Pennsylvania has a distinct four-season climate. Weather-wise, the best time to visit is autumn, especially from Labor Day through Columbus Day. Within the state, the climate varies significantly. The northwestern quadrant is considerably cooler than the southeastern part of the state. Places such as **Bradford, Kane,** and **Smethport** frequently record the coldest temperatures in the state, while the region from **Gettysburg** to **Philadelphia** is relatively mild.

Elevations also play a significant role in determining the weather. Pennsylvania's highest elevation is only 3,213 feet, but that's enough to make a major difference in summer and winter temperatures. **Philadelphia,** which is barely above sea level, is almost always warmer than **Eagles Mere,** which lies around 2,100 feet. Frost occasionally forms in June in the higher elevations of **Potter** and **McKean** counties. So, if you're looking to elude summer's heat, look for high elevations in the northern half of the state.

What's in a Name?

Pennsylvania places have interesting names. **Forty Fort, Eighty Four, Shy Beaver,** and **Slippery Rock** are a few favorites. Close to each other in Lancaster County are **Bird-In-Hand, Blue Ball, Intercourse,** and **Paradise.** The names of many other states also show up in Pennsylvania—**California, Delaware, Indiana, Oregon, Texas, Virginia,** and **Wyoming** are all city names on the Pennsylvania map.

Facts and Figures

- Pennsylvania joined the union on December 12, 1787 as the second state.
- Nicknames: **Keystone State** and **Quaker State**
- State bird: **Ruffed Grouse**
- State flower: **Mountain Laurel**
- State tree: **Eastern Hemlock**
- Area: 46,058 square miles (ranks 33rd among the states in size)

Distinctive Pennsylvania Features

Covered Bridges

Pennsylvania is the nation's leader in covered bridges and in covered-bridge history. Approximately 220 covered bridges are still standing in the state, and more than half of them are still open to cars. (If you have a motor home, don't try to drive through a covered bridge.) **Lancaster County** is the state leader in the number and condition of covered bridges. The county has 28 within its borders, and shares two others with Chester County. In addition, Lancaster County keeps its covered bridges in superb condition.

The first covered bridge built in North America spanned the Schuylkill in Philadelphia, and opened in 1806. The longest ever built, 5,690 feet, crossed the Susquehanna between Columbia and Wrightsville. A flood washed that one away, and its successor played a significant role in the Civil War. Union soldiers burned it to stop advancing Confederates from penetrating Lancaster County just a few days before the battle at Gettysburg, where the **Saks Covered Bridge** is still standing and has a historical past. Confederate soldiers retreated through it after the battle.

Most remaining covered bridges are in scenic rural spots, and these getaways will take you to many of them.

Tourist Railroads

Pennsylvania has a powerful railroad legacy, and the state's tourist railroads make it possible to enjoy a train ride. In fact, it's still possible to see Pennsylvania by train. Many of the state's most famous attractions are visible from the window of a train. Among them are:

• The Gettysburg Battlefield.
• The site of the world's first well.
• The nation's first Amish settlement.
• The site of the first trip by steam locomotive in North America.
• Fall foliage.

(For complete information on Pennsylvania's tourist railroads, see *Guide To Pennsylvania's Tourist Railroads*, also published by Pelican.)

Coal

If you want to know the complete history of Pennsylvania,

you have to learn about the coal industry and life in mining towns. More than half of Pennsylvania's counties have coal deposits, and in many small towns life revolved around coal for many decades.

In the northeastern part of the state, coal defined and dominated life for a century and a half, and Scranton was, at one time, the biggest mining town in the country. The work was dirty and dangerous, and life was hard. Boys as young as nine went to work in the mines, and deaths were common (among both children and adults). It's not always a pleasant story, but it is a fascinating one.

Pennsylvania coal comes in two varieties—**anthracite** and **bituminous.** The anthracite belt in the northeastern part of the state runs from **Forest City** in Susquehanna County southwest to **Lykens** in Dauphin County. Coal so dominated life in that region that many Pennsylvanians still refer to it as **"The Coal Region."**

Bituminous coal, which isn't as pure as anthracite, lies in many counties in the western half of the state. Anthracite is almost pure carbon, and it burns very cleanly, but mining it is more difficult than mining bituminous coal.

Today, anthracite mining continues on a much smaller scale than it did at its peak in the early part of the century, and the bituminous industry is going strong. Several large and productive mines have opened recently in the southwestern corner of the state.

In the northeast, many sites and museums remember the history of anthracite mining. As you drive through the region, you'll still see some mining operations. You'll also see reminders of past mining operations. Abandoned mines and huge slag piles dot the hillsides. They're not beautiful, but they are an integral part of Pennsylvania life. In **Ashland** and in **Scranton,** you can go into a real coal mine.

Bicycling

Pennsylvania has a large network of lightly-traveled rural roads that are excellent for bicycling. The state also has thousands of miles of trails for mountain bikers and 100 rail trails for those who like leisurely, flat rides. At the other extreme are thousands of miles of hilly roads.

If you think that Pennsylvania is a relatively flat place, the view from a bike will give you a different perspective. Pennsylvania's mountains aren't especially high, but they are steep, and they make many rides very challenging.

The best places for road biking are farm areas. Traffic is generally light, and the hills are only moderately steep. One good way to find enjoyable biking routes is to follow the **Amish.** They don't put any cars on the road.

So, if you have a bike, be sure to bring it along. If you don't, you'll find places to rent bikes near many of the rail trails. For information on Pennsylvania's rail trails, contact **Rails To Trails Conservancy,** 105 Locust Street, Harrisburg, PA 17105, (717) 238-1717.

Camping

Sleeping under the stars is a popular activity in Pennsylvania. Whether you have a tent or a RV, campgrounds have accommodations for you. For a list of Pennsylvania's campgrounds, contact the **Pennsylvania Campground Owners Association,** P.O. Box 5, New Tripoli, PA 18066, (610) 767-5026.

Caves

Limestone lies under much of Pennsylvania, and most caves develop in limestone that is permeable to water. Caves are common in Pennsylvania, and many are open to the public. Some of the more famous ones are **Penn's Cave** in Centre County (open 9 A.M.-5 P.M. daily, and 9 A.M.-7 P.M. June 1-August 31), **Indian Echo Caverns** near Hershey (open 10 A.M.-4 P.M. daily, and 9 A.M.-6 P.M. Memorial Day through Labor Day), and **Crystal Cave** near Kutztown (open 9 A.M.-5 P.M. daily, March through November). For a list of Pennsylvania's caves, write or call **Pennsylvania Caves Association,** RR #1, Box 220, Huntingdon, PA 16652, (814) 643-1358.

On The Waterfront

Pennsylvania doesn't border an ocean, but it has lots of water. Lakes cover thousands of square miles, and many rivers run through the state. Despite its lack of an ocean, Pennsylvania has many beaches and marinas. **Lake Erie** is actually an "inland" sea with sandy beaches. It won't work for surfing, but in other ways it's like the ocean.

Pennsylvanians flock to the water, and many of these getaway destinations feature bodies of water for swimming, boating, and fishing.

Meet Me at the Fair

The county fair is an important part of the social fabric of many Pennsylvania communities. Agricultural exhibits, harness racing, Ferris wheels, and food of every description fill fairgrounds and the streets of small towns during fair week. Most of the fairs are local events, but several have become large affairs that attract visitors from far away. The biggest and most famous fairs in Pennsylvania are in **York** and **Bloomsburg.** Both are in September, and both are big productions where you can enjoy local food and national entertainment acts. For a list of all Pennsylvania fairs, call the **Pennsylvania Department of Agriculture,** (717) 787-5342.

A Day in the Park

Pennsylvania has 116 state parks that range in size from 3 acres up to 21,122 acres. The parks provide places to enjoy nature, swimming pools, and many other recreational opportunities. For complete information on Pennsylvania's state parks, call **1-888-PA-PARKS.**

Climb Every Mountain

With the highest elevation only 3,213 feet, Pennsylvania doesn't appear to be a mountainous state, but that number is deceptive. Pennsylvania is rarely flat, and the word "mountain" is all over the map. In the 1850s, the **Allegheny Mountains** were an obstacle to westward expansion, and the opening of **Horseshoe Curve,** which took the Pennsylvania Railroad over the mountain at Altoona, was one of the most important events in the history of American railroads.

As you travel around the state, you'll do some serious climbing and descending, and at the top of many mountains you'll be able to pull off the road and enjoy scenic overlooks.

Days of Wine and Roses

Grapes grow well in Pennsylvania, and the state has 48 wineries. They're in all sections of the state, and they often stage weekend events such as lawn concerts and tastings. For a complete list of Pennsylvania's wineries, contact the **Pennsylvania Wine Association,** 2205 Oregon Pike, Lancaster, PA 17601, (717) 560-0250.

Tee It Up

Pennsylvania has an abundance of golf courses, with new ones opening every year, and they're not all on former cornfields. For instance, a new course in **Cornwall,** Lebanon County, lies on a reclaimed iron ore mine. Wherever you visit in Pennsylvania, you'll find a public golf course nearby. For a complete list of Pennsylvania's golf courses, call Pennsylvania Golf Course Owners at **(412) 751-3379.**

Down on the Farm

For a different sort of getaway, try a farm vacation. Farm owners around the state open up their homes to visitors who get a chance to experience life on the farm for a day or two. For a list of these farms, send a self-addressed stamped envelope to **Pennsylvania Department of Agriculture, Farm Vacations,** 2301 North Cameron Street, Harrisburg, PA 17110-9408, or call (888) 856-6622.

Fall Foliage

Since half of Pennsylvania is forest, when the leaves change in autumn, the hillsides come alive with colors. Reds, oranges, yellows, and golds replace the greens of summer, and the state is spectacular.

The leaves first show their colors in the northern mountains, and the color moves south through October. Many communities have foliage festivals, and some of the tourist railroads run extra trains. For weekly updates on the changing of the leaves, call **1-(800) FALL-IN-PA.**

Harvest Time

In agricultural communities, harvest time (September and October) is a time for celebration. Across the state, harvest festivals, apple festivals, and Oktoberfests fill the cities and small towns with a final outdoor celebration before winter sets in. For information on harvest festivals, call **1-(800) VISIT-PA,** or write the tourist office at 404 Forum Building, Harrisburg, PA 17120.

Winter Wonderlands

With lots of mountains and lots of snow, Pennsylvania is attractive to downhill skiers. The state has 31 ski resorts, with the highest concentration in the Poconos and the northeastern part of the state. When the snow doesn't fall, resorts make it. In fact, the first snow-making machine helped whiten Pennsylvania back in 1956.

For cross-country skiers, Pennsylvania has even more to offer. Every park, golf course, and corn field becomes a cross-country course when snow falls, and some of the ski resorts have cross-country areas. The resorts also have ski boarding areas, so think of Pennsylvania when you're looking for snow. For information on all of Pennsylvania's ski areas, call **1-(800) VISIT-PA,** or write the tourist office at 404 Forum Building, Harrisburg, PA 17120.

Whitewater Rafting

Pennsylvania's mountains create active water, especially in spring when the snow is melting. The most popular rafting destinations are **Ohiopyle** and **Jim Thorpe.** Check those entries for listings of tour companies.

So load up the golf clubs, the walking shoes, the binoculars, the camera, and the credit cards. Point the car to Pennsylvania, and you'll find a great getaway destination.

Getaway Themes

Pennsylvania offers many activities and "inactivities," and these general categories will give you an idea of what to expect when you arrive in each place (indicated at the beginning of each chapter).

(A)—Arts & Antiques

(H)—History

(N)—Nature

(PT)—Pure Tourism (wandering with a camera)

(R)—Recreation

(R&R)—Rest & Relaxation

(S)—Shopping

WEEKEND GETAWAYS
IN PENNSYLVANIA

1

ADAMSTOWN . . .
ANTIQUES CAPITAL, U.S.A.
(A)

Adamstown bills itself as **Antiques Capital, U.S.A.** That's a title that any town with three antiques shops can bestow on itself, but Adamstown does have a huge antiques presence, and thousands of eager buyers come to this small town every day. Antiques aren't the only reason why people come to Adamstown, but they are by far the biggest draw.

Adamstown is an easy place to reach, and the antique shops are easy to find. Adamstown is at Exit 21 of the Pennsylvania Turnpike, and the antiques and other attractions are all along a rather short stretch of PA Route 272 on both sides of the turnpike.

In addition to antiques, Adamstown is home to **Stoudt's Brewing Company,** a microbrewery that holds many events, such as beer festivals, on its grounds, and **Zinn's Park,** a recreational area.

Adamstown lies in the heart of **Pennsylvania Dutch Country,** and the "Plain People"—**Amish** and **Mennonites**—live nearby. Many of them travel in horse-drawn buggies, and they've become a tourist attraction in other parts of Lancaster County. The major highway through Adamstown is full of antique stores, motels, and restaurants, but if you turn off the highway and drive down a country road, you'll find quiet roads where one farm runs into another. One place where it's not so quiet, however, is the space around **Maple Grove Raceway,** where championship drag racing takes place during the warmer months.

Location is an important part of Adamstown's growth as an antiques mecca. People from Philadelphia, New York, and New Jersey can easily make a day trip to Adamstown, and Baltimore and Washington are also within easy driving distance. As a result, millions of people can get here rather quickly, and on weekends it often appears as though they've *all* arrived.

The antiques business began in 1962 at **Shupp's Grove,** which is still one of the big operations. In the mid-1960s, **Renninger's Farm Market** made a transition to antiques, giving dealers a place where rain and snow weren't problems. **Renninger's Antiques Market** became a permanent part of the Adamstown antiques scene, and it's probably the best-known name in the area. As Renninger's and Shupp's Grove grew and prospered, other dealers moved in, and today old things are the major industry in this little town.

So how big is the business? Well, the Exit 21 Tourist Association lists **22 antiques markets,** and some of them are co-ops that have many dealers. Renninger's has almost **800 dealers** indoors and out, and the total number of dealers at the 22 markets is above 2,700.

If you like antiques, this is definitely a great place to come for a weekend, because volume isn't the only attraction. The variety and the condition are also quite good. Many of the shops have specialties, such as advertising memorabilia, Victorian furniture, automobile antiques, and even Amish clothing.

In its early years, the antiques business operated primarily on weekends. Now, many of the shops are open daily, but Shupp's Grove operates only on weekends, and Renninger's is open only on Sundays. You can find lots of antiques every day, but only on Sundays will you find every shop open.

The success of the antiques business was part of the inspiration for **Stoudtburg,** a 23-acre village designed to capture the

Renninger's Antique Market

feel of a medieval German village. The model for Stoudtburg was **Rothenburg,** Germany.

In Stoudtburg, merchants conduct business on the ground floors of their buildings and live on the upper floors of the homes, which range from two stories to four. For a visitor, it's pleasant to imagine living in such a quiet little place, where automobile traffic is minimal. Stoudtburg has plenty of parking, but the design keeps them out of the shopping and living areas, so shoppers can enjoy car-free strolls around the village. That's part of the attraction to many of the shop owners who now measure their commutes in flights of stairs instead of miles.

The first building in the village was **Clock Towers Antiques Center,** and the clock tower is the most memorable building in the village. Stoudtburg is home to a wide variety of specialty shops that offer fine art, music boxes, antique toys, Bavarian coffee, ice cream, and Swiss chocolate.

Stoudtburg is not the first business here to carry the Stoudt name. Adjacent to Stoudtburg are the **Stoudt Brewing**

Clock Tower at Stoudtburg

Company, which has won awards for its beers, and **Stoudt's Antiques Mall.** The brewery makes some unusual brews, such as Apple Ale and Raspberry Weizen. The brewery also hosts beer tastings and festivals. In addition, a pub is open Friday, Saturday, and Sunday, beginning at noon.

When hunger calls after a long day of shopping, **Zinn's Diner** is a favorite stop. Located right beside the turnpike, it offers hearty Pennsylvania Dutch meals and many kinds of recreation. Miniature golf, water wars, an arcade, and picnic tables, grills, and a pavilion available for rental, as well as a playground, are on the grounds.

Antiques Capital, U.S.A. lives up to its reputation. For the best in antique shopping, take Exit 21 of the Pennsylvania Turnpike.

Attractions:

Antique shops all along Route 272.

Stoudtburg, on Route 272, (717) 484-4385, Sat. and Sun. 10 A.M.-5 P.M., changeable weekday hours.

Maple Grove Park and Raceway, Mohnton, (610) 856-7812, weekend racing.

Zinn's Recreational Park, Route 272 and Turnpike, (717) 336-3891, open 10 A.M. in season.

Dining:

The Black Horse Restaurant and Tavern, 2180 North Reading Road, Route 272, Denver, PA 17517, (717) 336-6555, Mon.-Sat., 4 P.M.-till, Sun., 11 A.M.-10 P.M.

Boehringer's Drive-In, Route 272, Adamstown, (717) 484-4227, Tues.-Sun., 11 A.M.-9 P.M.

Country Pride Restaurant, Route 272 south of Turnpike Exit 21, (717) 336-4010, 6 A.M.-10 P.M., seven days a week.

Silk City Diner, 1640 North Reading Road, Route 272, one mile south of Turnpike Exit 21, (717) 335-3833, Mon.-Thur., 6 A.M.-9 P.M., Fri. and Sat., 6 A.M.-10 P.M., Sun., 7 A.M.-9 P.M.

Stoudt's Black Angus Steak House & Brew Pub, Route 272, Adamstown, (717) 484-4385, Mon.-Sat., 5 P.M.-11 P.M., Sun., noon-9 P.M.

Weaver's Cafeteria Style Restaurant, located inside Weaver's Market, Route 272 and Route 897, (717) 336-7563, Mon.-Sat., 7 A.M.-9 P.M.

Zinn's Diner, Route 272 at Turnpike Exit 21, (717) 336-2210, 6 A.M.-11 P.M., seven days a week.

Lodging:

Black Forest Inn, Route 272, Adamstown, (717) 445-4526.

Black Horse Lodge & Suites, Route 272, Denver, (717) 336-7563.

Comfort Inn, Route 272, Denver, (800) 228-5150.

Holiday Inn, Route 272, Denver, (800) 437-5711.

Adamstown Inn, 62 West Main Street, Adamstown, (800) 593-4808.

Barnyard Inn Bed & Breakfast, 2145 Old Lancaster Pike, Reinholds, (888) 738-6624.

Belle Vista, 1216 East Main Street, Akron, (717) 859-4227.

Brownstowne Corner Bed & Breakfast, 590 Galen Hall Road, Reinholds, (800) 239-9902.

Cocalico Creek Bed & Breakfast, 224 South 4th Street, Denver, (717) 336-0271.

Living Spring Farm, 2614 Route 568, Mohnton, (610) 775-8525.

Hickory Run Family Campground, 285 Greenville Road, Denver, (800) 458-0612.

Lancaster/Reading KOA, 3 Denver Road, Denver, (800) 562-1621.

Maple Grove Park Campground, Road #3, Mohnton, (610) 856-9208.

Shady Grove Campground, Route 897 North, Adamstown, (800) 742-3947.

Sills Family Campground, Bowmansville Road, Adamstown, (800) 325-3002.

Sun Valley Campground, 451 East Maple Grove, Bowmansville, (800) 700-3370.

Shopping:

Shopping for antiques and collectibles is the entire story of Adamstown. The shops line Route 272. You can also buy specialty beers at Stoudt's Brewing Company on Route 272, and almost everything else at Weaver's, known to some locals as "The Mennonite Mall." The most famous antiques markets are:

Renninger's, Route 272, Adamstown, (717) 336-2177), Sun., 7 A.M.-4 P.M.

Shupp's Grove, Route 897 South, Adamstown, (717) 484-4115, Sat. and Sun., 7 A.M.-5 P.M.

Weaver's Store, Route 897, Fivepointville, (717) 445-6791, Mon., Tues., Thur., and Fri., 8 A.M.-9 P.M., Wed. and Sat., 8 A.M.-5 P.M.

Annual Events:

The calendar is full. Call (717) 336-7482 for information.

The antiques business and the Stoudt Brewing Company stage events on a regular basis, and many of the smaller businesses have one or two events.

The antiques extravaganzas are big draws. One motel owner spoke of having regular guests from Europe and Japan, so book your rooms early if you're coming for one of the big weekends. The biggest events are:

- **Spring Antique Extravaganza,** last weekend in April.
- **Summer Antique Extravaganza,** last weekend in June.
- **Fall Antique Extravaganza,** last weekend in September.
- **Summer Beer Festival,** weekends in August through Labor Day.
- **Oktoberfest,** Sundays in October.

The Active Life:

You'll put in plenty of miles walking among the antique shops, and if you want a great view of the countryside, bring your bike. Surrounding Adamstown are some of the fertile farmlands of the nation's most productive non-irrigated agricultural county.

The **Adamstown Community Pool** on West Main Street is open to the public. Prices are $5 for adults and $3 for children. Phone (717) 484-2175.

A Great Place to Relax:

The village of **Stoudtburg** is probably the most relaxing place in Adamstown.

Covered Bridges:

The nearest is Bucher's Mill, in Reamstown, about five miles south of Adamstown. The bridge is just east of Route 272 on Cocalico Creek Road. You can see the bridge from Route 272.

Tourist Information:

- **Exit 21 Tourist Association,** P.O. Box 457, Adamstown, PA 19501, (717) 336-7482.
- **Stoudtburg,** (717) 484-4385.

Where is it? Southeast, on U.S. 222 between Reading and Lancaster, at Exit 21 of the Pennsylvania Turnpike.

Getaway Rating: 2

Bucher's Mill Covered Bridge

2

ALTOONA/JOHNSTOWN . . .
"I'VE BEEN WORKIN'
ON THE RAILROAD . . . "
(H, R)

If you've never ridden a train, or if you consider trains loud, antiquated annoyances, then get to Altoona with all possible haste.

A visit to the **Railroaders Memorial Museum** and a ride on an Amtrak train through **Horseshoe Curve** will give you a new appreciation of the men who built the railroads that built America, as well as a delightful train ride. The route from Altoona to Johnstown is beautiful, and it will make you wonder just how they ever managed to get those trains over that big mountain.

If you already have a love and appreciation of trains, you'll find a trip to Altoona positively inspiring. Railroads and heavy industry built this region, and train-related sites are the primary attractions.

Altoona and Johnstown are on opposite sides of a mountain that was once an obstacle to the development of the American West. Outsiders often link the two cities, but they're distinct from each other. They're about 40 miles apart, and they're in different counties. For visitors, however, they're close enough to combine in the same visit, and the railroad links them.

Altoona Railroaders Memorial Museum

Each city has derived lasting fame from one event. Altoona became an immediate tourist attraction when **Horseshoe Curve** opened in 1854. Johnstown became forever linked to the ravages of flooding when a dam collapsed and buried the city beneath a wall of water in the **Johnstown Flood** of 1889.

Until Horseshoe Curve opened, the Allegheny Mountains made westward travel an ordeal. The driving of the golden spike at Promontory Point in Utah gets most of the ink as the most important event in American railroading, but the opening of "The Curve" was at least as important. Until then, covering the 300 miles from Philadelphia to Pittsburgh required at least four difficult days, so commerce and comfort improved greatly when the railroad finally conquered the Alleghenies.

Today, Horseshoe Curve is still in heavy daily use, and visitors come to watch trains struggle up and thunder down the mountain. A visitors' area puts spectators in the middle of trains. As they roll through the curve, the front is on one side of the area and the rear is on the other side. Because the curve is heavily wooded, train watching is better from November until April, when the leaves are off the trees.

In Johnstown, the **Flood Museum** remembers the events of May 31, 1889. Relentless rain had filled a man-made lake and weakened a dam. When the dam broke, a wall of water roared down the **Conemaugh Valley,** destroying everything in its path. Deaths totaled 2,209, and the water obliterated Johnstown.

When you visit, you'll see why Johnstown is prone to floods. Steep hills surround the city, and several creeks run through it. If you ride Amtrak between Johnstown and Altoona, you'll see where the water went, and why it did such damage—the valley is narrow, and it funnels water right into Johnstown.

The **Johnstown Flood Memorial** looks at the ruins of **South Fork Dam** and features a film and exhibits that recreate the flood experience. To reach the memorial, take Route 219 to the Sidman exit and follow the signs.

After the flood of 1889, the city didn't stay down. It quickly rebuilt and regained its place as a hub of the steel and rail industries. After the flood, a new suburb developed on top of a hill overlooking the city, and an inclined railroad linked downtown Johnstown with the new community of **Westmont.**

Today, the **Johnstown Incline** is still operating. It's the steepest incline in the world, at 71.9°, and also the only one that carries cars. The top is 634 feet higher than the bottom, and a ride up provides a great view. At the top is a visitors' area, and on a clear day, the view is spectacular.

Altoona developed as a rail hub at the eastern base of the mountain. The **Pennsylvania Railroad** built and repaired railcars there, and the city is still a railroad town. The Pennsy (the nickname of the now-defunct Pennsylvania Railroad) is gone, but it's still a big draw in Altoona. The **Railroaders Memorial Museum** tells the whole story of the Pennsy. The museum enjoyed a significant renovation and upgrading in 1998, and the new layout thrills train lovers.

An interactive format takes visitors into the shops where skilled craftsmen built locomotives and freight cars, and into the city of Altoona as it was 100 years ago. The tracks run right through the center of town, and they're still very busy. The 12th Street Bridge, which spans the tracks, is a great place to

Johnstown Incline

watch trains. Amtrak comes through a few times a day, and freights seem to run almost continuously.

Before Horseshoe Curve opened, the **Allegheny Portage Railroad** carried passengers over the mountains. The portage railroad used a combination of canal boats and rail cars. The portage railroad cut the travel time from 23 days to 4, but it still had flaws. The ropes that pulled cars up the mountains frequently broke, and when the canals froze, everything stopped.

Thus, Horseshoe Curve was a huge improvement, but the Allegheny Portage Railroad made a crucial contribution to American transportation during its short existence. A museum on the mountain shows how the portage railroad managed to get people and goods over the steep slopes.

For summer fun, Altoona has two theme parks. **Lakemont Park,** at the Frankstown Road exit of I-99, 700 Park Avenue, Altona, open 11 A.M.-9 P.M. daily, June through the end of August, has roller coasters, go-carts, and water rides, with prices as low as $6.95 for the whole day. Call (800) 434-8006 for details.

Allegheny Portage Railroad

Bland's Park, just north of Altoona beside 1-99, located at Old U.S. 220, Tipton, is an interactive water-park with miniature golf, go-carts, and rides. Call (814) 684-3538 for information. Opens at noon, Tues.-Dun., June through August. Closing hours vary.

For train lovers, a trip to Altoona and Johnstown is sure to make eyes grow wide and hearts beat fast.

Attractions:

Horseshoe Curve, Kittaning Point Road, Altoona, (814) 946-0834, visitors center open 10 A.M.-6 P.M. daily.

Altoona Railroaders Memorial Museum, 1300 9th Avenue, (814) 946-0834, 10 A.M.-6 P.M. daily.

Johnstown Flood National Memorial, Sidman/St. Michael exit of Route 219, (814) 495-4643, 9 A.M.-5 P.M. daily.

Johnstown Inclined Plane, 711 Edgehill Drive, (814) 536-1836, open seven days a week, early morning until late at night.

Johnstown Flood Museum

Johnstown Flood Museum, 304 Washington Street, (814) 539-1889, 10 A.M.-5 P.M. daily.

Dining:

Allegro, 3926 Broad Avenue, Altoona, (814) 946-5216, Mon.-Sat., 4 P.M.-9:30 P.M.

Altoona Hotel, 3830 Fifth Avenue, (814) 944-5521, 11:30 A.M. until evening.

Fazoli's Italian Restaurant, Plank Road Commons, 2550 Old Route 220 North, Altoona, (814) 949-8229, 11 A.M.-10 P.M., seven days a week.

Gingerbread Man, 206 East Plank Road, Altoona, (814) 942-2511, 11 A.M.-9 P.M., seven days a week.

Zach's Sociable Food & Spirits, 5820 Sixth Avenue, Altoona, (814) 943-9479, Mon-Sat., open noon-11 P.M.

Fazoli's Italian Restaurant, 1419 Scalp Avenue, Johnstown, (814) 269-3402, 11 A.M.-10 P.M. daily.

Incline Station Restaurant & Pub, 709 Edgehill Drive, Johnstown, opens at 11 A.M. Mon.-Sat., 10 A.M. on Sun.

Lodging:

The Station Inn, 827 Front Street, Cresson, (800) 555-4757. A bit of paradise for the train fan. The inn is about 70 feet from Conrail's triple track line to Pittsburgh. Visitors can sit on the porch and watch trains all day. Every room has a railroad theme.

Days Inn, 3306 Pleasant Valley Road, Altoona, (814) 944-9661.

Econo Lodge, 2906 Pleasant Valley Road, Altoona, (814) 944-3555.

Hampton Inn, 180 Charlotte Drive, Altoona, (814) 941-3500.

Holiday Inn, 2915 Pleasant Valley Road, Altoona, (814) 944-4581.

Ramada Inn, Plank Road exit, Route 220, Altoona, (814) 946-1631.

Comfort Inn, 455 Theatre Drive, Johnstown, (800) 228-5150.

Days Inn, 1540 Scalp Avenue, Johnstown, (800) 329-7466.

Hampton Inn, 129 Commerce Court, Johnstown, (814) 262-7700.

Holiday Inn, 250 Market street, Johnstown, (800) 433-5663.

Motel 6, 430 Napoleon Place, Johnstown, (800) 4-MOTEL-6.

Sleep Inn, 453 Theatre Drive, Johnstown, (800) 627-5337.

Super 8, 627 Solomon Run Road, Johnstown, (800) 800-8000.

Shopping:

The Galleria, Route 219 and Galleria Drive, Johnstown, (814) 266-6600, Mon.-Sat., 10 A.M.-9 P.M., Sun., noon-5 P.M.

Station Mall, 9th Avenue at 17th Street, Altoona, (814) 946-3088, Mon.-Sat., 10 A.M.-9 P.M., Sun., noon-5 P.M.

Logan Valley Mall, Route 220 and Goods Lane, Altoona, (814) 944-6128, Mon.-Sat., 10 A.M.-9 P.M., Sun., noon-6 P.M.

Annual Events:

Blair County Arts Festival, Altoona, mid-May, (814) 949-2787.

Johnstown Marathon, first Sunday in October, (814) 535-8381.

Cambria County Fair, Ebensburg, begins Sunday before Labor Day, (814) 472-7491.

Johnstown Folkfest, Labor Day weekend, (888) 222-1889.

The Active Life:

A hiking trail follows the route of the Johnstown Incline. It's a wild area right in the city, and walking up it is considerably easier than walking down. The hill is so steep that going down is a real challenge.

Canoe Creek State Park in Hollidaysburg offers a lake for swimming, boating, and fishing, as well as hiking trails and modern cabins. The area around the park is only moderately hilly and quite good for bicycling.

A Great Place to Relax:

At the top of the **Johnstown Incline** is a little park where you can sit and enjoy a spectacular view of the city. A stadium is at the base of the hill, and with really good binoculars you might be able to watch a baseball or football game.

Covered Bridges:

Shaffer's Bridge is two miles south of Johnstown, along Route 985. Follow 985 (Somerset Pike) out of the Johnstown area, then turn on Covered Bridge Road, which is visible from 985.

Tourist Information:

• (800) 84-ALTOONA or (800) 237-8590 (Johnstown).

Where is it? Southwest, on U.S. 22 and U.S. 219.

Getaway Rating: 2

3

ASHLAND/
SCHUYLKILL COUNTY . . .
WORKIN' IN A COAL MINE
(H)

Head deep into the earth. Learn about the lives of coal miners. Take a drive through a city that has burned down. Visit America's oldest brewery. In Ashland and the surrounding regions you can look at the past and taste the present.

Coal was one of the dominant forces that made Pennsylvania an industrial power, and Ashland is in the heart of the region that many Pennsylvanians call **"The Coal Regions."** It's a place of small towns and fascinating history. Away from the coal seams, it's an area of natural beauty, but mining has left scars.

Ashland isn't a major vacation destination, but it's a great place to learn about the history of coal mining in Pennsylvania and to walk the streets of a little mining town.

Across the valley from Ashland is a sad reminder that fire can be both friend and foe. **Centralia** was once a prosperous mining town, but now it's just eerie. In 1962, a fire broke out in a coal seam beneath the town. Efforts to put out the fire have been unsuccessful, and the fire has been burning for more than 37 years. Estimates say that the coal seam is big enough to burn for 100, or 1,000, years. Nobody really knows, but everybody knows that Centralia isn't really a town any more. Most of the

Pioneer Tunnel Coal Mine

residents have moved out as the fire has burned beneath their houses and lawns. The Catholic church fell in 1998, and just a few houses remain.

If you visit Centralia, the first thing you may notice is the smell. If you've ever ridden a steam train, you'll recognize the smell of burning coal. In Centralia, however, the smell doesn't come from a train—it comes from beneath the ground. In many places, puffs of steam rise up from the ground, and the scene is from another world. In cold weather, steam from the fire is visible in Ashland. Centralia isn't a place to spend a long time, but it's definitely worth a look.

Back in Ashland, you can experience the work of a miner at the **Pioneer Tunnel Coal Mine.** This was a real mine, but now it's a tourist attraction. A little engine pulls little cars into the mine and a guide, who actually worked in coal mines, describes the work of a miner.

As the door swings shut, the light of the sun disappears. For miners, the only light came from lamps on their helmets. Mining is hard work, and often dangerous. Mine owners were notorious for their mistreatment of their workers, and because of battles between labor and management, a group called **The Molly Maguires** sprang up in this area. The Mollies tried to achieve their goals of better pay and working conditions by many methods, including killing and terrorizing mine owners and foremen.

At least that's the generally accepted theory. Some local residents and historians question whether the Mollies ever actually existed. No hard evidence exists, the doubters say, to prove that the Mollies were real.

Whether the Mollies were real is a subject of debate, but no one has ever said that working in a mine was easy. Simply living in the towns was often dangerous. One resident of this area told a story of an explosion that sent a huge piece of debris into the air and through the roof of his house. It landed on the couch in the living room. Fortunately, no one was on the couch at the time.

The mine tour shows just how hard the work was. The conditions were cramped and narrow. The air was damp, and the work of digging coal was exhausting. Cave-ins and explosions were constant threats, and many miners lost their lives on the job. The term "canary in a coal mine" is a real reminder of coal mining's early days. Miners would send canaries into the mines, and if the birds didn't return, the miners knew that the mines held dangerous levels of gas.

Beside the Pioneer Tunnel Coal Mine is the **Anthracite Museum of Ashland.** There, you can learn about the work of miners. In the early days, their tools were crude, and human muscle provided most of the power needed to break coal loose from the mountain. Over the years the tools improved, but the work has always been hard.

Equally hard was the life of mining families. In many instances, the company owned everything in town—the mine, the houses, and the company store. Miners worked six days a week and lived in small houses. Wives had a set itinerary. Monday was laundry day. Tuesday was housecleaning, etc. Sunday was the one fun day of the week. Everyone went to church, and afterwards it was the day to socialize. In summer,

Centralia burning

baseball was big. Every town had its team, and competition was fierce, but after the game the people had a picnic.

Coal was the biggest part of life in Schuylkill County, but the coal fields are rather narrow, and the county has other identities. **Hawk Mountain,** near Kempton, was the world's first sanctuary for birds of prey. The preserve covers 2,400 acres and offers hiking trails, scenic views, and thousands of birds of prey flying by. Thousands of visitors come to watch the hawks, eagles, ospreys, and falcons. Call (610) 756-6961 for information, or write 1700 Hawk Mountain Road, Kempton, PA 19529.

Yuengling's, America's oldest brewery, operates at 5th and Mahantongo Streets in Pottsville. The brewery opened in 1829, and its location seems a bit surprising. Businesses that require large quantities of water often locate beside rivers and creeks, but Yuengling's is up on a hill in the middle of the city. It's an extremely steep hill, and it makes a visitor wonder just how trucks get up there when the streets are snowy.

The location hasn't been a hindrance to business, however. The brewery has prospered and recently expanded. Visitors can tour the plant Monday through Friday at 10 A.M. and 1:30 P.M.

all year, and also on Saturday from 11 A.M. to 1 P.M. during June, July, and August, and from Thanksgiving weekend until the weekend after Christmas. Call 570-628-4890 for information.

Shenandoah is a coal town that also produces perogies (potatoes, cheese, etc., wrapped in dough and cooked—yum!). **Mrs.T's** makes them in large quantities on East Center Street. Many years ago, Shenandoah gave the world music. The Dorsey brothers, Jimmy and Tommy, grew up in Shenandoah and chose careers outside the mines.

The coal regions aren't one of Pennsylvania's major vacation destinations, but they tell a fascinating story, and a visit here is a good way to get away from crowds and congestion.

Attractions:

Pioneer Tunnel Coal Mine, 19th Street, follow signs from Route 61, Ashland, (570) 875-3850, open April-October. Check for daily hours.

Museum of Anthracite Mining, 17th and Pine Streets, follow signs from Route 61, Ashland, (570) 875-4708, Mon.-Sat., 9 A.M.- 5 P.M., Sun., noon-5 P.M.

The remains of **Centralia,** along Route 54.

Yuengling Brewery (America's oldest), 5th and Mahantongo Streets, Pottsville, (570) 628-4890, tours Mon.-Fri. at 10 A.M. and 1:30 P.M., Sat. in June, July, and August, 11 A.M. and 1 P.M., gift shop Mon.-Fri., 9 A.M.-4 P.M.

Mrs. T's Perogies, East Center Street, Shenandoah, (570) 462- 2745, call for tour appointment 30 days in advance. From Memorial Day through Labor Day tours begin at 10 A.M., and in April, May, September, October, and November they begin at 11 A.M.

Hawk Mountain Sanctuary, 1700 Hawk Mountain Road, Kempton, (610) 756-6961, Visitors' Center open 9 A.M.-5 P.M. daily.

Dining:

Dutch Kitchen, 433 South Lehigh Avenue, Frackville, (570) 874-3265, 8 A.M.-8 P.M. daily.

Henry's Family Restaurant, 1120 Centre Street, Ashland, (570) 875-1234, 7 A.M.-9 P.M. daily.

Holahan's Food and Spirits, 114 Centre Street, Pottsville, (570) 622-1444, Mon.-Fri., 11 A.M.-11 P.M., Sat., 11 A.M.-9 P.M.

New Garfield Diner, Garfield Square in downtown Pottsville, (570) 628-2199, open 24 hours a day, seven days a week.

Quality Hotel, 100 South Centre Street, Pottsville, (570) 622-4600, breakfast, lunch, and dinner daily.

Lodging:

Budget Host Inn, Route 61 and I-81, Frackville, (570) 874-0408.

Fairlane Motor Inn, Route 61, Pottsville, (570) 429-1696.

Pottsville Motor Inn, Route 61, Pottsville, (570) 622-4917.

Quality Hotel, 100 South Centre Street, Pottsville, (570) 622-4600.

River Inn, Route 61, Pottsville, (570) 385-2407.

Kaier Mansion Bed & Breakfast, 729 East Centre Street, Mahanoy City, (570) 733-3040.

Stone House Bed & Breakfast, 16 Dock Street, Schuylkill Haven, (570) 385-2115.

Rosemont Camping Resort, RR 1, Tamaqua, (570) 668-2580.

Shopping:

Renninger's Farmer's Market, Route 61, Schuylkill Haven, (570) 385-3720, open Sat. and Sun. at 7 A.M.

Schuylkill Mall, Route 61 and Route 81, Frackville, (570) 874-3660, Mon.-Sat., 9:30 A.M.-9 P.M., Sun., noon-5 P.M.

Fairlane Village, Route 61, Pottsville, (570) 429-2449, Mon.-Sat., 10 A.M.-6 P.M., Sun., noon-5 P.M.

Cressona Mall, Route 61 and Route 183, (570) 385-5657, Mon.-Sat., 9:30 A.M.-9 P.M., Sun., noon-5 P.M.

Pioneer Tunnel Coal Mine Gift Shop, (570) 875-3850, daily at 10 A.M.

Big hunk of coal

Annual Events:

Pottsville Area Winter Carnival, January and February, (570) 628-2702.

American Way Street Fair, Pottsville, third Sunday in May, (570) 628-2702.

Molly Maguire Weekend, thired weekend in June, Pottsville, (570) 622-7700.

Coal Cracker 10K & Festival, second Saturday in June, Shenandoah, (570) 622-7700.

Pennsylvania Dutch Kutztown Folk Festival, Summit Station, late June and early July, (570) 622-7700.

Irish Weekend, Pottsville, last weekend in July, (570) 544-5753.

Schuylkill County Fair, Summitt Station, first week in August, (570) 754-FAIR.

Pioneer Day, Higher Up Park, Ashland, August, (570) 875-3850.

Ashland Boys Association Mummers Parade, Labor Day, (570) 622-7700.

Fall Festival & Craft Show, Summit Station, second weekend in October, (570) 622-4124.

The Active Life:

Locust Lake State Park and Tuscarora State Park offer activities such as swimming, boating, fishing, and picnicking. Both are accessible from Route 81 via Route 54. Hawk Mountain is excellent for hiking, and the Appalachian Trail passes nearby.

Mountain Valley Golf Course is at Exit 37 of I-81, near Locust Lake State Park. Call (570) 467-2242 for times and rates. White Birch Golf Course is at the same exit. Call (570) 467-2525.

A Great Place to Relax:

Walk the trails at Hawk Mountain, find a perch, and watch the Schuylkill River meander through the valley far below. Or just find a comfortable bench in Higher Up Park in Ashland, right beside the Pioneer Tunnel Coal Mine.

Covered Bridges:

Schuylkill County has two. They're both near Rock, in the southern part of the county, near Route 895, and both cross the Little Swatara Creek. Rock Bridge is on Township Route 452, north of 895, and east of the village of Rock. Zimmerman's Bridge is on Township Route 661, south of 895, and west of Rock.

Tourist Information:

• Schuylkill County Visitors Bureau, (570) 622-7700.

Where is it? Southeastern quadrant, on Route 61, west of interstate 81.

Getaway Rating: 2

4

BEDFORD . . .
GEORGE WASHINGTON
SLEPT HERE
(A, H, R, S)

Bedford's history dates back to the 1750s when Robert MacRay established a trading post on what was then America's western frontier. Settlers attempted to move in, but hostile Indians drove many away, and in 1758 the British established **Fort Bedford** to protect settlers against Indian attack. Fort Bedford lies on the Juniata River on the edge of downtown, and it's now a museum.

The British built the fort on a bluff above the Juniata River, giving soldiers control over the river. The original Fort Bedford lasted until the 1770s, and the **Fort Bedford Museum** is a replica of the original, but it still conveys the hardships that soldiers and settlers endured on the frontier. If you enjoy the comforts of modern life, a visit to Fort Bedford will make you glad that you didn't have to cross the country on a horse and catch or shoot your meals every day.

The British established Fort Bedford during the time of the French-Indian War, and they planned an assault on Fort Duquesne (now Pittsburgh) to establish control of the region. To do that, the Brits needed a road to transport supplies, and they hired settlers to widen an existing walking path into a

Old fashioned gas station

usable road. Travel became an important part of the regional economy, and at one time one of every three houses along the road was a tavern. Eventually, that road became part of the **Lincoln Highway,** or Route 30.

Bedford is right in the middle of the **Lincoln Highway Heritage Corridor,** a 145-mile stretch of Route 30 that works to preserve the road's historic past. Before the turnpike and Interstate 70, Route 30 was the major road across southern Pennsylvania. The Lincoln Highway was the first road to cross the United States, and it helped spark the idea of tourism. The gas stations, motels, and restaurants that sprang up beside the highway transformed the look of the country, and the road initiated the idea of driving from coast to coast. In many places, bypasses have taken Route 30 around cities, but the old sections of highway, such as the section of Route 30 that runs through downtown Bedford, are more interesting routes than the new superhighways.

Today, Bedford County is a major transportation hub. In the small town of Breezewood, I-70, the Pennsylvania Turnpike, and U.S. Route 30 come together, and Breezewood bills itself as **"The Town of Motels."** It's a good place to eat, sleep, and buy gasoline.

Back in 1794, when the roads were still pretty rough, **President Washington** led an army of 13,000 into western Pennsylvania to quell the **Whiskey Rebellion,** an uprising in which farmers were refusing to pay taxes. The **Espy House,** now a National Historic Landmark, served as Washington's headquarters during the first crucial test of the American constitution.

Over the years, agriculture became a large segment of the local economy, and Bedford grew into the biggest town for miles around, as well as the county seat. The **Bedford County Fair,** held the second week in August, has been displaying local livestock and produce for more than 125 years.

Downtown Bedford is a pleasant little place filled with historic sites, antique shops, restaurants, and bed & breakfast inns. The downtown is compact enough to allow visitors to walk comfortably from end to end. Weekend visitors can park the car on arrival and not need it for their entire stay.

Shoppers will enjoy strolling through downtown and browsing at the many antique shops. Bunched close together are six shops with antiques of many varieties. Mingled with the shops are seven notable historic sites, including the Espy House, Fort Bedford Museum, and the **Bedford County Court House,** which is the oldest court house still in use for judicial purposes in Pennsylvania. A brochure available at the visitors' bureau will guide you on a walking tour of downtown.

If you want to experience a bit of Americana, stop at the **Bedford Fairgrounds Speedway** on a Friday night. You don't have to be a fan of auto racing to enjoy one visit to a track. The action is fast, the sounds are loud, and the crowds are into it. This track is a half-mile dirt oval that hosts a variety of different racing cars. A night of racing is certainly an interesting way to begin a weekend getaway.

Outside the town, Bedford County is forests and farms, and the county's 14 covered bridges are scenic attractions. Bicycles provide an excellent way to see the region, and the local visitors bureau has created a series of six bike rides that will take you around the county. The rides range up to 46 miles, and the toughest are quite strenuous, while some of the shorter ones are relatively easy. For a brochure describing the rides, contact the Bedford County Visitors Bureau at 141 South Julianna Street in Bedford, PA 15522, (800) 765-3331.

If Bedford seems a little crowded, head east on Route 30 to **McConnellsburg** in Fulton County. The county has only about 15,000 residents, and McConnellsburg is the county's biggest town. Like Bedford, McConnellsburg is a historic place with many old buildings, and an easy walking tour will take you to many of them. Additionally, a driving tour will take you to many historic and recreational attractions around Fulton County, such as the **last Confederate Bivouac.** After burning Chambersburg on July 30, 1864 (a year after Gettysburg), Confederate soldiers camped for the night along Cove Creek and demanded 2,600 meals from the town's 550 people. This was the last Confederate camp on Union soil.

Bedford is a nice, small town, and McConnellsburg is a nice smaller town. For a country getaway with history and good shopping, take a drive along the Lincoln Highway in the center of Pennsylvania.

Attractions:

Fort Bedford Museum, Fort Bedford Drive, (800) 259-4284, open daily 10 A.M.-5 P.M.

Old Bedford Village, Route 220 North, Thur.-Tues., May to October, 9 A.M.-5 P.M.

Downtown shopping and **Historic District.**

Covered Bridges.

Dining:

Baker's Loaf, Pitt Street, Bedford, (814) 623-1108, open 8 A.M. daily.

Carriage House Restaurant, Route 220 North, Bedford, (814) 623-1174, Sun.-Thur., 11 A.M.-9 P.M., Fri., 11 A.M.-10 P.M., and Sat., 4 P.M.-10 P.M.

Espy House

Clara's Place, Route 220 North, Bedford, (814) 623-9006, open 6:30 A.M. daily.

Ed's Steak House, Route 220 North, Bedford, (814) 623-8894, open 7 A.M. daily.

Landmark Restaurant, South Juliana Street, Bedford, (814) 623-5488, open 7 A.M. daily.

Landmark Restaurant, East Pitt Street, Bedford, (814) 623-6762, open 7 A.M. daily.

Jean Bonnet Tavern, Route 30 and Route 31, Bedford, (814) 623-2250, open 11 A.M. daily, except 10 A.M. on Sundays.

Oralee's Golden Eagle Inn, East Pitt Street, Bedford, (814) 624-0800, open for lunch and dinner.

Lodging:

Best Western Bedford Inn, Route 220 North, (800) 752-8592.

Econo Lodge, Route 220 North, Bedford, (814) 623-5174.

Haven Rest Motel, Route 220 North, Bedford, (800) 932-8634.

Janey Lynn Motel, Route 220 North, Bedford, (814) 623-9515.

Judy's Motel, Route 220 North, (814) 623-9118.

Midway Motel, Route 220 North, Bedford, (814) 623-8107.

Quality Inn, Route 220 North, (814) 623-5188.

Bedford House Bed & Breakfast, 203 West Pitt Street, Bedford, (814) 623-7171.

Covered Bridge Inn, ½ mile from Route 30, west of Bedford, (814) 733-4093.

Jean Bonnet Tavern, Route 30 and Route 31, Bedford, (814) 623-2250.

Miss Charlotte's Victorian Bed & Breakfast, Penn Street, Bedford, (814) 624-0642.

Oralee's Golden Eagle Inn, Pitt Street, Bedford, (814) 624-0800.

Friendship Village Campground & RV Park, 548 Friendship Village, Bedford, (814) 623-1677.

Living Waters Hostel, Route 30, Schellsburg, (814) 733-4212.

Johnnie's Motel, 709 Lincoln Way East, McConnellsburg, (717) 485-3116.

Market Street Inn, 131 West Market Street, McConnellsburg, (717) 485-5495.

Shopping:

Candles 'N Things, 108 East Pitt Street, Bedford, (814) 623-8034, Mon.-Sat., 9 A.M.-5 P.M.

Deepwood Gallery, 102 East Pitt Street, Bedford, (814) 623-9175, 9 A.M.-6 P.M. daily, except Fridays, till 7 P.M., and Sundays, noon-4 P.M.

Elaine's Wearable Art, 104 East Pitt Street, Bedford, (814) 623-7216, daily 9 A.M.-7 P.M., Sun., noon-4 P.M.

Fisher's Country Store, Route 220, Cessna, (814) 623-2667, Mon.-Thur., 8 A.M.-5 P.M., Fri., 8 A.M.-8 P.M., and Sat., 8 A.M.-4 P.M.

Founder's Crossing, Julianna & Pitt Streets, Bedford, (814) 623-9120, Mon.-Sat., 10 A.M.-5 P.M., Sun., noon-4 P.M.

Little Barn Bake Shop, Route 30 West, Bedford, (814) 623-2603, Tues., Thur., and Fri., 8 A.M.-6 P.M., and Sat., 8 A.M.-4 P.M.

Graystone Galleria, Richard & Pitt Streets, Bedford, (814) 623-1768, daily 10 A.M.-5 P.M.

Heirlooms of Tomorrow, 138 East Pitt Street, Bedford, (814) 623-7970, Mon.-Thur., 9 A.M.-6 P.M., Fri., 9 A.M.-7 P.M., and Sat., 9 A.M.-5 P.M.

Lin's Touch of Elegance, 238 East Pitt Street, Bedford, (814) 623-2673, Mon.-Fri., 8 A.M.-5 P.M., Sat., 9 A.M.-5 P.M.

Annual Events:

Art Show & Sale, last three weeks of January and all of February, Art Center, Pitt Street, Bedford, (814) 623-1538.

Snow Board Weekend & Races, late January, Blue Knob Ski Area, (814) 239-5111.

Civil War Living History, late May, Old Bedford Village, (800) 238-4347.

Country Music Festival, second weekend in June, Old Bedford Village, (800) 238-4347.

Live Theater, Old Bedford Village Opera House, weekends in June, July, August, and September, (800) 238-4347.

Garden Art Show & Sale, July, Arts Center, Pitt Street, Bedford, (814) 623-1538.

Gospel Music Festival, Old Bedford Village, early August, (800) 238-4347.

Fulton County Fair, McConnellsburg, last week of August, (717) 485-4111.

Bedford County Fair, second week in August, (814) 623-9011.

Civil War Reenactment, Old Bedford Village, (800) 238-4347.

Juried Arts Exhibit, October, Arts Center, Pitt Street, (814) 623-1538.

Fall Foliage Festival, downtown Bedford, (800) 765-3331.

Apple Harvest Festival, early November, Old Bedford Village, (800) 238-4347.

Old Fashioned Country Christmas, Old Bedford Village, (800) 238-4347.

The Active Life:

The county's lightly traveled country roads are ideal for bicycling, and the tourist bureau has mapped out six routes of varying difficulties and distances.

Call the tourist bureau for a brochure or stop in the office at 141 South Juliana Street. Canoeing on the Juniata River is popular. **Adventure Marine** rents and sells canoes. Call (814) 623-1821 for information. Golfers can play at Down River Golf Course on Route 30 in Everett. Call (814) 652-5193 for information.

In winter, snow comes and skiers, snowmobilers, and sleigh riders take to the woods and fields. **Blue Knob State Park, Shawnee State Park,** and **Warriors Path State Park** are popular places for these activities.

A Great Place to Relax:

Beside Fort Bedford Museum is a little park where ducks swim in the lazy Juniata River. It's a nice place to sit and watch the river flow.

Covered Bridge

Covered Bridges:

Bedford County has 14, and they outnumber the traffic lights. The easiest to find is the Claycomb/Reynoldsdale Bridge at the entrance of Old Bedford Village. For a covered bridge guide, call the tourist bureau at (800) 765-3331.

Tourist Information:

• Bedford County Visitors Bureau, (800) 765-3331.

Where is it? Southwest quadrant, at the intersection of the Pennsylvania Turnpike, U.S. Route 30, and U.S. 220.

Getaway Rating: 3

5

BELLEFONTE/
STATE COLLEGE . . .
THE CENTRE OF IT ALL
(A, R, H, R&R)

Bellefonte is a lovely Victorian town that's the county seat of Centre County. Governors were one of its major products. Seven of them called Bellefonte home, and before Pennsylvania State University (Penn State) grew to prominence, Bellefonte was the most important town in the county.

Today, Bellefonte and State College are opposites in the pace of life. Bellefonte moves at a pleasant pace. Life at State College is hectic, and it reaches a level of congestion and excitement unmatched in Pennsylvania when the **Nittany Lions** attract 100,000 fans to **Beaver Stadium** on autumn Saturdays. On football weekends, the congestion doesn't stay exclusively in State College. Any lodging in the county sells out quickly, and hotel and motel employees recommend making reservations a year in advance if you want to stay in Centre County on a football weekend.

Bellefonte received its name from the famous French statesman Prince Talleyrand. He viewed Big Spring and remarked "La Belle Fonte," meaning "beautiful fountain." Big Spring is the third largest in Pennsylvania, producing 11.5 million gallons of water every day, and Spring Creek runs right through Bellefonte, where the downtown district has earned a place on the National Register of Historic Places.

Talleyrand Park

Bellefonte's early prosperity came from its iron industry. Nearby deposits of limestone, coal, and iron ore fueled the industry, and the limestone quarries are still flourishing. As a result of the early prosperity, mansions and hotels sprang up in town. Many are still in excellent condition, and they're some of the attractions on the self-guided walking tour. Several are now bed & breakfast inns, and a map available at the railroad station provides directions to the major attractions. Bellefonte has a rather compact downtown area. It's easy to walk around the entire shopping area and to the park and the railroad.

Adam of Art at 126 South Allegheny Street is a distinctive art galley in the downtown area. **Temple Court Crafters** at 114 South Allegheny Street sells items made by local artisans and crafters. The **Bellefonte Arts & Crafts Fair** in mid-August fills the streets with paintings and sculptures.

The atmosphere in Bellefonte will invite you to relax and take a leisurely walk. **Talleyrand Park,** beside Spring Creek, in the center of town, is an excellent place to do nothing. On the bridge across the creek is a vending machine that sells fish

Old Main, Penn State University

food, and many visitors delight in feeding the ducks and the large fish that live in the creek.

The **Bellefonte Historical Railroad** operates on weekends from the train station, which is in Talleyrand Park. The railroad operates on several different routes, and it's the only railroad in Pennsylvania that uses rail diesel cars (RDC's), which are the self-propelled passenger cars frequently used on commuter railroads.

State College came into existence when the state legislature picked a spot in the center of the state for **Penn State University,** which opened in 1855. Football is Penn State's most visible activity, but the 40,000+ students also go to class, and a primary economic activity in State College is supplying food and other necessities to the students. State College isn't a warm weather spot, but it has become a retirement community, and many older citizens enjoy the activities provided by the huge university.

The shopping is good in downtown State College. Penn State T-shirts are the most popular items, and you'll find much more. Restaurants of all descriptions and specialty shops line the downtown streets. The "must go" dining place is **The Corner Room** at College & Allen streets, right across College Avenue from **The Wall,** where college students sit and talk about the state of the world and other topics. The Corner Room is a casual place that's been in business since 1855.

Without question, the liveliest weekends in State College occur when the football team has a home game. Beaver Stadium holds about 100,000 fans, and getting that many people into a college town creates traffic jams on the roads, on the sidewalks, and in the restaurants. The game also brings a special excitement to the town. Many fans arrive a day or two before the game and stay in their RV's throughout the weekend. It's an enjoyable weekend, unless you don't like crowds.

Almost as lively, but with an entirely different atmosphere, is the weekend of the **Central Pennsylvania Festival of the Arts** in July. As many as 200,000 people crowd the streets to enjoy the art, music, fun, and food, and the whole region is extremely crowded for those three days. If you want an entirely different view of State College, practically a "private viewing," come in late July or early August when school isn't in session. For those few weeks, State College is a quiet place.

If you choose to go to Centre County on a football weekend, a good piece of advice is to **avoid Route 322** from Harrisburg to State College. That road often becomes a big parking lot, so it's good to take any other route. When traffic isn't a problem, that section of Route 322 is one of the most scenic roads anywhere. It runs beside the **Juniata River** for many miles and provides numerous scenic views.

Outside State College and Bellefonte, Centre County is small towns, farms, and forested mountains. An intriguing natural landmark is **Penn's Cave,** America's only all-water cavern. Stalactites and stalagmites in mysterious formations such as curtains, cascades, and pillars fill the cavern. The grounds of Penn's Cave are also home to a wildlife sanctuary where North American animals such as deer, elk, mountain lions, and wolves live. Penn's Cave is on Route 192 east of State College.

Beaver Stadium, Penn State University

Call (814) 364-1664 for information or visit the web site at http://www.pennscave.com.

East of State College on Route 322 is **Boalsburg,** home of the **Pennsylvania Military Museum.** The museum honors Pennsylvania's soldiers, beginning with Benjamin Franklin's first military unit, "The Associators." Shrines and monuments cover the museum's 66 acres.

The 28th Division Shrine honors members of the Pennsylvania National Guard who died during World War I, and Route 322 carries the name "28th Division Highway."

Six state parks provide plenty of opportunities for outdoor activities. **Bald Eagle State Park** has a 1,730 acre lake, as well as an environmental center, hiking trails, and bike rentals. **Black Moshannon State Park** has a 250-acre lake, trails, and modern cabins that visitors can rent.

Like many counties in Pennsylvania, Centre County has a strong **Amish** presence. Their farms fill many of the fertile valleys in the eastern part of the county along Routes 45 and 192. In summer and fall you can buy fresh farm goods from many roadside stands.

Centre County is a land of pleasing contrasts. The quiet of

the countryside, the relaxed atmosphere of Bellefonte, and the frenzied feeling of a football weekend in State College all make enjoyable getaways.

Attractions:

Victorian Bellefonte

Curtin Village, Route 150, Bellefonte, (814) 355-1982, Memorial Day-Labor Day, Wed.-Sat., 10 A.M.-5 P.M., Sun., 1 P.M.-5 P.M., weekends only Labor Day through mid-October.

Bellefonte Historical Railroad, High Street, (814) 355-0311, Sat. and Sun., 1 P.M. and 3 P.M., occasional dinner trains.

Talleyrand Park in Bellefonte, High Street. (See also "A Great Place to Relax")

Pennsylvania Military Museum, Route 322, Boalsburg, (814) 466-6263, Tues.-Sat., 9 A.M.-5 P.M., Sun., noon-5 P.M.

Penn's Cave, Route 192, Centre Hall, (814) 364-1664, 9 A.M.-5 P.M. daily, June 1 through August 31, 'till 7 P.M.

Downtown State College, 1402 South Atherton Street, State College, PA, (800) 358-5466.

Penn State football games

Dining:

Allen Street Grill, 100 West College Avenue, State College, (814) 231-4745, 11 A.M.-2 A.M. daily.

Autoport, 1405 South Atherton Street, State College, (814) 238-2333, 6 A.M.-midnight daily.

Bonfatto's, 213 West High Street, Bellefonte, (814) 355-2638, breakfast, lunch, and dinner daily.

Cafe 210 West, 210 West College Avenue, State College, (814) 237-3449, lunch and dinner daily.

Corner Room, College & Allen, State College, (717) 237-3051, open all day.

Duffy's Boalsburg Tavern, 113 East Main Street, Boalsburg, (814) 466-6241, dinner daily at 5 P.M.

The Gamble Mill Tavern, Lamb Street Bridge along Spring Creek, Bellefonte, (814) 355-7764, Mon.-Sat., 11:30 A.M. for lunch, 5 P.M. for dinner.

India Pavilion, Calder Square, State College, (814) 237-3400, 11 A.M.-2:30 P.M. and 5 P.M.-10 P.M. daily.

Original Italian Pizza, 222 West Beaver Avenue, State College, (814) 231-1202, Mon.-Sat., 11 A.M.-midnight, Sun., noon-11 P.M.

Panda House, 1880 South Atherton Street, State College, (814) 238-1070, 11:30 A.M.-10 P.M. daily.

Schnitzel's Tavern, 315 West High Street, Bellefonte, (814) 355-4230, Sun.-Thur., 11:30 A.M.-9 P.M., Fri. and Sat., 11:30 A.M.-10 P.M.

Spats Café, 142 East College Avenue, State College, (814) 238-7010, Mon.-Sat., lunch and dinner.

The Tavern Restaurant, 220 East College Avenue, State College, (814) 238-6116, opens at 4 P.M. daily.

Waffle Shop, 127 West Bishop Street, Bellefonte, (814) 355-7761, Mon.-Sat., 6 A.M.-3 P.M., Sun., 7 A.M.-3 P.M.

Whistle Stop Restaurant, Route 144, Centre Hall, (814) 364-2544, opens at 11 A.M. daily, 8 A.M. on Sat.

Lodging:

Bush House Hotel, 315 West High Street, Bellefonte, (814) 355-8400.

Dartt House, 252 North Allegheny Street, Bellefonte, (814) 353-0408.

Garrett, 217 West Linn Street, Bellefonte, (814) 355-3093.

Knights Inn, 476 Benner Pike, Bellefonte, (814) 355-5561.

Natt House, 127 West Curtin Street, Bellefonte, (814) 353-1456.

Reynolds Mansion Bed & Breakfast, 101 West Linn Street, Bellefonte, (800) 899-3929.

Selgate House, 176 Armagast Road, Bellefonte, (814) 353-1102.

Yocum's Victorian, 313 East Linn Street, Bellefonte, (814) 355-5100.

Atherton Hotel, 125 South Atherton Street, State College, (814) 231-2100.

Autoport, 1405 South Atherton Street, State College, (800) 932-7678.

Hampton Inn, 1101 East College Avenue, State College, (814) 237-6300.

Nittany Lion Inn, 200 West Park Avenue, State College, (800) 233-7505.

Sleep Inn, 111 Village Drive, State College, (814) 235-1020.

Stevens Motel, 1275 North Atherton Street, State College, (814) 238-2438.

Toftrees Resort, 1 Country Club Lane, State College, (800) 252-3551.

Windswept Farm, 1000 Filmore Road, State College, (814) 355-1233.

Bellefonte KOA Kampground, Route 26 North, (814) 355-7912.

For a brochure on **Bed & Breakfasts** in this region, call **Rest & Repast,** (814) 238-1484.

Shopping:

A Basket Full, 105 West Main Street, Boalsburg, (814) 466-7788, Mon.-Sat., 10 A.M.-5 P.M., Sun., noon-4 P.M.

Adam & Art, 126 South Allegheny Street, Bellefonte, (814) 353-1450, Tues., Thur., and Sat., 11 A.M.-5 P.M.

Apple Hill Antiques, 105 Gerald Street, State College, (814) 238-2980, 10 A.M.-6 P.M. daily.

Balleywicks, 122 East Main Street, Boalsburg, (814) 466-6320, Mon.-Sat., 10 A.M.-5 P.M., Sun., noon-5 P.M.

Country Sampler, Village Square, Boalsburg, (814) 466-7402, Mon.-Sat., 9:30 A.M.-5 P.M., Sun., noon-4 P.M.

Hayloft Antiques, 660 Benner Pike, Bellefonte, (814) 355-7588, Wed.-Mon., 10 A.M.-5 P.M.

Ken's Boot Shop, 123 South Allegheny Street, Bellefonte,

(814) 355-3202, Mon., Wed., Fri., and Sat., 9 A.M.-5 P.M., Tues. and Thur., 9 A.M.-8:30 P.M.

Lindsay's On The Diamond, 104 West Main Street, Boalsburg, (814) 466-7775, Mon.-Sat., 10 A.M.-5 P.M.

Nittany Mall, Routes 26 and 150, State College, (814) 238-8037, Mon.-Sat., 10 A.M.-9 P.M., Sun., 11 A.M.-5 P.M.

Rapid Transit Sportswear, 115 South Allen Street, State College, (814) 238-3831, Mon.-Sat., 8 A.M.-9 P.M., Sun., 9 A.M.-6 P.M.

Serendipity Valley Farm, 122 East Main Street, Boalsburg, (814) 466-7282, Mon.-Sat., 10 A.M.-5 P.M.

Seven Mountain Books, 111 South Pugh Street, State College, (814) 234-9712, Mon.-Sat., 9:30 A.M.-7 P.M., Sun., 11 A.M.-5 P.M.

Temple Court Crafters, 114 North Allegheny Street, Bellefonte, (814) 353-1631, Tues., Wed., and Fri., 10 A.M.-5 P.M., Thur., 10 A.M.-7 P.M., and Sat., 9 A.M.-5 P.M.

Annual Events:

Penn State football games are the most famous happenings in Happy Valley, but they don't put any more people on the streets of State College than the Central Pennsylvania Festival of the Arts does. Held in July, it turns the downtown into a big party for five days.

Blue & White football game, April, Beaver Stadium.

Civil War Encampment, May, Curtin Village, (814) 355-1982.

Big Fish Feed, third Saturday in May, Bellefonte, (814) 355-2917.

Nittany Antique Machinery Association, June, Penn's Cave, (814) 364-9855.

Penn's Woods Summer Music Festival, June and July, Penn State, (814) 863-1118.

Crafts & Collectibles, June, Curtin Village, (814) 355-1982.

Central Pennsylvania Festival of the Arts, July, State College, (814) 237-3682.

Ag Progress Days, August, Rock Springs, (814) 865-2081.

Bellefonte Arts & Crafts Fair, August, (814) 355-2917.

Football, September, October, and November, Penn State.

Apple Butter Day, second Saturday in October, Curtin Village, (814) 355-1982.

Bellefonte Victorian Christmas, December, (814) 355-2917.

The Active Life:

You can do something here that you can't do many other places in Pennsylvania. You can go "gliding" in a glider (an airplane without an engine). You can do this at the **Keystone Gliderport** in Julian. For information, call (814) 355-2483.

Penn State has a huge recreational complex, with swimming pools, skating rinks, and running tracks. Many are open to the public at different times. Call (814) 863-1311 for information.

In the valleys, bicycling is enjoyable. One good place to start a ride is **Penn's Cave** on Route 192 in Centre Hall. Golfers and skiers can enjoy their favorite sports at **Tussey Mountain Ski Area & Golf Course** on Route 322 in Boalsburg. Golfers can also try the courses at Penn State. Call (814) 865-1833 for information.

A Great Place to Relax:

Talleyrand Park, in the center of Bellefonte, is excellent for feeding fish and ducks. Bring a collection of quarters for the little vending machines that sell food for the fish and ducks. Then there is **The Wall,** along College Avenue in State College. The Wall and the adjacent **Old Main** are major hangouts for Penn State students.

Covered Bridges:

There's one on private property on Route 144, South of Bellefonte.

Tourist Information:

• Call (800) 358-5466 for information.

Where is it? In the exact center of the state, along U.S. 322 and Interstate 80.

Getaway Rating: 3

A Note on Football Weekends:

The roads in the area can't handle the traffic—it starts on Friday and continues until game time. The worst road is Route 322, which is the primary route for fans coming from the east.

Also, it's impossible to get a room anywhere in Centre County when Penn State has a home game if you don't make reservations well in advance.

If you do have reservations, or a motorhome, football weekends are great times to visit. If you don't go to the game, you'll find the streets empty during the game and jammed both before and after.

Talleyrand Park

6

BIRD-IN-HAND/ INTERCOURSE . . . AMISH COUNTRY
(R, PT)

Bird-In-Hand and Intercourse are in the heart of Amish Country, and a visit to the small towns will give you a good look at the agrarian lifestyle of the Amish. The Amish own most of the farms in this region. Their buggies are frequent sights on the roads, and their horse-drawn equipment is frequently visible in farm fields. The Amish also work in many local businesses. Many attractions have "Amish" in their names, but the Amish don't own any business that says "Amish."

About the Names. Nobody's really sure how **Intercourse** got its name. It was formerly Cross Keys, and theories abound on how that name became Intercourse. **Bird-In-Hand** takes its name from an old tavern. In the nation's early days, many people couldn't read, so commercial establishments often had distinctive signs. The sign on a tavern here showed a man with a bird in his hand, and that's how this name came about.

About 10 miles from Bird-In-Hand is the village of **Blue Ball,** which got its name from a blue ball that graced a tavern, and if you think that taverns are common around here, you're right. The nation's first turnpike opened in 1794 and extended

Conestoga Wagon at Bird-In-Hand Farmer's Market

68 miles from Lancaster to Philadelphia. Along that route were 62 taverns, and at least one of them, **The White Horse Inn,** in eastern Lancaster County on Route 340, is still operating.

On many farms in this area you'll see "cottage" industries. To supplement their farm incomes and to stay busy during the winter, the Amish make quilts, crafts, and woodwork. If you're looking to buy any of these items, you'll save significantly by buying directly from the makers.

The biggest attraction in Bird-In-Hand is the **Bird-In-Hand Farmers Market.** At this air-conditioned market you can buy produce fresh from the farm, as well as many other foods and crafts. At the **Bird-In-Hand Bakery,** Pennsylvania Dutch baked goods, such as shoo-fly pies and breads, are available for purchase and for shipping to friends in places where they can't buy shoo-fly pies.

The best way to experience the Amish country is to get off the main highways. The real Amish country lies on the quiet country roads where one farm runs into another, and the best way to see the area is to ride a bike. On a 10-mile ride from

Bird-In-Hand you can see the Amish at work in their fields, roadside stands bursting with fresh produce and baked goods, a covered bridge, and many places that sell quilts and wooden goods. The area around Bird-In-Hand is relatively flat, and anyone who can ride a bike at all can handle a ride there.

One cottage business with a strong and loyal following is **Miller's Natural Foods,** located on an Amish farm on Monterey Road, just north of Bird-In-Hand. At Miller's, prices are considerably lower than at natural foods stores in suburban malls, and customers drive many miles to shop there.

To reach Miller's from Bird-In-Hand, go to the traffic light at the intersection of Route 340 and North Ronks Road. Go north to the T-intersection, then go right. At the next intersection, turn left. Miller's is about a quarter of a mile ahead, on the right.

Several attractions offer insights into Amish life. The **Amish Country Homestead,** on Route 340, is an authentically furnished Old Order Amish home of today. "Old Order" Amish are the most conservative. They favor retaining the old customs, meaning those maintained before 1878, when major divisions occurred.

The **Weavertown One Room Schoolhouse** depicts life in a one-room schoolhouse, like those still used by the Amish. If you travel through the region, you'll see many one-room Amish schools. Amish children go to school for eight years, and their own school system is a relatively new concept, whose origins weren't entirely religious. It didn't begin until the early 1940s, when bussing threatened to take Amish children far from home. In response, the Amish established their own school system.

Just east of Bird-In-Hand is the equally small village of Intercourse, which has more tourist attractions than Bird-In-Hand. The biggest is **Kitchen Kettle Village,** a collection of food, craft, and collectibles shops. Beside Kitchen Kettle Village is **The People's Place,** an attraction that offers objective insights into the lives of the Amish and Mennonites. The People's Place has a museum, and it shows a documentary film called *Who are the Amish?*

Quilt Museum in Intercourse

Also in Intercourse is **The Old Country Store,** where you'll often see the cars of tourists parked beside the horse-drawn buggies of local Amish residents who shop here for the basics, such as the fabrics to make their clothes and quilts.

Intercourse has a large food presence, and the dining is casual. The **Intercourse Pretzel Factory** makes soft pretzels, hard pretzels, stuffed pretzels, and chocolate pretzels. You can sit and eat at the factory. **Harvest Drive Family Restaurant** offers large portions and a view of the farmlands. **Stoltzfus Farm Restaurant** does the same.

Along Route 340 are many shops that sell Amish quilts and crafts. You can buy them there, or you can attend a "mud sale." These are sales held to benefit volunteer fire companies, and they offer a look into the local culture that you won't get from the tourist attractions. The most famous mud sale takes place at the **Gordonville Fire Company** on a Saturday in early March. Amish women make quilts and donate them. Also for sale are Amish buggies and many other items. Many outsiders find it interesting that some Amish buggies have radios on the dashboards.

At the intersection of Stumptown and 772 is the **Mascot Roller Mill**. This 19th-century mill is now a tourist attraction where visitors can see corn ground into flour. The mill is open from May through October, and admission is free.

Roadside Stands

For an unusual and pleasant shopping experience, seek out a roadside stand or two. There, you'll find produce fresh from the field, as well as baked goods, crafts, and maybe even some home-brewed root beer. Stands are everywhere in this region. Many farms operate them in summer, and some are open almost all year.

One good and interesting stand is on an Amish farm on Stumptown Road, just north of Route 772. In addition to produce, this stand sells baked goods, homemade root beer, and souvenirs such as painted milk cans. To reach the stand, take 772 West from Intercourse. At the intersection with Stumptown Road, turn right. The stand is about a quarter mile ahead on the right.

One intriguing place to shop is **Riehl's Quilts & Crafts** at 247 Eby Road, right at the end of Stumptown Road, just a quarter of a mile from the roadside stand. Riehl's sells quilts made right on the Amish dairy farm, as well as smaller items such as pillows. Visitors can talk to the proprietor and the seamstresses, and the shop takes credit cards.

For other good places to shop, simply take a ride down a country road. Almost every Amish farm has a stand or a shop, and you'll find many items that you won't find in the malls.

About the Amish

The first thing to know is that they're not actors. Local lore is full of stories of visitors who walked onto Amish farms and became angry because the "actors" wouldn't pose for pictures.

Amish is a religion, and a very conservative one. To a true Amish believer, material goods have no inherent value. Acquiring wealth for wealth's sake is not a goal in Amish life. God, family, and work are the things of importance to the Amish.

The Amish don't own cars and many other modern conveniences, but that doesn't mean that they believe that those things are inherently evil. Instead, the Amish fear that cars and other worldly goods will pull families apart, so they generally don't allow their use.

However, many of these rules have some apparent contradictions. Take telephones. At the end of many Amish farm lanes are little sheds with phones. The Amish use the phones for business purposes, but housewives won't sit and talk for hours. And young "Amish" people may own cars. Actually, these young people aren't officially Amish. The Amish are Anabaptists, which means that they have adult baptism. Thus, a person isn't officially Amish until he or she joins the church. So, it's okay for someone who hasn't joined the church to own a car and to do many of the things that other Americans do.

Ultimately, the Amish are not intrinsically different from anyone else. They're looking for happiness in this life and salvation in the next. They dress differently, and they work very hard, but they're just people. To them, nothing is harder to understand than their role as tourist attractions.

The Amish live in many areas in Lancaster County, and the area around Bird-In-Hand and Intercourse is an Amish stronghold and a good place to learn something about them and to buy the things that they produce.

Amish Names

Most Amish in Lancaster County have one of five names— Beiler, Glick, King, Lapp, and Stoltzfus. If you see one of these names on a business, especially a small business on a country road, it's probably Amish. One exception is **King Buffet** on Route 30. That's a Chinese restaurant.

Common Mennonite names are Martin, Weaver, and Zimmerman. On some roads, you'll see mailbox after mailbox with one of these names.

Attractions:

Bird-In-Hand Farmers Market, Route 340 and Maple Avenue,

(717) 393-9674, Wed.-Sat., 8:30 A.M.-5:30 P.M., April-November, and Fridays and Saturdays all year.

Weavertown One Room Schoolhouse, Route 340 between Bird-In-Hand and Intercourse, (717) 768-3976, opens daily at 9 A.M., Good Friday through the end of October.

Amish Country Homestead, Route 340, (717) 768-3600, Mon.-Sat., 10:30 A.M.-4:30 P.M.

Scenic farms, everywhere.

One-room schoolhouses, everywhere.

Bird-In-Hand Bake Shop, 542 Gibbons Road, (717) 656-7947, Mon.-Sat., 9 A.M.-5 P.M.

Kitchen Kettle Village, Intercourse, (800) 732-3538, Mon.-Sat., 9 A.M.-5 P.M.

Miller's Natural Foods, Monterey Road, Mon.-Fri., 7 A.M.-5 P.M., Sat., 7 A.M.-4 P.M. (No phone number.)

Dining:

Amish Barn, Route 340 between Bird-In-Hand and Intercourse, (717) 768-8886, 8 A.M.-9 P.M. daily.

Bird-In-Hand Family Restaurant, 2760 Old Philadelphia Pike, (717) 768-8266, Mon.-Sat., 6 A.M.-8 P.M.

Good 'N Plenty, Route 896, Smoketown, (717) 394-7111, Mon.-Sat., 11:30 A.M.-8 P.M.

Harvest Drive Family Restaurant, 3370 Harvest Drive, Intercourse, (717) 768-4510, hours vary by season.

Kling House Restaurant, Route 340, Intercourse, (717) 768-7300, Mon.-Wed., 8 A.M.-4 P.M., Thur.-Sat., 8 A.M.-8 P.M.

Plain & Fancy Farm, Route 340 between Bird-In-Hand and Intercourse, (717) 768-4400, open daily, hours vary by season.

Shady Maple Farm, Route 23, Blue Ball, (717) 354-8222, Mon.-Sat., 8 A.M.-8 P.M.

Stoltzfus Farm Restaurant, Route 772 East, Intercourse, (717) 768-8156, Mon.-Sat., 11:30 A.M.-8 P.M.

Lodging:

Amish Country Motel, 3013 Old Philadelphia Pike, Bird-In-Hand, (800) 538-2535.

Best Western Intercourse, Routes 340 and 772, (717) 768-3636.

Bird-In-Hand Inn, 2740 Old Philadelphia Pike, (800) 537-2535.

Comfort Inn of New Holland, 624 West Main Street (Route 23), (717) 355-9900.

Harvest Drive Motel, 3370 Harvest Drive, Intercourse, (717) 768-7186.

Smoketown Motor Lodge, 190 East Brook Road, Smoketown, (717) 397-6944.

Traveler's Rest Motel, 3701 Old Philadelphia Pike, Intercourse, (800) 626-2021.

Artist's Inn & Gallery, 117 East Main Street, Terre Hill, (717) 445-0219.

Carriage Corner Bed & Breakfast, 3705 East Newport Road, Intercourse, (800) 209-3059.

Churchtown Inn Bed & Breakfast, Route 23, Churchtown, (800) 637-4446.

Greystone Manor Bed & Breakfast, 2658 Old Philadelphia Pike, Bird-In-Hand, (717) 393-4233.

Intercourse Village Bed & Breakfast, Route 340, (800) 664-0949.

Mill Creek Homestead Bed & Breakfast, 2758 Old Philadelphia Pike, Bird-In-Hand, (717) 291-6419.

Shopping:

Amishland Prints, 3504 Old Philadelphia Pike, Intercourse, (717) 768-7273, Mon.-Sat., 10 A.M.-5 P.M.

Bird-In-Hand Bake Shop, 542 Gibbons Road, (717) 656-7947, Mon.-Sat., 9 A.M.-5 P.M.

Bird-In-Hand Farmers' Market, Route 340, (717) 393-9674, Wed.-Sat., 8:30 A.M.-5:30 P.M., April-November, and Fridays and Saturdays all year.

Crafts of the World, Route 340, Intercourse, (717) 768-7171, Mon.-Sat., 9 A.M.-5 P.M.

Family Creations, 3453 Old Philadelphia Pike, Intercourse, (717) 768-8651, Mon.-Sat., 9 A.M.-5 P.M.

Glick's Quilts & Crafts, 333 Monterey Road, Bird-In-Hand, Mon.-Sat., 8 A.M.-5 P.M.

Intercourse Pretzel Factory, 3614 Old Philadelphia Pike, (717) 768-3432, Mon.-Sat., 9 A.M.-6 P.M.

Kitchen Kettle Village, Route 340, Intercourse, (800) 732-3538, Mon.-Sat., 9 A.M.-5 P.M.

Lapp's Coach Shop, Route 772, Intercourse, (717) 768-8712, Mon.-Sat., 9 A.M.-5 P.M.

Moore Bears, 2685 Old Philadelphia Pike, Bird-In-Hand, (717) 391-1081, Mon.-Sat., 9 A.M.-5 P.M.

Marian Stoltzfus Quilts, 3066 Irishtown Road, Bird-In-Hand, (717) 768-8690, Mon.-Sat., 9 A.M.-5 P.M.

The Old Candle Barn, 3551 Old Philadelphia Pike, Intercourse, (717) 768-3231, Mon.-Sat., 9 A.M.-5 P.M.

The Old Country Store, Route 340, Intercourse, (717) 768-7101, open 9 A.M.-8 P.M. Memorial Day through Halloween, 9 A.M.-5 P.M. the rest of the year.

The Old Village Store, Route 340, Bird-In-Hand, (717) 397-1291, Mon.-Sat., 9 A.M.-5:30 P.M.

Riehl's Quilts & Crafts, 247 Eby Road, Bird-In-Hand, Mon.-Sat., dawn to dusk.

Somewhere In Tyme, 2680 Old Philadelphia Pike, Bird-In-Hand, (717) 295-9224, Mon.-Sat., 9 A.M.-5 P.M.

Speedway Express Wagons, 1090 Mondale Road, Bird-In-Hand, (717) 656-9605, Mon.-Fri., 9 A.M.-5 P.M.

Susquehanna Glass, Route 340, Bird-In-Hand, (717) 393-5670, Mon.-Sat., 9 A.M.-5:30 P.M.

Village Peddler, 3520 Old Philadelphia Pike, Intercourse, (717) 768-3414, Mon.-Sat., 9 A.M.-5:30 P.M.

Wild Goose Gallery, Route 340, Intercourse, (717) 768-8611, Mon.-Sat., 10 A.M.-5:30 P.M.

Witmer's Quilt Shop, 1070 West Main Street, New Holland, (717) 656-9526, Mon.-Sat., 9:30 A.M.-5:30 P.M.

Notes:

• *Some businesses owned by the Amish don't have phones.*
• *Route 340 and Old Philadelphia Pike are the same road.*

Annual Events:

Gordonville Fire Company Sales, March and September, (717) 768-3869.

Rhubarb Festival, May, Kitchen Kettle Village, Intercourse, (800) 732-3538.

Route 340 Food & Folk Fair, third weekend in June, Bird-In-Hand, (717) 768-8272.

The Active Life:

You won't find any recreational areas in Bird-In-Hand or Intercourse, but the country roads are superb for bicycling. The region is reasonably flat, and if you get off the highways, the traffic isn't bad. On a pristine autumn morning, the scenery is spectacular, as Amish children walk through the canyons of corn to their one-room schoolhouses. The **Lancaster Host Resort** is the nearest golf course. Call (717) 299-5500 for information.

A Great Place to Relax:

Head over to the **Bird-In-Hand Bake Shop** on Gibbons Road, get something to eat, such as ice cream, sit on a picnic table, and watch the corn grow. To reach the bake shop from Route 340, turn north on Beechdale Road, just east of the railroad bridge. Go about half a mile and turn right on Gibbons Road.

Covered Bridges:

Many are nearby. The easiest to find is on Belmont Road,

south of Intercourse and about ½ mile north of Route 30. From Intercourse, go east on Route 772, and then immediately right on Queen Lane. Go right on Harvest Road and left on Belmont to the bridge. Then make a left on Queen Lane and you'll come back to Intercourse without encountering busy Route 30.

Tourist Information:

• (800) PA-DUTCH.

Where is it? Southeastern quadrant, on PA Route 340.

Getaway Rating: 3

Advertisement for fire company sale

7

THE BRANDYWINE VALLEY . . .
THE DUPONTS
AND THE WYETHS
(A, H, R)

Perched on the edge of Philadelphia, The Brandywine Valley is a land of gracious estates, beautiful horse farms, and many historic sites. The best known attraction is **Longwood Gardens,** which is home to one of the world's great collections of flowers and plants. On the western edge of the valley is an industry that doesn't seem to match the character of the estates and the gardens—around Kennett Square, the primary industry is mushroom growing, which gives the air a different aroma than the roses at Longwood Gardens.

Something is always blooming at Longwood Gardens. The estate dates back to 1798 when the descendants of George Pierce began planting an arboretum that, by 1850, had become one of the best in the nation. In 1906, Pierre du Pont purchased the farm to preserve the trees, and from then until his death in 1954 he personally designed most of the gardens that are still in operation today.

Longwood covers 1,050 acres of gardens, woodlands, and meadows, with expansive indoor gardens and greenhouses. More than 11,000 different types of plants grow here, and one of the major attractions is Longwood's ability to fool Mother

Longwood Gardens

Nature. Tropical plants grow profusely in controlled environ-
ments, and when snow covers the grounds, the blooming continues indoors.

Throughout the year, Longwood offers festivals, concerts,
and educational programs. You can learn how to grow your
own bonsai trees, enjoy a chamber music concert, and watch a
Festival of Fountains. Longwood is open all year, and you can
easily spend an entire day here.

A few miles down Route 1 from Longwood is the **Brandywine
River Museum,** a showcase for American art. Originally a Civil
War-era grist mill, the museum is famous for its collection of
art works by members of the **Wyeth** family, who live nearby.

Works by Andrew, N.C., and Jamie Wyeth highlight the collection. Examples are *The Hunter* by N.C. Wyeth and *Roasted
Chestnuts* by Andrew Wyeth. Other important artists represent-
ed here are Howard Pyle, Jasper Cropsey, Trost Richards, and
Harvey Dunn.

The **Andrew Wyeth Gallery** houses approximately 40 water-
color, dry brush, and tempera paintings by Andrew Wyeth,
including some of his recent works. At the museum, visitors

can dine in a restaurant in a glass tower that overlooks the Brandywine River. Native wildflower gardens and a trail beside the river allow visitors to enjoy the tranquil beauty of the area.

Also on Route 1 is the **Brandywine Battlefield Park.** The Battle of the Brandywine, fought on September 11, 1777, was a victory for the British during the American Revolution. Intending to capture Philadelphia, Gen. William Howe landed on Chesapeake Bay with 15,000 men and moved north toward the city.

George Washington met him at Brandywine Creek with an army of 11,000. Howe successfully used a flanking movement to drive the Americans from the field, but Washington managed to withdraw most of his troops safely.

From there, the British moved to comfortable winter quarters in Philadelphia while the Americans headed for a brutal winter at Valley Forge.

Throughout the Brandywine area, deer are common sights. The large estates are perfect grazing grounds for deer, but horses are the stars in this valley, and horse shows allow them to strut their stuff. The most famous of the shows takes place in Devon during the last week of May. Jumpers, hunters, and many other categories of horses are the attractions, and the show is also a costume party. No one would think of mounting up without exactly the right outfit, especially the right hat.

The **Devon Horse Show** (last week in May) also includes a country fair, so there's fun for everyone with rides, games, and an abundance of food. The Devon Horse Show grounds are on Route 30. Call (610) 688-2554 for information.

At Devon the emphasis is on jumping, style, and show, and at the **Radnor Hunt Steeplechase Races** (third Sunday in May), speed counts. Held in mid-May, the steeplechases are real races run over difficult courses for attractive purses. Post is at 1:30 P.M. For information call (610) 647-4233.

Downtown West Chester is attracting new antique and furniture shops, as well as restaurants. The town is home to West Chester University and the **Chester County Historical Society.** One business that operates in West Chester now finds its way into most American homes. **QVC,** a television shopping network, operates 24 hours a day, seven days a week, and a studio tour allows visitors to see how the operation functions. The tours run from 10 A.M. to 4 P.M., and QVC's address is Studio Park, West Chester, PA. Call (800) 600-9900 for details.

Farther north is Downingtown, home of the **Struble Trail,** a 3-mile rail trail that's ideal for easy exercise. Walkers and leisurely bicyclists will enjoy a trek over this flat course.

Valley Forge National Historical Park is the site where the American army spent six harsh months in 1777 and 1778. It was the campground of 11,000 troops of George Washington's Continental Army from December 19, 1777, to June 19, 1778. Because of the suffering endured by the hungry and badly housed troops, 2,500 of whom died during the harsh winter, Valley Forge came to symbolize the heroism of the American revolutionaries.

Today, Valley Forge is an oasis of tranquility in an area of suburban sprawl. The Pennsylvania turnpike and many other busy roads, office parks, and shopping centers are nearby, but the park is quiet. A network of trails runs through the park, and the trails are popular with walkers, bicyclists, and runners. Down by the Schuylkill is the **Schuylkill River Trail,** a rail trail that goes for almost 25 miles and ends at Fairmont Park in Philadelphia.

On the Brandywine Valley's western edge, it takes on an agricultural air. Mushrooms are Pennsylvania's biggest cash crop, and this is the biggest mushroom-growing region in the state.

At the **Phillips Mushroom Museum** on Route 1 near Kennett Square, you can see how the mushroom-growing process works. Because they're fungi, mushrooms don't grow the way other crops grow. Mushrooms grow inside under controlled conditions. Mushrooms of many varieties are for sale here. Call (610) 388-6082 for information. They are open daily, 10 A.M.-6 P.M.

To see how potatoes become potato chips, visit **Herr's** on Route 272 in Nottingham. There, a tour will show you the mass production of chips. Trucks loaded with tons of potatoes dump their spuds to start the process, and it's not long until they

Phillips Mushroom Museum

become potato chips. The tour is free and you can sample warm chips right off the line. Call (800) 284-7488 for information. They are open Mon.-Thur., 9 A.M.-3 P.M., and Fri., 9 A.M.-11 A.M.

The Brandywine River empties into the Delaware near Wilmington, and the Brandywine Valley includes part of northern Delaware. **Winterthur Museum** has one of the world's best collections of American decorative arts, made or used in the United States before 1860. Henry Francis du Pont assembled the collection, which is now in two buildings. The property also includes almost 1,000 acres of gardens that visitors can explore on foot or by tram.

The Brandywine Valley is a gracious place where you can always vacation in style.

Attractions:

Longwood Gardens, Route 1, Chadds Ford, (610) 388-1000, opens at 9 A.M. daily all year long.

Brandywine River Museum, Route 1, Chadds Ford, (610) 388-2700, 9:30 A.M.-4:30 P.M. daily.

Longwood Gardens

Phillips Mushroom Museum, Route 1, Kennett Square, (610) 388-6082, 10 A.M.-6 P.M. daily.

Herr's Snack Food Factory Tour, Route 272, Nottingham, (800) 284-7488, Mon.-Thur., 9 A.M.-3 P.M., Fri., 9 A.M.-11 A.M.

Brandywine Battlefield Park, Route 1, Chadds Ford, (610) 459-3342, Tues.-Sat., 9 A.M.-5 P.M., Sun., noon-5 P.M.

Dining:

Alberto's Newtown Square, 191 South Newtown Street, Newtown Square, (610) 356-9700, lunch and dinner daily.

Chadds Ford Café, 95 Baltimore Pike, Chadds Ford, (610) 558-3960, lunch, dinner, and Sunday brunch.

Chadds Ford Inn, Route 1, Chadds Ford, (610) 388-2613, lunch Mon.-Sat., dinner daily.

Chadds Ford Tavern, Route 1, Chadds Ford, (610) 459-8453, opens daily at 11 A.M.

Dilworthtown Inn, 1390 Old Wilmington Pike, West Chester, (610) 399-1390, dinner daily from 5:30 P.M., Sun., 3 P.M.-9 P.M.

The Gourmet's Table, 2 Waterview Road, West Chester, (610) 696-2211, lunch and dinner daily.

Hank's Place, Route 1, Chadds Ford, (610) 388-7061, Mon.-Sat., 5 A.M.-7 P.M., Sun., 7 A.M.-3 P.M.

Hugo's Inn, 940 East Baltimore Pike, Kennett Square, (610) 388-1144, lunch and dinner daily.

Kennett Square Inn, 201 East State Street, Kennett Square, (610) 444-5688, lunch and dinner daily.

Lenape Inn, 1333 Lenape Road, West Chester, (610) 793-2005, lunch and dinner, Tues.-Sun.

Marshalton Inn, Route 162, Marshalton, (610) 692-4367, dinner daily.

Mendenhall Inn, Route 52, Mendenhall, (610) 388-1181, lunch and dinner daily.

The Restaurant & Bar, 18 West Gay Street, West Chester, (610) 431-0770, lunch and dinner daily.

Spence Café, 29 East Gay Street, West Chester, (610) 738-8844, lunch and dinner daily.

Lodging:

Best Western, Route 1 and Route 322, Concordville, (610) 358-9400.

Brandywine River Hotel, Route 1, Chadds Ford, (610) 388-1200.

Chadds Ford Ramada Inn, Route 1 and Route 202, (610) 358-1700.

Fairville Inn, Route 52, Mendenhall, (610) 358-5900.

Hotel Dupont, 11th and Market, Wilmington, Delaware, (302) 594-3100.

Longwood Inn, Route 1, Kennett Square, (610) 444-3515.

Mendenhall Hotel, Route 52, Mendenhall, (610) 388-1181.

1810 House of Marshalton, 1280 West Strasburg Road, West Chester, (610) 430-6013.

Cornerstone Bed & Breakfast, 300 Buttonwood Road, Landenberg, (610) 274-2143.

Franklin House, 339 North Franklin Street, West Chester, (610) 696-1665.

Harlan Log House, 205 Fairville Road, Chadds Ford, (610) 388-1114.

Hedgerow Bed & Breakfast, Route 52, Kennett Square, (610) 388-6080.

Meadow Spring Farm, 201 East Street Road, Kennett Square, (610) 444-3903.

Old Mill Bed & Breakfast, 680 Haines Road, West Chester, (610) 793-1633.

Pennsbury Inn, Route 1, Chadds Ford, (610) 388-1435.

Scarlett House, 503 West State Street, Kennett Square, (610) 444-9592.

Philadelphia/West Chester KOA Campground, Unionville, (610) 486-0447.

Shopping:

American Christmas Museum & Country Store, Route 1, Chadds Ford, (610) 388-0600, Tues.-Sat., 9:30 A.M.-5:30 P.M., Sun., noon-5 P.M.

Antiquus, 120 West State Street, Kennett Square, (610) 444-9892, Tues.-Sat., 10 A.M.-4:30 P.M.

Baldwin's Book Barn, 865 Lenape Road, West Chester, (610) 696-0816, Mon.-Fri., 9 A.M.-9 P.M., Sat. and Sun., 10 A.M.-5 P.M.

Brandywine Flags, 142 Wallace Avenue, Downingtown, (610) 269-5800, Mon., Wed., and Fri., 10 A.M.-5:30 P.M., Thur., 10 A.M.-6 P.M., and Sat., 10 A.M.-4 P.M.

The Brandywine Gourmet, 126 East Gay Street, West Chester, (610) 430-1999, Mon.-Sat., 10 A.M.-5:30 P.M.

Brandywine River Antiques Market, Route 1, Chadds Ford, (610) 388-2000, Wed.-Sun., 10 A.M.-5 P.M.

Chadds Ford Gallery, Route 1, Chadds Ford, (610) 459-5510, Mon.-Sat., 10 A.M.-5 P.M., Sun., noon-5 P.M.

Dilworthtown Country Store, 275 Brinton's Bridge Road, West Chester, (610) 399-0560, Mon.-Sat., 9:30 A.M.-5:30 P.M.

Longwood Art Gallery, Route 1, Kennett Square, Tues.-Fri., 11 A.M.-5 P.M., Sat., 11 A.M.-4:30 P.M., and Sun., noon-5 P.M.

Military History Shop, 110 West State Street, Kennett Square, (610) 444-2883, call for hours.

Northbrook Orchards, 6 Northbrook Road, West Chester, (610) 793-1210, seasonal hours.

Olde South Brittle Company, 516 Kennett Pike, Chadds Ford, (610) 388-9179, Wed.-Sat., 10 A.M.-5 P.M., Sun., noon-4 P.M.

Pennsbury-Chadds Ford Antique Mall, Route 1, Chadds Ford, (610) 388-1620, Thur.-Mon., 10 A.M.-5 P.M.

Visual Expansion Gallery, 126 North High Street, West Chester, (610) 436-8697, Mon.-Fri., 9 A.M.-6 P.M., Sat., 9 A.M.-5 P.M.

Wendy's Corner Antiques, Route 202, Chadds Ford, (610) 358-4077, Tues., 1 P.M.-5 P.M., Wed.-Sat., 11 A.M.-5 P.M.

Wooden Knob Antiques, Route 1 and Route 100, Chadds Ford, Mon.-Sat., 10 A.M.-5 P.M., Sun., noon-4 P.M.

Annual Events:

Welcome to Spring, Longwood Gardens, January through April, (610) 388-1000.

Radnor Hunt Steeplechase Races, May, (610) 388-2700.

Devon Horse Show, May, (610) 647-4233.

Mother's Day Specials, Brandywine Scenic Railway, (610) 793-4433.

Father's Day Specials, June, Brandywine Scenic Railway, (610) 793-4433.

Festival of Fountains, May through September, Longwood Gardens, (610) 388-1000.

Bonsai Show, Brandywine River Museum, June, (610) 388-2700.

Good Neighbor Day, July 4, Downingtown, (610) 289-0344.

Mushroom Festival, September, Kennett Square, (610) 444-4951.

Revolutionary Times, Brandywine Battlefield Park, September, (610) 459-3342.

Autumn's Colors, October, Longwood Gardens, (610) 388-1000.

Apple Wine Weekend, October, Chaddsford Winery, (610) 388-6221.

Longwood Gardens Chrysanthemum Festival, November, (610) 388-1000.

A Brandywine Christmas, December, Brandywine River Museum, (610) 388-2700.

The Active Life:

French Creek State Park [(610) 582-9680] covers 11 square miles, and it's an ideal place to do something or to do nothing. The park has a lake and an extensive system of trails. The **Struble Trail** in Downingtown [(610) 924-2450] is about three miles long. It's flat and excellent for walks or leisurely bike rides.

The rural roads of Chester County provide miles and miles of pleasant bicycling, and **Northbrook Canoe Company** rents canoes for rides on the Brandywine. Call (610) 793-2279 for information.

A Great Place to Relax:

Take a stroll through the native wildflower meadows at Longwood Gardens. Sit and watch the fountains.

Covered Bridges:

Chester County has more than a dozen, including several shared with neighboring counties. **Harmony Hill Bridge** is on

Harmony Hill Road, northeast of Route 322, about two miles south of Downingtown.

Tourist Information:
 • (800) 228-9933

Where is it? Southeast quadrant, along Route 1.

Getaway Rating: 3

Longwood Gardens

8

COUDERSPORT . . . GOD'S COUNTRY

(A, R, R&R)

Called **God's Country** because of its natural splendor, **Potter County** is a rural area where many of the homes are vacation homes and hunting cabins. Because the mountains are rugged and steep, the population of Potter County is only about 17,000 in 1,072 square miles, an area the size of Rhode Island.

An indication of the friendly, small town atmosphere in Potter County often shows up in the weekly newspaper, *The Leader-Enterprise,* which carries reports from many of the small communities in the county. These reports will frequently state that Mabel and Fred from Olean visited Jim and Ethel in Germania. The paper also publishes a picture and a brief biography of every graduating senior from the county's high schools.

One famous name who enjoyed the quiet of Coudersport was Eliot Ness, the famous crime fighter. After his hectic years in Chicago and Cleveland, he moved to Coudersport, where he spent the last year of his life in these lightly populated woods.

While people are few, wildlife is abundant. Deer, bears, beavers, birds of prey, and trout are species that attract visitors. The county has 800 miles of trout streams, and many miles of hiking trails. In Coudersport, it also has a comfortable

Victorian town where visitors with no interest in mud or water can enjoy a relaxing weekend.

Pennsylvanians flock to Potter County throughout the year to enjoy the woods and waters, and the influx peaks in late November for deer hunting season. By then, the trees are bare, and snow often covers the ground, especially at higher elevations. By Pennsylvania standards, Potter County has a very cold climate, and many visitors come to enjoy the snow. In summer, those same visitors will find cooler temperatures here than in other parts of the state. In 1997, for instance, the year's official high temperature was only 88°.

The **Eastern Continental Divide** passes through Potter County, and on a hill in the northern part of a county are the headwaters of streams that flow east, west, and north to the Susquehanna, the Mississippi, and Lake Ontario. On Route 6 between Galeton and Coudersport, the elevation reaches 2,424 feet, and at that site is **Ski Denton,** which features one of the steepest slopes in the east and facilities for other snow sports. In June, **God's Country Marathon** takes runners from Galeton to Coudersport, and **Denton Hill** is a serious challenge for runners who have already run 16 miles. It's no surprise that the race has a reputation as one of the toughest anywhere.

The race ends at **Coudersport Area Recreation Park** in the borough of 3,000, whose population makes it the biggest in the county. It's a busy little town, and a good base for adventures in the woods. In Coudersport, you'll find a movie theater, restaurants, an old hotel, motels, and a town square with a gazebo that hosts community concerts. On Saturdays from April through October, from 9 A.M. to 2 P.M., a farmers' market operates on the square. The Allegheny River runs through Coudersport, but you may not associate this stream with the mighty river that reaches Pittsburgh. In Coudersport, the Allegheny is just a trickle, and its banks are concrete.

A century ago, the lumber industry was the dominant economic and social force in Potter County, and on a smaller scale lumber is still important today. The **Pennsylvania Lumber Museum** preserves the heritage of the era with tools, a logging

Pennsylvania Lumber Museum

locomotive, and the weathered buildings of a lumber camp and sawmill. Throughout the year, the museum offers workshops and events such as the Bark Peelers Convention.

On a map, most of Potter County is green, which means forests, and much of the land is state parks, forests, and game lands that are open for public use. Potter County has six state parks and shares two others with Cameron County. At **Lyman Run,** you can swim in a lake that often feels as though it was ice just a few minutes earlier. The water is much warmer in July and August than when the lake opens for swimming around Memorial Day.

Mountain bikers and ATV riders will receive a welcome in Potter County. The **Susquehannock Forest** covers over 400 square miles, and it contains 43 miles of ATV trails.

Anyone wishing a leisurely weekend will enjoy a stay in downtown Coudersport. You can sleep and dine at the **Hotel Crittenden,** which is right in the center of downtown. More than 100 years old, the Crittenden has the atmosphere of an old hotel and the smell of history, and it makes relaxing easy.

Coudersport Theatre

Down the street from the Crittenden is the **Coudersport Theatre.** The theater turned 75 in 1998, and it's received many updates since it was built, but it still has the feel of an old theater. In the downtown shopping district are some interesting stores, such as **The Right Stuff Consignment Shop, Morgart's Trash & Treasures,** and **J.C. Penney,** which more commonly has stores in malls than in downtowns.

At **City News** you can pick up a magazine, and across the street you can sit on the town green and read. Occasionally, the gazebo in the green is the site of community band concerts and other activities.

Across the continental divide from Coudersport is **Galeton,** another small town that many visitors use as a base for outdoor adventures. In the center of Galeton is **Center Town Lake,** created by damming **Pine Creek,** the stream that flows through Pennsylvania's Grand Canyon.

At the beginning of the 20th century, tanneries, lumber mills, and railroads made this a busy place. Thirty-five trains a day passed through town, and in spring hundreds of loggers would come out of the mountains and into town for food and entertainment. Drunken brawls were regular events. Today, Galeton is a pretty quiet place that's excellent for relaxing, and a self-guided walking tour will take you to more than 50 of the town's historic sites.

Twenty-five miles west of Coudersport on Route 6 is the Victorian village of **Smethport,** where it's always Christmas season. **America's First Christmas Store** opened in 1935. Today, it is four rooms filled with Christmas gifts, and it's open all year. If you enjoy Christmas shopping, you can always do it in Smethport. Also in Smethport is **The Christmas Inn,** a large Victorian home with nine fireplaces and original woodwork in oak, maple, and mahogany.

Coudersport is a pretty little town in the woods. It's a good place to take in a movie at the old theater, to relax on the town square, and to enjoy walking the streets of a downtown that's still the primary shopping district.

Attractions:

Pristine mountains and clear streams, small town with pleasant downtown shopping district.

Coudersport Theatre, 11 North Main Street, (814) 274-8580, evening shows.

Pennsylvania Lumber Museum, Route 6 between Galeton and Coudersport, (814) 435-2652, 9 A.M.-5 P.M. daily, April through November.

Rainbow Paradise Trout Farm, Route 6 East, Coudersport, (814) 274-8309, daily, 9 A.M. till.

Coudersport Golf Club, Route 44 South, (814) 274-9122, open daily (when weather allows).

Ski Denton, Route 6 between Galeton and Coudersport, (814) 435-2115, open daily (when it snows).

Dining:

Fox's Pizza, 2 West Street, Galeton, (814) 435-8874, Mon.-Sat., 11 A.M.-9:30 P.M., Sun., noon-9:30 P.M.

Coudersport Bandstand

Fox's Pizza, Route 6 West, Coudersport, (814) 274-8160, Mon.-Sat., 11 A.M.-9:30 P.M., Sun., noon-9:30 P.M.

Hotel Crittenden, 133 North Main Street, Coudersport, (814) 274-8320, lunch and dinner, Mon.-Sat.

Laurelwood Inn, Route 6, Coudersport, (814) 274-9220, dinner seven days a week.

Potato City Country Inn, Route 6 at the Eastern Continental Divide, (814) 274-7133, open for dinner seven days a week, and breakfast and lunch in the busy seasons (i.e. Summer, "Hunting," and October).

McDonald's, 104 South Main Street, Coudersport, (814) 274-9111.

The Northern Pub & Eatery, Route 6 and Route 872, Coudersport, (814) 274-8930, lunch and dinner daily.

Original Italian Pizza, 18 East Second Street, (814) 274-0455, Mon.-Thur., 11 A.M.-9 P.M., Fri. and Sat., 11 A.M.-10 P.M.

Ox Yoke Family Inn, Route 6, Galeton, (814) 435-6522, 6 A.M.-9 P.M. daily.

Lodging:

Hotel Crittenden, 133 North Main Street, Coudersport, (814) 274-8320.

Potato City Country Inn, Route 6 at the Eastern Continental Divide, (814) 274-7133.

Ox Yoke Family Inn, Route 6, Galeton, (814) 435-6522.

Lindy Motel, Route 6 East, Coudersport, (814) 274-0327.

Susquehannock Lodge, Route 6 West, Galeton, (814) 435-2163.

Laurelwood Inn, Route 6 East, Coudersport, (814) 274-9220.

Lush Victorian Bed & Breakfast, 201 Cartee Street, Coudersport, (814) 274-7557.

J.T.'s Motel, Route 6 East, Galeton, (800) 289-0648.

Sweden Valley Motel, Route 6 East, Coudersport, (814) 274-8770.

Village Inn, 61 Germania Street, Galeton, (814) 435-2127.

Paul's Exxon, Route 6 East, Coudersport, (814) 274-8700. (Yes, it's a hotel and a gas station!)

West Pike Motor Lodge, Route 6 West, Galeton, (814) 435-6552.

The Christmas Inn, 911 West Main Street, Smethport, (800) 841-2721.

Kenshire Kampsite, Route 6 East, Galeton, (814) 435-6764.

Denton Hill State Park (cabins), (814) 435-2115.

Ole Bull State Park (cabins), (814) 435-500.

Sinnemahoning State Park (cabins), (814) 647-8401.

Note: Potter County is a popular getaway, and the region has a rather small number of hotel and motel rooms. The "No Vacancy" signs often light up on weekends, so always call ahead and make reservations.

Shopping:

Potter County has no big shopping malls, but it does have many interesting shops and stores. Hours of operation vary from season to season, and sometimes proprietors will close for a day to go fishing. That's the relaxed atmosphere of Potter County.

America's First Christmas Store, 101 West Main Street, Smethport, (814) 887-5792, call for hours.

Black Forest Trading Post, Route 6 and Route 449, west of Galeton, (814) 435-6754, opens at 9 A.M. daily.

Country Stuff, Route 6, west of Coudersport, (814) 274-7840, Mon.-Sat., 10 A.M.-5 P.M.

Kline's Gift Shop, Route 6 East, Galeton, (814) 435-2853, Mon.-Sat., 9:30 A.M.-5 P.M.

Hauber's, 115 North Main Street, Coudersport, (814) 274-9825, Mon.-Sat., 9 A.M.-5 P.M.

Halloran's Hardware & Sporting Goods, 201 North Main Street, Coudersport, (814) 274-9494, Mon.-Sat., 10 A.M.-5 P.M.

Morgart's Trash & Treasures, 131 North Main Street, Coudersport, (814) 274-2210, Mon.-Sat., 10 A.M.-5 P.M.

J.C. Penney, North Main Street, Coudersport, (814) 274-8111, Mon.-Sat., 9 A.M.-5 P.M.

The Right Stuff Consignment Shop, 364 East Second Street, Coudersport, (814) 274-4200, Mon.-Sat., 10 A.M.-5 P.M.

Annual Events:

Hunting Seasons, spring and fall.

God's Country Marathon, Galeton to Coudersport, first Saturday in June.

Fireworks, July 4, Center Town Lake, Galeton.

Woodsmen's Show, late July, Cherry Springs State Park.

Potter County Fair, last week of July, Millport.

Fall Foliage, early October.

Skiing, winter, Ski Denton, Route 6.

The Active Life:

It's always the right season for outdoor activities in Potter County. Hiking, biking, hunting, fishing, swimming, and boating are favorite activities. Mountain bikers love the area. Road bikers are somewhat less enthusiastic because of the steep hills. The area north of Coudersport is much better for road biking than the southern part of the county.

A Great Place to Relax:

Just about anywhere—from the square in Coudersport to the solitude of a mountain top, Potter County is a good place to sit back and watch the world go by.

Covered Bridges:

Potter County has one. It's on private property along Route 6, about a mile west of Coudersport, and it carries traffic from Route 6 into a farm.

Tourist Information:

- (888) POTTER2; http://www.pavisnet.com

Where is it? North central, along U.S. 6.

Getaway Rating: 4

Climb every mountain or sit on a bench on the town green. Walk in the woods or shop in a country store. Coudersport is a charming little town where you can enjoy the pleasures of the wilderness or the "city."

A residence in Eagles Mere

9

EAGLES MERE . . .
THE TOWN THAT
TIME FORGOT
(A, R&R)

Eagles Mere isn't just far from the beaten path. Eagles Mere is far from the path to the beaten path. Nobody just happens to be passing through this little town. You have to make a choice to follow Route 42 into Eagles Mere, and you'll have no choice but to get away from it all up here.

With **no traffic lights** and a listed population of 123, Eagles Mere is a tiny place that's a long, long way from the noise and congestion of modern life. Dushore, 16 miles away and the largest town in Sullivan County, has a listed population of 728 and the county's only traffic light. **Forests** cover most of the county (94 percent), and it's almost impossible to find a view that doesn't include a wooded mountain.

Eagles Mere sits on top of a mountain at an elevation of 2,126 feet, but despite its setting, it's hardly a wilderness outpost. Instead, it's a genteel Victorian town with comfortable lodging, gracious dining, a community center with musical and stage productions, a lake, and an extensive series of paths through the surrounding woods. And, right in the center of town, there is a casual little restaurant that's a great gathering place after a day on the water.

Besides traffic lights, Eagles Mere **doesn't have** supermarkets, department stores, or manufacturing. Residents have to

The town clock

drive a distance to do any serious shopping, and their inconvenience makes the little town a great getaway.

The most visible landmark in Eagles Mere is the **town clock,** which is ironic in a place that calls itself **"The town that time forgot."** Life moves at a gentle pace, and relaxation and recreation are the main businesses. The bank is open only on Mondays, Wednesdays, and Fridays, and nobody seems to be in a great hurry to get anywhere.

The atmosphere in Eagles Mere is similar to that at a beach resort. Elegant homes ring the lake, and everybody is here either to relax or to cater to the visitors. One major difference between Eagles Mere and a beach resort is scale. The numbers are much smaller here, and day-trippers can't use the lake or the golf course. Only members and guests at any of the town's lodging establishments may use those facilities. The **David A. Dewire Center** presents plays and music during the summer.

Eagles Mere's history dates to 1794 when an Englishman named George Lewis purchased the lake and 10,000 acres. By 1803 he had built a glass factory, and from Eagles Mere he shipped his products to Philadelphia by horse-drawn wagons.

What's hard to believe is that anything could reach Philadelphia intact after 170 miles on dirt roads. Nevertheless, Lewis's business flourished for about a decade, but went bankrupt after the War of 1812. It was then that Eagles Mere began its transition to a resort.

By the middle of the 19th century, Eagles Mere was home to a small collection of summer cottages. Serious development began in 1885 with the formation of the **Eagles Mere Land Company,** and in 1892 the railroad came to Eagles Mere. When you see how the town sits on top of the mountain, you'll appreciate the engineering feat involved in getting trains here.

When the railroad came, it brought with it affluent families. They stayed with their servants and nannies in hotels or their own cottages. Summer life revolved around tennis parties, picnics, boating, swimming, regattas, and golf at the country club. It was a leisurely life for the affluent and a hard-working time for the servants.

The Catholic church in Eagles Mere is the result of the affluent families' desire to keep their servants working on Sunday. A century ago, the nearest Catholic churches were down the mountain in distant towns, and going to church took up most of Sunday for the servants. To keep them closer to home, the wealthy people in town, most of whom were Protestants, built a Catholic church.

At the last turn of the century, Eagles Mere had three large hotels and several smaller ones, but they're all gone now. In their place is a collection of inns and bed & breakfasts. Eagles Mere doesn't have the facilities to handle masses of people, and everyone likes it that way. The people who are here spend most of their time relaxing in one way or another, whether it's **swimming in the lake** or **sitting in the park.** The **Eagles Mere Village Shoppes,** in the center of town, offer specialty shopping and souvenirs.

When summer ends, Eagles Mere takes on a different character. The green mountains turn orange and red and gold, and the view is spectacular. On clear autumn days, the colors reflect off the waters of the lake and create beautiful photo opportunities.

Crestmont Inn and condos above the lake

Because of the elevation, autumn comes earlier to Eagles Mere than to most other places in Pennsylvania. The first signs of autumn color show up in mid-September, and the colors last well into October. And, because 94 percent of Sullivan County is wooded, the whole place looks like a postcard when the leaves are bright.

In winter, the snow comes and life slows even more. A walk in the woods is an exercise in tranquility, and an evening by a fireplace is a warm way to end a relaxing day.

Eagles Mere is a surprise sitting high on a mountain. Come to Eagles Mere and you'll get away from everything but comfort.

Attractions:

Eagles Mere Lake.

Green woodlands.

Fall foliage.

Sweatshirts in July.

Toboggan Run in winter.

Dining:

The Sweet Shoppe, Eagles Mere Avenue and Pennsylvania Avenue, in the center of town, open 10:30 A.M.-10 P.M. in the summer.

Crestmont Inn, Crestmont Avenue, (570) 525-3519, open for dinner.

Eagles Mere Inn, Mary Avenue, (800) 426-3273, open for breakfast and dinner.

Lodging:

Crestmont Inn, Crestmont Avenue (570) 525-3519.

Eagles Mere Inn, Mary Avenue, (800) 426-3273.

Flora Villa Bed & Breakfast, Eagles Mere Avenue, (570) 525-3245.

Shady Lane Bed & Breakfast, Allegheny Avenue, (800) 524-1248.

Endless Mountains Bed & Breakfast Reservation Service (covers surrounding 4-county area), (888) 365-7686.

Shopping:

You won't find any outlet stores or huge malls around here, but you will find a collection of specialty shops and a general store on the town square.

The Eagles Mere Village Shoppes are on Eagles Mere Avenue, in the center of town. They offer crafts, sweaters, gifts, books, jewelry, pottery, antiques, and general merchandise (open daily from 10 A.M. to 5 P.M.). Call (570) 525-3503 for information.

Annual Events:

Summer Antique Market, second Saturday in July.

Fine Art Show & Sale, last weekend in July.

Arts & Crafts Festival, second weekend in August.

Fall Antique Market, Saturday before Labor Day.

Fall Festival, last weekend in September.

Grace's Run, 3.4 miles, second Saturday in October.

Sullivan County Fair, Forksville, Labor Day week, (570) 924-3843.

Victorian Christmas, first weekend in December.

The **David A. Dewire Center** on Laporte Avenue offers music and cultural events. Write to Box 217, Eagles Mere, PA 17731 or call (570) 525-3503 for information.

The Active Life:

Everything in Eagles Mere is close enough to everything else to let you park your car and walk everywhere you go. Besides walking, opportunities are ample for hiking, swimming, biking, golf, boating, and cross-country skiing.

If you want to head out on a long bike ride, expect to do some serious climbing. Traffic in the region is generally light, but the hills are frequent and steep. It's about a 10-mile round trip from Eagles Mere to Laporte, with one big climb and a number of smaller ones. Be sure to bring your bike, though. You can always ride around the lake a few times.

The woods around town are full of marked trails, and a brochure describing them is available many places around town. The longest trail is about 2 miles, so just about everyone can enjoy a pleasant walk in the woods.

The biggest recreation center is the **Beach Club,** on the northern end of the lake. It's a private facility, and everyone staying at any of the lodging facilities in town may use it. At the beach club you can swim, canoe, and relax.

The **Eagles Mere Country Club** offers 18 holes of golf and tennis courts to everyone staying at any of the town's lodging establishments.

In winter, Eagles Mere turns white. Snow is frequent, and it doesn't melt for months. For cross-country skiers, that's great news. In good winters, members of the fire department cut blocks of ice and create a toboggan slide. Riders start at the top of Lake Avenue, zoom down the steep street, and hit the frozen lake at high speed. Sometimes they can slide all the way across the lake.

You can rent mountain bikes at **Eagles Mere Mountain Bikes** on Route 42, south of town. Call (570) 525-3368 for information.

A Great Place to Relax:

This whole town is perfect for relaxation.

Covered Bridges:

Sullivan County has three. The most photographed is at **Forksville.** The easiest to find is at **Sonestown,** just off Route 220.

Tourist Information:

• Eagles Mere Village, (570) 525-3503.

Where is it? On PA Route 42, West of U.S. 220, Northeast of Williamsport.

Getaway Rating: 5

The Eagles Mere Song, sung to the tune of *Camelot*:

A law was made a distant moon ago here,
July and August cannot be too hot.
And there's no legal limit to the fun here.
In Eagles Mere.

The winter is forbidden till December,
And ends on April 1 when spring is here.
By order summer lingers through September,
In Eagles Mere.

Eagles Mere! Eagles Mere!
I know it sounds a bit bizarre.

But in Eagles Mere, Eagles Mere,
That's how conditions are.

There's sailing, fishing, swimming in the lake,
And at the beach mermaids oft appear.
In short there's simply not a more congenial spot,
For happily ever aftering than here in Eagles Mere.

Eagles Mere! Eagles Mere!
I know it gives a person pause.
But in Eagles Mere, Eagles Mere.
Those are the legal laws.

The sun must brightly shine till seven o'clock,
By 9 P.M. the moonlight must appear.
In short there's simply not a more congenial spot,
For happily ever aftering than here in Eagles Mere.

The pond

10

ERIE . . .
ISLE TAKE YOU THERE
(H, R)

Erie grew up as a harbor town. Lake Erie connects to the other great lakes, and much of Erie's commerce has always centered on the lake. The downtown shopping district is just a few blocks from the water, and the waterfront has recently enjoyed a revitalization.

The best way to see Erie, Lake Erie, and everything nearby is to take a ride up the 138-foot high **Bicentennial Tower.** From the top, you can see land and water, and local promoters say that you can even see Canada on a clear day. Sixteen stations on the observation deck point out geographic, historic, and modern points of interest.

Close to the tower is the **Erie Maritime Museum,** whose star performer is the *Brig Niagara.* This *Niagara* is a reconstruction of the ship that Commodore Oliver Perry captained when he encountered and defeated the British in the 1813 Battle of Lake Erie. At the end of that battle, Perry sent his famous victory proclamation—"We have met the enemy and they are ours."

The *Niagara* stayed in Erie until 1820, when it was scuttled (sunk) in Presque Isle's Misery Bay. Raised to celebrate the centennial of the battle in 1913, the *Niagara* received major

The beach at Presque Isle State Park

renovations. Eventually it was dismantled and rebuilt from mostly new materials. In 1990, the ship received the designation "Flagship of Pennsylvania."

The disappointing news about the *Niagara* is that people can't sail on the *Niagara* unless they're members of the **Flagship Niagara League.** In addition, the ship sometimes sails around the Great Lakes, so if it's the highlight of your visit, call ahead [(814) 452-2744] to make sure it's in port. You can, however, tour the harbor area aboard a variety of different ships.

The *Victorian Princess* offers sightseeing and dinner cruises aboard this 149-passenger sidewheeler. The *Presque Isle Express* carries passengers from Dobbins Landing to Presque Isle. The *Little Toot* offers 45-minute tours from Dobbins Landing, and the *Appledore IV* is an 85-foot schooner equipped with modern conveniences and private cabins.

The biggest attraction in Erie is **Presque Isle State Park,** a 7-mile peninsula that's an ideal place to walk, swim, bike, run, and just relax. Presque Isle is a recreational area for people, and it's home to hundreds of species of wildlife. Birds, squirrels, turtles, foxes, raccoons, clams, and eels are some of the wildlife that lives on the isle. Spotters have identified 321 species of birds on the isle, making it one of the best birding spots in the country.

The multi-use trail around the park is 13 miles long, and at the 6-mile mark is the **Perry Monument,** dedicated to Commodore Perry. From there, you can board the *Lady Kate* for a 90-minute cruise. Presque Isle even has the honor of being named one of the nation's "100 Best Swimming Holes" by *Conde Nast Traveler* magazine.

For an education on the isle's ecology, stop at the **Stull Interpretive Center.** Exhibits there explain how the constant washing away and building up of sands give the land beaches, dunes, grasslands, savannas, mature forests, marshes, and a lagoon.

The name Presque Isle is French for "almost an island," and the isle has actually been an island several times. Storm waves have broken through the neck to isolate the rest of the spit four times since 1819.

For modern visitors, the list of activities is long. On summer weekends, the park draws large crowds, but there's still room to find quiet, if not complete, solitude. The crowds thin out as you get farther away from the park's entrances, and the most distant beaches are usually the least congested.

Presque Isle doesn't allow visitors to stay overnight, but there are many hotels and motels just outside the park. Also outside the park is **Waldameer Park & Water World.** The highlighted ride of this theme park is **Thunder River,** a log flume ride that resembles a roller coaster with a watery ending.

Downtown has good attractions. **Discovery Square** contains the **Erie Art Museum,** the **Erie History Center,** and the **ExpERIEnce Children's Museum.** The **Firefighters Historical Museum** is a former fire station that houses more than 1,000 pieces of firefighting memorabilia, such as a collection of helmets and a 19th-century horse-drawn fire engine.

Arts and culture are strong in downtown Erie, with a base at the **Warner Theatre,** originally commissioned by the Warner

Brothers from Hollywood. The **Erie Philharmonic** and the **Erie Civic Music Association** perform here. The **Lake Erie Ballet Company** shares the Warner stage, and the **Erie Playhouse** offers comedies, musicals, and dramas.

Sports fans will enjoy catching a game of the **Erie Sea Wolves** minor league baseball team. The Sea Wolves play in **Jerry Uht Stadium,** which is just east of downtown. The impressive stadium opened in 1995, and the team moved from the A New York-Penn League in 1998 to the AA Eastern League in 1999.

Shoppers flock to the **Millcreek Mall,** which has over 200 stores and advertises tax-free clothing. That's true, but it's also true of every other clothing outlet in Pennsylvania because the state doesn't tax clothing.

Outside the city, Erie County is a rich agricultural area. Grapes grow well here, and around the small city of **North East** are four wineries. Throughout the county, the hills are smaller and less steep than they are in adjacent counties, and the land is good for farming, and also for bicycling. Riding in Erie County is pleasant and not terribly strenuous.

Presque Isle can keep you occupied for the weekend, and Erie has many more attractions. Erie is a fine spot for an active weekend.

Attractions:

Lake Erie, an inland sea and the biggest great lake.

Presque Isle State Park, (814) 833-7424, no overnight stays.

Bicentennial Tower, on the waterfront, (814) 471-4596.

Discovery Square, 417 State Street, (814) 454-1813, Tues.-Thur., 9 A.M.-5 P.M.

Waldameer Park, beside entrance to Presque Isle State Park, (814) 838-3591.

ExpERIEnce Children's Museum, 420 French Street, (814) 453-3743, Tues.-Sat., 10 A.M.-4 P.M., Sun., 1 P.M.-4 P.M.

Erie Playhouse, 13 West 10th Street, (814) 454-2851.

Erie History Center, 419 State Street, (814) 454-1813, Mon.-Sat., 10 A.M.-4 P.M.

Erie skyline

Erie Art Center, 411 State Street, (814) 459-5477, Tues.-Sat., 11 A.M.-5 P.M., Sun., 1 P.M.-5 P.M.

Erie Historical Museum & Planetarium, 356 West Sixth Street, (814) 871-5790, Museum, Tues.-Sun., 1 P.M.-5 P.M., Planetarium, Sun., shows at 2 P.M. and 3 P.M.

Erie SeaWolves Baseball, Jerry Uht Field, East 12th Street, (800) 456-1304, call for schedule.

Warner Theatre, 811 State Street, (814) 453-7117, call for schedule.

Erie Maritime Museum/*Brig Niagara,* 150 East Front Street, (814) 455-6067, Mon.-Sat., 9 A.M.-5 P.M., Sun., noon-5 P.M.

Dining:

Ali Baba, 3602 West Lake Road, (814) 838-7197, Mon.-Thur., 11 A.M.-9 P.M., Fri. and Sat., 11 A.M.-10 P.M.

Asian Palace Buffet, 4125 Peach Street, (814) 868-8615, open 11 A.M.-11 P.M. daily.

Avalon Hotel, 16 West 10th Street, (800) 822-5011, lunch and dinner daily.

Calamari's, 1317 State Street, (814) 459-4276, open 11 A.M.-2 A.M. daily.

Colony Pub & Grille, 2670 West 8th Street, (814) 838-2162, opens Mon.-Sat. at 4 P.M., Sun. at noon

Damon's Clubhouse, 7165 Peach Street, (814) 866-7427, lunch and dinner daily.

Dominick's 24 Hour Eatery, 123 East 12th Street, (814) 465-6891, always open.

The Downs OTB, 7700 Peach Street, (814) 866-3678, call for schedule.

The Elephant Bar, 2826 West 8th Street, (814) 838-3613, Mon.-Sat., 11 A.M.-2 A.M.

Fox & Hound, 250 Millcreek Plaza, (814) 864-5589, opens at 11 A.M. daily.

George's Restaurant, 2614 Glenwood Park Avenue, (814) 465-0660, Mon.-Fri., 7 A.M.-8 P.M., Sat., 7 A.M.-3 P.M.

Hopper's Brewpub, 123 West 14th Street, (814) 838-6718, Mon.-Sat., 11:30 A.M.-1 A.M.

Las Cazuelas Tortilla Factory, 524 West 18th Street, (814) 455-4588, open 11 A.M.-9 P.M. daily.

Lucchetti's Pizza, 1042 West 26th Street, (814) 452-4413, open 11 A.M.-1 A.M. daily.

Mamma Mia's Pizza-Ria, 5154 Peach Street, (814) 864-3718, Mon.-Thur., 11 A.M.-11 P.M., Fri. and Sat., 11 A.M.-midnight, and Sun., 4 P.M.-11 P.M.

Maximillian's At The Bel-Aire Hotel, 2800 West 8th Street, (814) 838-9270, Sun.-Thur., 6 A.M.-11 P.M., Fri. and Sat., 6 A.M.-midnight

Marketplace Grill, 319 State Street, (814) 455-7272, Mon.-Sat., 11:30 A.M.-10 P.M.

Old Country Buffet, 7200 Peach Street, (814) 866-5671, lunch and dinner daily.

Olive Garden, 5945 Peach Street, (814) 866-1105, opens at 11 A.M. daily.

1000 French, 25 East 10th Street, (814) 464-2896, lunch and dinner daily.

Pio's Italian Restaurant, 815 East Avenue, (814) 456-8866, open 11:30 A.M.-9 P.M. daily.

Pufferbelly Restaurant, 414 French Street, (814) 454-1557, lunch and dinner daily.

Riverside Inn, Cambridge Springs, (800) 964-5173, lunch and dinner daily, April through December.

Roadhouse Restaurant, Millcreek Mall, (814) 868-0841, Mon.-Thur., 11:30 A.M.-10:30 P.M., Sat. and Sun., 11:30 A.M.-11:30 P.M., and Sun., 11:30 A.M.-9 P.M.

Scully's Pub, 408 State Street, (814) 454-0067, Mon.-Sat., 11 A.M.-1 A.M.

Serafini's, 2642 West 12th Street, (814) 838-8111, opens at 11 A.M. daily.

Spinner McGee's Steakhouse, 4940 Peach Street, (814) 866-7746, opens at 4 P.M. daily.

Sullivan's Pub, 301 French Street, (814) 838-2977, Mon.-Sat., 11:30 A.M.-midnight

Waterfront Seafood & Steakhouse, 4 State Street, (814) 459-0606, open 11 A.M.-2:30 P.M. and 4 P.M.-10 P.M. daily.

Lodging:

Avalon Hotel, 16 West 10th Street, (814) 459-2220.

Bel Air Hotel, 2800 West 8th Street, (800) 888-8781.

Best Western Presque Isle, I-90 and PA 832, (814) 838-7467.

Comfort Inn, 8501 Peach Street, (814) 866-6666.

Days Inn, 7400 Schultz Road, (814) 868-8521.

El Patio Motel, West 8th Street and Peninsula Drive, (814) 838-9772.

Glass House Inn, 3202 West 26th Street, (814) 833-7751.

Hampton Inn, 3041 West 12th Street, (814) 835-4200.

Holiday Inn Downtown, 18 West 18th Street, (814) 456-2961.

Downtown Erie

Lin Lee Motel, 3425 Lake Road, (814) 533-5235.

Peninsula Motel, 1002 Peninsula Drive, (814) 838-1938.

Riverside Inn, Cambridge Springs, (800) 964-5173.

Scott's Beachcomber Inn, 2930 West Sixth Street, (814) 838-1961.

Carroll Inn, 401 Peach Street, (814) 455-2022.

Spencer House Bed & Breakfast, 519 West 6th Street, (814) 454-5984.

Cassidy's Presque Isle Campground, 3749 Zimberly Road, (814) 833-6035.

Sara Coyne Campgrounds, 50 Peninsula Drive, (814) 833-4560.

Hills Family Campground, 6300 Sterrettania Road, (814) 833-3272.

Kelso Beach Summer Rentals, 1903 West 8th Street, (814) 254-1900.

Shopping:

Amish Buggy Gift Shop, 7870 West Ridge Road, (814) 474-3003, Mon.-Sat., 10 A.M.-5 P.M., Sun., noon-5 P.M.

Celtic Imports, 1656 West 8th Street, (814) 454-3362, Mon.-Sat., 10 A.M.-5 P.M.

The Collector's Choice, 3402 West Lake Road, (814) 838-6833, Tues.-Sat., 11 A.M.-5 P.M., Sun., noon-5 P.M.

Cover To Cover Books, 3350 West 26th Street, (814) 836-8800, Mon.-Fri., 10 A.M.-6 P.M., Sat., 10 A.M.-5 P.M.

For Old Times Sake Antique Mall, 6821 Buffalo Road, Harborcreek, (814) 899-9590, Sun., 10 A.M.-5 P.M.

Interstate Antique Mall, 11019 Sidehill Road, Northeast, (814) 725-1603, Mon.-Fri., 10:30 A.M.-5 P.M., Sat. and Sun., noon-5 P.M.

Millcreek Mall, Exit 6, Peach Street, I-90, (814) 868-9000, Mon.-Sat., 10 A.M.-9 P.M., Sun., 11 A.M.-6 P.M.

PJ's Gift World, 407 East 10th Street, (814) 455-8223, Mon.-Sat., 10 A.M.-5 P.M.

Waterford Flea Market, Route 19, Waterford, (814) 796-1018, Sat. and Sun., 9 A.M.-5 P.M.

Wooden Nickel Buffalo Shop, 5970 Koman Road, Edinboro, (814) 734-2833, open 11 A.M.-5 P.M. daily.

Annual Events:

Winter Carnival and Ice Sculpting, late January, on the Bayfront, (814) 454-7191.

PBA Tour Flagship City Open, February, Eastway Lanes, (814) 899-9855.

St. Patrick's Day Parade, downtown, (814) 456-5300.

Spring Show, April, Erie Art Museum, (814) 459-5477.

Erie Sea Wolves baseball, Spring and Summer.

Spring Highland Festival, early May, Edinboro University, (814) 732-2672.

Memorial Day Fireworks, Waldameer Park, (814) 838-3591.

Erie Summer Festival of Arts, late June, (814) 833-0812.

4th of July Fireworks, Waldameer Park, (814) 838-3591.

North East Cherry Festival, July, (814) 725-1537.

Summer Theatre, Erie Playhouse, (814) 398-4645.

Blues & Jazz Festival, early August, Frontier Park, (814) 459-5477.

We Love Erie Days, mid-August, (814) 454-7191.

Hamot 10K/Mayor's Cup, mid-August, (814) 452-1026.

Erie County Fair, late August, Wattsburg Fairgrounds, (814) 739-2952.

Albion Fair, September, (814) 756-4833.

Oktoberfest, mid-September, Hopper's Brewpub, (814) 453-4000.

Zooboo, October, Erie Zoo, (814) 864-4091.

Jingle Bell 5K, Presque Isle, early December, (814) 452-1026.

First Night Erie, New Year's Eve, downtown, (814) 977-7097.

The Active Life:

Presque Isle offers a full list of activities. The country roads throughout Erie County range from flat to rolling hills, and they're ideal for bicycling. Golfers can work on their games at Lake Pleasant Golf Club on Lake Pleasant Road, (814) 825-7839.

A Great Place to Relax:

Find a comfortable piece of beach in Presque Isle State Park or a nice bench along the waterfront in Erie. Sitting by the water is an excellent way to relax.

Covered Bridges:

Erie County has four. The closest to Erie is the Gudgeonville Bridge. To reach the bridge from the town of Girard, go south on Walnut street two miles to Beckman Road. Then go 0.8

miles southeast on Beckman Road and 0.7 miles south on Gudgeonville Road to the bridge.

Tourist Information:
- (814) 454-7191

Where is it? In the northwestern corner of Pennsylvania, on Lake Erie.

Getaway Rating: 2

A Note on the Weather:

Winter comes early, and the city receives frequent "Lake Effect" snows. They occur when cold air moves across the lake, absorbs moisture, freezes it, and drops it as snow. Because of the "Lake Effect" snows, Erie receives the white stuff much more frequently than places just a few miles from the lake do.

Gudgeonville Bridge

11

GETTYSBURG . . .
FOUR SCORE AND SEVEN . . .
(H, PT, R)

Gettysburg gained a permanent place in American history and a perpetual economic engine from the events that took place July 1 to July 3, 1863. On that sultry weekend, the forces of **General Robert E. Lee** encountered the Union Army of the Potomac, under **General George G. Meade,** on the outskirts of this small farming town. Lee challenged the Union right (July 1) and then, in an assault led by General James Longstreet, the left (July 2). On July 3, **General George Pickett** mounted the most famous charge in American military history against the Union center. Only 5,000 of his original force of 15,000 survived the repulse.

Lee watched the survivors return and confessed, "It is all my fault." Gettysburg cost Lee 20,000 men (fatalities and injuries) and 30,000 weapons. Meade lost almost as many men. The battle deeply moved both sides and it inspired President Lincoln's **Gettysburg Address.** Occurring in the same week that Vicksburg **fell to General Ulysses S. Grant,** Gettysburg put the Confederates on the defensive in the east. Despite the toll the battle extracted from the South, Gettysburg did nothing to hasten the end of the war, which dragged on for another 21 months.

Battlefield scene

Today, Gettysburg is a town of about 8,000, and the battlefield is its primary economic force and the source of its identity. Say "Gettysburg," and the battle comes to the mind of almost every American.

The preserved battlefield surrounds the town and occupies most of the ground. It's hard to go anywhere in Gettysburg without going through the battlefield. Adjacent to the battlefield is the farm of **Dwight D. Eisenhower.** A few miles farther down the road is a covered bridge through which Confederate soldiers retreated after the battle.

For visitors, one choice is how to see the battlefield. Cars are the most popular option, but they're not necessarily the best. Walking, bicycling, buses, horses, towers, and a train also provide excellent views. Each offers a different outlook at a slower pace than a car, and tour guides can answer all your questions.

Away from the battlefield, **Adams County** is largely an agricultural community. The **Peach Orchard** is an important part of the battlefield, and the orchards around nearby **Biglerville** make Adams County Pennsylvania's largest fruit-growing region.

Gettysburg has more attractions than anyone can possibly see in a weekend. One choice that you have is whether to visit the free attractions or the ones that charge admission. The battlefield is officially **Gettysburg National Military Park** (open 6 A.M.-10 P.M. daily), and you can spend days without spending a penny. The **Visitor's Center** (open 8 A.M.-5 P.M. daily) tells the story of the battle very well, and the adjacent **Cyclorama Center** (open 9 A.M.-5 P.M. daily) has a free movie and a sound and light program that you can pay to see.

To get a real feel of what happened here, you have to go out on the battlefield, and the best way to do that is to take a walk. Park the car anywhere and go for a stroll. Somehow, it's hard to visualize the blood that flowed on this now hallowed ground.

The battlefield was a loud and violent place for three days, but now a reverent hush seems to hang over it. For many, a visit to Gettysburg is emotionally painful as they think of the young men from both sides who died here.

The biggest attractions in Gettysburg are the battle re-enactments. They usually happen around the dates of the battle, but they aren't on a set schedule. Call the visitors' bureau for information, and if you don't like crowds, don't come near Gettysburg when any of the battle-related events are going on. It's a small town, and a small number of cars can jam things up considerably.

In Gettysburg, you can take a **Civil War Walking Tour.** Brochures are available at the visitors bureau, and this tour will take you to many sites in the town that were there before the battle.

Railroads were operating in Gettysburg at the time of the battle, and the trains are still running today. **Gettysburg Scenic Rail Tours** takes passengers on leisurely rides through part of the battlefield and the scenic farmlands of Adams County. The regular ride is 16 miles and 90 minutes between Gettysburg and Biglerville. One Saturday a month, the train makes a 34-mile trip to the Aspers Fire Hall for a catered early dinner, and in October passengers can enjoy a 40-mile "Fall Foliage" ride.

Battlefield monument

Near the battlefield is former President Dwight D. Eisenhower's **Gettysburg Farm,** which is now the **Eisenhower National Historic Site.** Eisenhower purchased the 189-acre farm in 1952, and when he became president, the farm became his retreat.

Today, the farm is much as it was when Mamie Eisenhower died in 1979. The house retains its original furnishings, and cattle still graze in the pastures. Tickets are necessary to visit the farm, and they're available at the visitors' center in the national park (adjacent to the battlefield, and open 9 A.M.-4 P.M. daily, April-October, and 9 A.M.-4 P.M., Wed.-Sun., November-March).

For a look at more of Adams County, follow the **Scenic Valley Tour,** for which you can pick up a brochure at the visitors' bureau or you can just follow the signs. The tour is 36 miles long, and it takes visitors to historic sights and the county's orchards. In some spots, fruit trees are all that are visible. The most beautiful time is late April and early May, when most of the tees are in blossom. Apples, peaches, cherries, pears, and plums are the most popular fruits, and the trees are a pretty amazing sight.

On the tour is the **South Mountain Fairgrounds,** home of the annual fair in September, as well as apple festivals in spring and fall. The tour reaches an elevation of 1,350 feet, which is about 1,000 feet higher than Gettysburg, so you'll be doing some climbing. If you're planning to do the tour on a bike, bring your climbing gears and legs. If you want to enjoy a less taxing ride, just stay down in the valley. The hills are modest, and the roads are quiet. Biglerville is home to **Musselman's,** a large producer of fruit products such as applesauce.

West of Gettysburg on Route 30 is **Caledonia State Park,** which has a Civil War connection. **Thaddeus Stevens,** a famous abolitionist, operated an iron furnace here. Because of the conflict and because of Stevens' views on slavery, Confederate soldiers destroyed the furnace in June of 1863. After the battle, pastures served as field hospitals for soldiers wounded at Gettysburg.

Today, the park is rather small, but it has a large list of attractions. Perhaps most notable is the "B," a summer stock theater that offers daily performances during the summer months. Beside the theater is an 18-hole golf course that is open to the public. The park has a swimming pool, hiking trails, and environmental education programs. In addition, modern cabins are available for rental.

Attractions:

Gettysburg Battlefield.

Eisenhower National Historic Site, (717) 334-9114, open 9 A.M.- 4 P.M. daily.

Gettysburg Battle Theatre, 571 Steinwehr Avenue, (717) 334-6100.

Gettysburg Railroad, 106 North Washington Street, (717) 334-6992, call for schedule.

Lincoln Room Museum, in the Wills House on Lincoln Square, (717) 334-8188.

National Tower, opposite battlefield, (717) 334-6754.

Battlefield scene

National Civil War Wax Museum, 297 Steinwehr Avenue, (717) 334-6245, opens daily at 9 A.M.

Lincoln Train Museum, 425 Steinwehr Avenue, (717) 334-5678.

Dining:

Altland House, Route 30, Abbottstown, (717) 259-9535, Tues.-Sun., opens at 5 P.M., Sun., 11:30 A.M.-2 P.M.

Avenue Restaurant, 21 Steinwehr Avenue, (717) 334-3235, opens at 7 A.M. daily.

Gettysburg Hotel, Lincoln Square, (717) 337-200, breakfast, lunch, and dinner daily.

Dobbin House Tavern, 89 Steinwehr Avenue, (717) 334-2100, 5 P.M.-9 P.M. daily.

Ernie's Texas Lunch, 58 Chambersburg Street, (717) 334-1970, Mon.-Fri., 6 A.M-7:30 p.m., Sat., 6 A.M.-8:30 P.M.

General Pickett's Buffet Restaurant, 571 Steinwehr Avenue, (717) 334-7580, 11 A.M.-9 P.M. daily.

Gettysburg Pub & Brewery, 348 Hunterstown Road, (717) 337-1001, Mon.-Fri., 4 P.M.-10 P.M., Sat. and Sun., noon-10 P.M.

Lincoln Diner, 32 Carlisle Street, (717) 334-3900, 24 hours a day.

Lupita's Mexican Restaurant, 51 West Street, (717) 337-9575, Sun.-Thur., 11 A.M.-9 P.M., Fri. and Sat., 11 A.M.-10 P.M.

Plaza Restaurant, Lincoln Square, (717) 334-1999, lunch and dinner daily.

Thistlefield's, 29 Chambersburg Street, (717) 338-9131, Mon.-Sat., 11:30 A.M.-4:30 P.M., Sun., noon-4:30 P.M., closed Tuesdays.

Lodging:

Gettysburg Hotel, 1797 landmark on Lincoln Square, (800) 528-1234.

Blue Sky Motel, Route 34, (717) 677-7736.

Budget Host, 205 Steinwehr Avenue, (800) 729-6564.

College Motel, 345 Carlisle Street, (800) 367-6731.

Colonial Motel, 157 Carlisle Street, (800) 336-3126.

Colton Motel, 232 Steinwehr Avenue, (800) 262-0317.

Comfort Inn, Route 30 East, (717) 337-2400.

Criterion Motor Lodge, 337 Carlisle Street, (717) 334-6268.

Gettysburg Inn, Route 34 North, (717) 334-2263.

Days Inn, Route 30 East, (717) 334-0030.

Eisenhower Inn, Route 15 South, (717) 334-8121.

Econo Lodge, Route 97, (800) 553-2666.

Hampton Inn, Route 30 East, (717) 338-9121.

Holiday Inn Battlefield, Route 97, (717) 334-6211.

Holiday Inn Express, Route 30 East, (717) 337-1400.

Home Sweet Home Motel, 593 Steinwehr Avenue, (800) 440-3916.

Howard Johnson Lodge, 301 Steinwehr Avenue, (800) 446-4656.

James Gettys Hotel, 27 Chambersburg Street, (717) 337-1334.

Homestead Motor Lodge, Route 30 East, (717) 334-3866.

Lincolnway East Motel, Route 30 East, (717) 334-4208.

North Ridge Motel, Route 34 North, (800) 550-2392.

Quality Inn, 380 Steinwehr Avenue, (800) 228-5151.

Red Carpet Inn, Route 15 South, (800) 336-1345.

A Tannery Bed & Breakfast, 449 Baltimore Street, (717) 334-2454.

Baladerry Inn, 40 Hospital Road, (717) 334-1342.

Battlefield Bed & Breakfast, 2264 Emmitsburg Road, (717) 334-8804.

Brafferton Inn, 44 York Street, (717) 334-3423.

Doubleday Inn Bed & Breakfast, on the battlefield, (717) 334-9119.

Brierfield Bed & Breakfast, 240 Baltimore Street, (717) 334-8725.

Gaslight Inn, 33 East Middle Street, (717) 337-9100.

Gettystown Inn, 89 Steinwehr Avenue, (717) 334-2100.

Herr Tavern & Publick House, Route 30 West, (800) 362-9849.

Keystone Inn, 231 Hanover Street, (717) 337-3888.

Gettysburg Campground, 2030 Fairfield Road, (717) 334-3304.

Gettysburg KOA Campground, 20 Knox Road, (800) KOA-1869.

Round Top Campground, 180 Knight Road, (717) 334-9565.

Shopping:

The most interesting shopping in Gettysburg is for souvenirs and Civil War artifacts, and the best places are in downtown Gettysburg and right around the battlefield.

American Crafters & Artists, 1919 Steinwehr Avenue, (717) 337-9186, Thus.-Mon., 10 A.M.-6 P.M.

An Early Elegance, 61 Steinwehr Avenue, (717) 338-9311, opens at 9 A.M. daily.

Antique Center of Gettysburg, 7 Lincoln Square, (717) 337-3669, Mon., Wed., Thur., and Sat., 10 A.M.-6 P.M., Fri., 10 A.M.-8 P.M., Sun., 11 A.M.-6 P.M.

Farnsworth Military Gallery, 415 Baltimore Street, (717) 334-8838, Tues.-Sun., 10 A.M.- 5 P.M.

Battlefield scene

Fiddle Faddles, 54 Chambersburg Street, (717) 334-8270, Mon.-Sat., 10 A.M.-5 P.M., Sun., 11 A.M.-4 P.M.

Gallon Historical Art, 9 Steinwehr Avenue, (717) 334-8666, Wed.-Mon., 10 A.M.- 5 P.M.

The Great T-Shirt Company, 65 Steinwehr Avenue, (717) 334-8611, open 9 A.M.- 5 P.M. daily.

Gettysburg Candle Company, Route 30 West, McKnightstown, (717) 334-0094, open 10 A.M.-5 P.M. daily.

Gettysburg Frame Shop & Gallery, 25 Chambersburg Street, (717) 337-2796, Mon.-Thur., 9 A.M.-6 P.M., Fri. and Sat., 9 A.M.- 8 P.M., Sun., noon-4 P.M.

Gettysburg Gift Center, in National Civil War Wax Museum, 291 Steinwehr Avenue, (717) 334-2996, open 9 A.M.- 5 P.M., 9 A.M.- 7 P.M., April through June, and 9 A.M.- 9 P.M., June through Labor Day.

Gettysburg Historical Prints, 219 Steinwehr Avenue, (888) 447-2515, Mon.-Sat., 9 A.M.-5 P.M., Sun., 11 A.M.-3 P.M.

The Horse Soldier, 777 Baltimore Street, (717) 334-0347, open daily except Wednesdays.

Annual Events:

Gettysburg Spring Bluegrass Festival, first weekend in May, (717) 642-8749.

Apple Blossom Festival, first weekend in May, (717) 334-6274.

Gettysburg Spring Antique Show, third Saturday in May, Lincoln Square, (717) 334-6274.

Memorial Day Parade, (717) 334-6274.

Gettysburg Civil War Heritage Days, last weekend in June and first week in July, (717) 334-6274.

Gettysburg Civil War Collectors Show, first weekend in July, (717) 334-6274.

GPBA Civil War Book Fair, first weekend in July, (717) 334-6274.

Gettysburg Firemen's Festival, week of July 4, (717) 334-6274.

South Mountain Fair, five days before Labor Day, (717) 677-8409.

National Apple Harvest Festival, first two weekends in October, (717) 334-6274.

Anniversary of the Gettysburg Address, November 19, (717) 334-6274.

Remembrance Day, mid-November, (717) 334-6274.

Gettysburg Yuletide Festival, first two weekends in December, (717) 334-6274.

The Active Life:

Touring the battlefield usually involves a significant amount of walking. If you do a full day as a tourist, you'll get a good workout. For a better way to see the battlefield travel by bike. A bike tour map is available at the visitors' center. The bike tour is about 18 miles, and a bike is really a better way to get around the battlefield than a car. On a bike, it's much easier to pull over to see the monuments and artifacts. You can rent bikes at **Artillery Ridge Campgrounds,** 610 Taneytown Road. Call (717) 334-1288 for information.

Battlefield Tours:

You can choose one of many different ways to get around the battlefield. Methods other than your own car are good because they come with guides who can answer all your questions.

Association of Licensed Battlefield Guides (the guide rides with you in your car), 97 Taneytown Road, (717) 334-1124.

Battlefield Bicycle Tours, (800) 830-5775.

Gettysburg Battlefield Bus Tours, 778 Baltimore Street, (717) 334-6296.

Gettysburg Trolley Living History Tours, (717) 334-2070.

Ghosts of Gettysburg Candlelight Walking Tours, 271 Baltimore Street, (717) 334-0445.

Historic Tours, 55 Steinwehr Avenue, (717) 334-8000.

Gettysburg Scenic Rail Tours, 106 North Washington Street, (717) 334-6992.

A Great Place to Relax/Covered Bridges:

Saks Covered Bridge lies just off Millerstown Road, southwest of town. Follow signs to the Eisenhower Farm and continue on Millerstown Road. After crossing the second concrete bridge across a stream, turn left and you'll see the bridge, which was standing during the battle.

After the battle, retreating soldiers from Virginia passed through the bridge. In 1996, a flood lifted the bridge off its foundations. Subsequent restorations have created a beautiful bridge in a beautiful setting. The bridge is open to pedestrians and bicycles, but not to cars, although you can drive right to it. Picnickers can relax near the bridge or in its shade. In fact, you could set up a picnic table inside the bridge.

The stream is a favorite with fishermen, and this is just a nice place to sit and relax.

Tourist Information:

• Gettysburg Convention and Visitors Bureau, (717) 334-6274.

Where is it? South central, at the intersection of U.S. 30 and U.S. 15.

Getaway Rating: 3

A Great Time to Visit:

Try November. The crowds are smaller, and the weather is still comfortable.

Saks Covered Bridge

12

HERSHEY . . .
CHOCOLATE TOWN, U.S.A.
(PT, R)

"ChocolateTown, U.S.A." says it all, or almost all of it. Candy is Hershey's best known product, but candy isn't Hershey's only attraction. For a small town, Hershey has a huge entertainment presence. Candy and entertainment make up most of its economy, and they come together at **HersheyPark,** where visitors can eat chocolate and ride roller coasters all day and all night.

One interesting aspect of Hershey is that it is the beneficiary of all the money that pours into the Hershey empire. **Milton Hershey School** is a legacy of Milton Hershey, and the school provides a free education and housing for socially and financially needy children in grades from kindergarten through high school. The school's campus is big and beautiful, and it covers 3,200 acres, or five square miles.

Milton Hershey School has about 1,000 students, but HersheyPark draws many more than that, as does **Chocolate World.** Milton Hershey founded HersheyPark in 1907, and since then it's been a favorite summer destination. HersheyPark isn't the world's biggest amusement park, but it has plenty of rides and enough activities to keep you busy (and dizzy) all day.

Streetlamp in shape of Hershey kiss

For years, the **Superdooperlooper** was HersheyPark's most famous ride. Now a new roller coaster, the **Great Bear,** is getting all the attention. The Great Bear goes through all sorts of rolls, turns, twists, and spirals, and it lasts for almost three minutes.

If you survive the roller coasters, gentler rides such as the **Kissing Tower** and a **ferris wheel** both offer scenic views of the surrounding countryside.

Entertainment is also an important part of a visit to HersheyPark. Dance reviews, a dolphin show, and famous country and rock 'n roll acts play in the amphitheater. And, of course, you can snack on Hershey candy all day as you move from ride to ride.

Beside HersheyPark is Chocolate World, where you can see how cocoa beans move from tropical jungles to a vat of milk chocolate in Pennsylvania to a candy bar in your local market.

Also nearby are **HersheyPark Arena** and **HersheyPark Stadium.** HersheyPark Arena is the site where Wilt Chamberlain scored 100 points in a NBA game on March 2, 1962. Now the arena is home to the **Hershey Bears** minor league team and to the Pennsylvania high school championships in basketball and wrestling, which take place in March.

The arena also hosts events such as the **Ice Follies** and **WWF** professional wrestling.

HersheyPark Stadium holds about 20,000 for football and soccer. The **Hershey Wildcats** soccer team is the main tenant in the stadium, and the Pennsylvania high school football championships also take place there. Within the stadium is the **Star Pavilion,** where rock 'n roll acts such as Live and Hanson entertain crowds of 20,000 and more.

Milton Hershey built this entire town from a meadow, and one of his later additions was the **Hotel Hershey,** a Mediterranean-style palace that bestows just about every luxury on its guests.

The hotel sits high on a hill, and it hosts many special events and theme weekends such as **Warm Winter Nights** and **Big Band Weekends.** Hershey also has a strong cultural presence. The **Hershey Theatre** hosts operas, stage productions, movies, and band concerts.

Also on the grounds are the **Hershey Museum** and **ZooAmerica.** Hershey Museum displays early Hershey products and items owned by Catherine and Milton Hershey. ZooAmerica covers 11 acres and allows visitors to walk through habitats that are home to over 200 animals from different regions of North America.

Across Hotel Road from the Hotel Hershey are **The Hershey Gardens.** Hershey Gardens houses the world's largest outdoor butterfly garden, as well as a 23-acre botanical garden founded by Milton Hershey in 1937.

On the campus of Milton Hershey School is **Founder's Hall,** the largest rotunda in the Western Hemisphere and the second largest in the world. The building is a tribute to the Hersheys, and it serves as the administrative headquarters for the school. In the rotunda, visitors can watch a video about Milton Hershey and his building of his empire.

If those attractions aren't enough to keep you occupied, you can do a little shopping . . . a little outlet shopping. **The Factory Stores at Hershey, PA** is an outlet of more than 50 stores practically beside the park and other attractions. T-shirts,

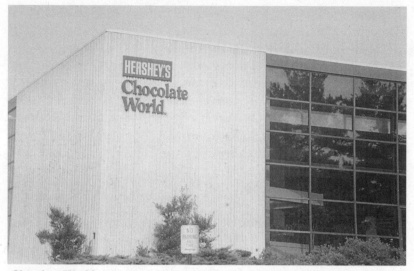

Chocolate World

sunglasses, cosmetics, and Hershey's sweets are just a few of the things that you can buy there.

South of Hershey on Route 743 is **Adventure Sports,** where everyone can have some fun with go-karts, batting ranges, bumper boats, a driving range, and a video arcade.

Close to Hershey is one of the country's most infamous attractions—**Three Mile Island.** On March 28, 1979, this nuclear power plant broke and threatened a meltdown, an event which would have vaporized everything within 25 miles. That radius includes such important places as the state capital of Harrisburg, Lancaster, and York. People were scared, but the final meltdown never happened, and life continued, although lawsuits are still ongoing against the owners of TMI because of the incident. No one has ever proved that the accident did anything harmful to people nearby. Today, the undamaged nuclear reactor at TMI is still operating, and a visitors' center tells the story of the accident. The center is on Route 441, south of Middletown.

In Middletown is the **Middletown and Hummelstown Railroad,** which operates excursion trains to **Indian Echo**

Middletown & Hummelstown Railroad

Caverns. Passengers can combine a train ride with a visit to the caverns. The train departs from downtown Middletown.

Harrisburg, the state capital, is about 10 miles west of Hershey. The biggest attraction in Harrisburg is **City Island,** an island in the middle of the Susquehanna River that's home to the **Harrisburg Senators** AA Eastern League baseball team. Also on City Island are many entertainment options, such as miniature golf, amusement rides, and paddleboat rides on the river.

The **Museum of Scientific Discovery,** in **Strawberry Square** in downtown Harrisburg, explains scientific concepts, and Strawberry Square is a large shopping mall directly beside the state capitol. At Third and North Streets in Harrisburg is the **State Museum of Pennsylvania,** which has four floors of exhibits and activities that explain Pennsylvania's colorful history.

Horse lovers can visit **Penn National,** a thoroughbred race track in Grantville that operates Monday, Wednesday, Friday, and Saturday nights, and Sunday afternoons all year.

Hershey is a place of entertainment and candy. For a getaway, Pennsylvania has no sweeter destination.

Attractions:

Adventure Sports, Route 743 South, (717) 533-7479, open 10 A.M.-10 P.M., Memorial Day through Labor Day, call other times.

HersheyPark, 100 West HersheyPark Drive, (717) 534-3090, opens at 10 A.M., closings vary.

Hershey's Chocolate World, Park Boulevard, (717) 534-4900, open 9 A.M.-5 P.M. daily, later in the summer.

HersheyPark Arena, 100 West HersheyPark Drive, (717) 534-3911.

Hershey Gardens, 170 Hotel Road, (717) 534-3492, opens at 10 A.M. daily, April through October.

Hershey Museum, 170 West HersheyPark Drive, (717) 534-3439, open 10 A.M.-5 P.M. daily.

Middletown & Hummelstown Railroad, 136 Brown Street, Middletown, (717) 944-4435, runs at 11 A.M., 1 P.M., and 2:30 P.M. on Tues. and Thur., and 11 A.M., 1 P.M., 2:30 P.M., and 4 P.M. on Sat. and Sun.

Indian Echo Caverns, off U.S. 322, Hummelstown, (717) 566-8131, open 9 A.M.-6 P.M. Memorial Day through Labor Day, and 10 A.M.-4 P.M. the rest of year.

Harrisburg Senators baseball, City Island, Harrisburg, (717) 231-4444.

Penn National Race Course, Route 743, Grantville, (717) 469-2211, Mon., Wed., Fri., and Sat. post time is 7:30 P.M., and 1:30 P.M. on Sundays.

Pride of the Susquehanna Riverboat, City Island, Harrisburg, (717) 234-6500, seasonal, call for times.

Pennsylvania State Capitol, 3rd and State Streets, Harrisburg, (800) TOUR-N-PA, Mon.-Fri., 9 A.M.-5 P.M.

Three Mile Island, Route 441, Middletown, (717) 948-8829, Thur.-Sun., noon-4:30 P.M..

Dining:

Al Mediterraneo, 288 East Main Street, Hummelstown, (717) 566-5086, Mon.-Thur., 5 P.M.-10 P.M., Fri. and Sat., 4 P.M.-11 P.M.

Kissing Tower

Alfred's Victorian, 38 North Union Street, Middletown, (717) 944-5373, lunch from noon, Mon.-Fri., dinner at 5 P.M., Mon.-Sat., and at 3 P.M. on Sundays.

Fenicci's, 102 West Chocolate Avenue, (717) 533-7159, opens at 4 P.M., Mon.-Sat.

Lucy's, 267 West Chocolate Avenue, (717) 534-1045, Mon.-Sat., 4 P.M.-10 P.M.

Hotel Hershey, Hotel Road, (717) 533-2171, call for hours.

The Restaurant on Chocolate, 814 East Chocolate Avenue, (717) 534-2734, Mon.-Fri., 11 A.M.-2:30 P.M., Mon.-Sat., 5 P.M.-10 P.M.

New York Steak & Seafood, 202 West Chocolate Avenue, (717) 533-7747, open 11:30 A.M.-9 P.M. daily.

Pavone's, Route 39 and Manor Drive, (717) 545-2338, Tues.-Sat., 11 A.M.-till, Sun., 1 P.M.-8 PM.

RY's Bagels & Deli, Hershey Square, HersheyPark Drive, (717) 533-2222, Mon.-Fri., 6:30 A.M.-4 P.M., Sat. and Sun., 7 A.M.-3 P.M.

Spinners, 845 East Chocolate Avenue, (717) 533-9050, Tues.-Sat., 5 P.M.-10 P.M.

Lodging:

Best Western Hershey, Route 422, (717) 533-5665.

Chocolatetown Motel, 1806 East Chocolate Avenue, (717) 533-2330.

Cocoa Motel, 914 Cocoa Avenue, (717) 534-1243.

Cocoa Nights Motel, 1518 East Chocolate Avenue, (717) 533-2384.

Conewago Valley Motor Inn, Route 743, Elizabethtown, (717) 367-4320.

Comfort Inn Hershey, 1200 Mae Avenue, Hummelstown, (717) 566-2050.

Econo Lodge, 115 Lucy Avenue, (717) 533-2515.

Hershey Lodge, West Chocolate Avenue and 7 University Drive, (717) 533-3311.

Hershey Travel Motel, 905 East Chocolate Avenue, (717) 533-7950.

Hotel Hershey, Hotel Road, (717) 533-2171.

Milton Motel, 1733 East Chocolate Avenue, (717) 533-4533.

Rodeway Inn, 43 West Areba Avenue, (717) 533-7054.

Simmons Motel, 355 West Chocolate Avenue, (717) 533-9177.

Spinner's Motor Inn, 845 East Chocolate Avenue, (717) 533-9157.

Union Canal House, 107 South Hanover Street, (717) 566-0054.

Pinehurst Inn Bed & Breakfast, 50 Northeast Drive, (717) 533-2603.

Hershey Highmeadow Campground, 300 Park Boulevard, (717) 566-0902.

Hen-Apple Bed & Breakfast, 409 South Lingle Avenue, Palmyra, (717) 838-8282.

Mottern Bed & Breakfast, 28 East Main Street, Hummelstown, (717) 566-3840.

Founder's Hall, Milton Hershey School

Shopping:

Factory Stores at Hershey, 46 Outlet Square, Hershey, (717) 520-1236, Mon.-Sat., 9:30 A.M.-9 P.M., Sun., 11 A.M.-5 P.M.

Zieglers in the Country, Route 743 South, (717) 533-1662, 10 A.M.-5 P.M. daily.

Cross Your Stitches, 8 Briarcrest Square, (717) 533-4010, Mon.-Sat., 10 A.M.-6 P.M.

Toys on the Square, Briarcrest Square, (717) 534-1970, , Mon.-Sat., 10 A.M.-6 P.M.

Maplenut Creations, 5 Briarcrest Square, (717) 533-5689, Mon.-Sat., 10 A.M.-6 P.M.

Annual Events:

With all the indoor and outdoor attractions, you'll find something special happening just about every week in Hershey. Call for a complete calendar. Here are a few of the highlights:

January, February, March, April—**Ice shows, Harlem Globetrotters, WWF Wrestling,** and **Hershey Bears hockey** at the HersheyPark Arena, (717) 534-3911.

March—Pennsylvania **high school wrestling and basketball championships,** HersheyPark Arena, (717) 534-3911.

Spring and Summer—**Wildcats professional soccer,** HersheyPark Arena, (717) 534-3911.

July—**Nike Tour Golf Tournament,** Country Club of Hershey, (717) 533-2360.

November and December, **Ride The Train with Santa,** Middletown and Hummelstown Railroad, (717) 944-4435.

December, **HersheyPark Christmas Candylane,** (717) 534-3900.

The Active Life:

Hershey is hectic, but the surrounding country roads are good for bicycling. Hershey is also a good place to play golf, with 72 holes available to the public. For golf reservations, call (800) 533-3131.

A Great Place to Relax:

Harrisburg has walking paths and picnic tables all along the river. It's a good place to sit and watch the water flow.

Covered Bridges:

None nearby.

Great Bear roller coaster

Tourist Information:
- (800) HERSHEY

Where is it? Southeast quadrant, on U.S. 322 and U.S. 422.

Getaway Rating: 2

13

HONESDALE . . .
MAIN STREET HIGHLIGHTS
(A, H, R)

Main Street is still a major shopping area in Honesdale. The district is about eight blocks long, and as you walk down Main, you'll quickly notice that one of the town's nicest characteristics is that drivers stop at marked crosswalks to let pedestrians cross the street. Stroll down Main Street and you'll find some stores that you might not expect in a town of 5,000, such as a health food store, a Chinese restaurant, and "His" and "Her" clothing stores.

Main Street is a nice place to eat and shop, and it's not the only reason visitors come. Local publications refer to the region as **"Lake Country,"** and many lakes lie around Honesdale. The largest is **Lake Wallenpaupack,** which is the biggest attraction in the area. Pennsylvania's third largest man-made lake offers 52 miles of shoreline, and it's a very popular spot for fishing, swimming, and boating. Around the lake are many types of attractions, such as water parks, golf courses, and summer camps. This area is home to a multitude of summer camps. Thousands of children come to enjoy a week or a summer in the woods, and their parents can make motel rooms hard to find on visiting weekends.

Honesdale has an important place in the history of American railroads, and the **Wayne County Museum** on Main Street

The Town Green in Honesdale

celebrates that history. In August of 1829, Horatio Allen took the throttle of a locomotive named the **Stourbridge Lion** and made the first trip by steam locomotive in North America.

Allen rolled about three miles over flimsy tracks and rails, and the Lion proved to be too heavy for the rails on which it rolled. Its time in service was brief, but it proved that the idea of steam locomotives would work.

Within a few years, improved rails came to the region, and Honesdale became an important port on the Delaware & Hudson Canal. From Honesdale, coal mined in Carbondale and Scranton took a 108-mile journey to New York. Railroads eventually made the shipping process much easier. At the museum, you can sit in a real railroad car and watch a video that tells the story of the rails and the region. Inside the museum is an authentic reproduction of the original Stourbridge Lion. The **Stourbridge Line** is a tourist railroad that operates in downtown Honesdale. It takes passengers on scenic rides through Wayne and Pike counties along the Lackawaxen River.

Highlights magazine has its offices in an old home on Church Street in Honesdale but its not much of a tourist attraction. Watching writers, editors, and artists create magazines and books isn't nearly as interesting as reading them.

The home of Highlights

Central Park in downtown Honesdale, in front of the **Wayne County Courthouse,** is an ideal place to sit and watch the water fountain, and in summer the park hosts a series of events such as barbershop singers, fiddlers, and dancers. The events take place on Monday and Thursday evenings.

The region around Honesdale is attractive to bicyclists. The drawback is that Honesdale lies at the bottom, so any ride out of town will involve a climb. The good news is that traffic is light on the rural roads.

Honesdale offers the kinds of getaways that seem typical to an area of rural Pennsylvania, and the region also has a getaway destination that's rather unusual by local standards. The **Himalayan Institute,** located six miles north of downtown, offers programs in yoga, meditation, Eastern philosophy, and holistic health. Founded by Swi Swami Rama in 1971, the institute covers 400 acres and provides programs throughout the year, including holiday retreats. The institute focuses on healthful eating, and it also offers supervised fasts to cleanse the body and mind.

On the north side of town, along Route 191, are the **Wayne County Fairgrounds.** The county fair takes place there beginning in early August, and the grounds host activities throughout the year, including a 5K run in mid-July that gives competitors the unusual thrill of running on a track normally used for horse racing. In rural communities, fairs are big social events, and Wayne County brings in musical acts, demolition derby, woodsmen's competitions, and harness racing.

In **Hawley,** east of Honesdale on Route 6, antiques are big business. The **Castle Antiques** building is the largest bluestone building in the world, and nearby are lovely waterfalls that provided power for the buildings when they were mills in the 1800s.

In White Mills, also along Route 6, are the **Dorflinger Glass Museum** and the **Dorflinger-Suydam Wildlife Sanctuary.** The glass museum houses an extensive collection of glass made by Dorflinger Glassworks. Beginning in 1852, Christian Dorflinger's factories made lead crystal for presidents and kings. The museum was Christian Dorflinger's home, and it houses the largest public display of Dorflinger glass.

The wildlife sanctuary covers 600 acres with five miles of walking trails and **Trout Lake.** In summer, the grounds are host to musical performances where squirrels, chipmunks, and rabbits are always in attendance, and where deer occasionally stop by for a favorite song.

Along the **Lackawaxen River** are remnants of the Delaware & Hudson Canal, which closed in 1898. Working on a canal may seem like an exciting job now, but it was a grueling life for the entire family. Father steered the vessel. Mother ran the household, older children drove the mules, and younger children often found themselves tied to the deck to keep them out of the water.

Sometimes, the workday lasted up to 20 hours, so the families who lived and worked on the canal probably weren't too unhappy when the canal froze in November or December.

The Lackawaxen River joins the Delaware River at the small village of Lackawaxen. Some of the Stourbridge Line's excursion trains travel to Lackawaxen, and on those rides visitors can walk around and visit the **Zane Grey Museum,** the home of the former dentist turned Western author.

Whether you're looking for fun on the lake and in the woods or a gentle weekend in town, Honesdale has what you need.

Attractions:

Main Street shopping district.

Stourbridge Line Railroad, 700 Main Street, (800) 433-9008, call for schedule.

Lake Wallenpaupack, Route 6, Hawley.

Wayne County Historical Society Museum, 810 Main Street, (570) 253-3240, Wed.-Sat., 10 A.M.-4 P.M.

Maple Drive-In, Route 6, (570) 253-2800, shows start at dusk.

Dorflinger Glass Museum, Long Ridge Road, White Mills, (570) 253-1185, Wed.-Sat., 10 A.M.-4 P.M., Sun., 1 P.M.-4 P.M., May through October.

Ritz Company Playhouse, 512 Keystone Street, Hawley, (570) 226-9752, open 11 A.M.-10 P.M., Memorial Day through Labor Day.

Himalayan Institute, Route 670, (800) 822-4547, call to arrange a visit (it's a retreat).

Carousel Water Park, Route 652, Beach Lake (570) 729-7532, open 11 A.M.-10 P.M., Memorial Day through Labor Day.

Beach Lake Water Park, Route 652, (570) 729-7532, open in summer.

Costa's Family Fun Park, Route 6, east of Lake Wallenpaupack, (570) 226-8585, open in summer.

Zane Grey Museum, Scenic Drive, Lackawaxen, (570) 685-4871, seasonal hours, call ahead for times.

Dining:

The Alpine, Route 6, (570) 253-5899, Tues., 8 A.M.-5 P.M., Wed. and Thur., 8 A.M.-8 P.M., Fri. and Sat., 8 A.M.-9 P.M., and Sun., 9 A.M.-5 P.M.

Lake Wallenpaupack

Antique & Craft Café, 1050 Main Street, (570) 251-8738, Sun.-Thur., 11 A.M.-7:30 P.M., Fri. and Sat., 11 A.M.-10 P.M.

Bagels Gourmet, 110 7th Street, (570) 253-3566, 6 A.M.-2 P.M. daily.

Bartans, Route 6 and Route 652, (570) 253-3186, Mon., 6 A.M.-4 P.M., Tues. and Thur., 6 A.M.-8 P.M., Fri. and Sat., 24 hours, and Sun., 7 A.M.-3 P.M.

Brill's Restaurant, 503 Main Street, (570) 253-4355, Tues.-Sat., 7 A.M.-9 P.M, SUN., 7 a.m.-2 P.M.

China Castle, 1143 Main Street, (570) 253-2030, 11:30 A.M.-9 P.M. daily.

Coffee Grinder, 526 Main Street, (570) 253-2285, Mon.-Sat., 6 A.M.-7 P.M., Sun., 7 A.M.-6 P.M.

Cordaro's Restaurant, Route 6 East, (570) 253-3713, Mon.-Sat., 6 A.M.-10 P.M., Sun., 7 A.M.-10 P.M.

Donut Connection, Route 6, Honesdale, open 5 A.M.-10 P.M. daily.

Erhardt's Lakeside, Route 507 on Lake Wallenpaupack, (570) 226-2124, Mon.-Thur., 11 A.M.-9 P.M., Fri. and Sat., 11 A.M.-11 P.M., and Sun., 9 A.M.-9 P.M.

Elegante Restaurant, 851 Main Street, (570) 253-3244, 11 A.M.-9 P.M. daily.

Falcone's Pizzeria, 503 Main Street, (570) 253-4755, open 11 A.M.-11 P.M. daily.

Falls Port Inn, 330 Main Avenue, Hawley, (570) 226-2600, lunch and dinner daily.

The Fireside, Route 191 North, (570) 253-0141, Tues.-Sun., 11 A.M.-9 P.M.

The Hamlin Diner, Route 590, Hamlin, (570) 689-0424, open 8 A.M.-8 P.M. daily.

Main Street Beanery, 1139 Main Street, (570) 253-5740, breakfast, lunch, and dinner.

Maple City Restaurant, 734 Main Street, (570) 253-2462, Mon.-Thur., and Sat. 6:30 A.M.-7 P.M., Fri., 6:30 A.M.-8 P.M.

Nature's Grace, 947 Main Street, (570) 253-3469, Mon.-Thur., and Sat., 10 A.M.-6 P.M., Fri., 10 A.M.-8 P.M.

Towne House Diner, 920 Main Street, (570) 253-1311, open 7 A.M.-9 P.M. daily.

Jack Trainor's Restaurant, 760 Terrace Street, (570) 253-3733, Tues.-Sun., 11:30 A.M.-8 P.M..

Wayne Hotel, 1202 Main Street, (570) 253-3290, lunch and dinner daily.

Lodging:

Brookside Country Cabins, Route 191, (570) 253-1038.

Deer Lodge Motel, Route 191, (570) 253-3629.

Fife & Drum Motor Inn, 100 Terrace Street, (570) 253-1392.

Grandview Motel, Route 6 East, (570) 253-4744.

Oliver's Bed & Breakfast, 1415 Main Street, (570) 253-4533.

Park Hotel, 118 8th Street, (570) 253-0121.

Wayne Hotel, 1202 Main Street, (570) 253-3290.

Willow Pond Inn, Route 191, (570) 253-3930.

Falls Port Inn, 330 Main Avenue, Hawley, (570) 226-2600.

Sandy Beach Motel, Route 6, Hawley, (570) 226-3858.

Settlers Inn, 4 Main Avenue, Hawley, (570) 226-2993.

Keen Lake Camping/Cottage Resort, Route 6, Waymart, (570) 488-6161.

Shopping:

Antique & Craft Café, 1050 Main Street, (570) 251-8738, Sun.-Thur., 11 A.M.-7:30 P.M., Fri. and Sat., 11 A.M.-10 P.M.

Art's For Him/Art's For Her, 823 & 843 Main Street, (570) 253-2710, Mon.-Thur. and Sat., 9:30 A.M.-5 P.M., Fri., 9:30 A.M.-8 P.M.

Castle Antiques, 515 Welwood Avenue, Hawley, (570) 226-8550, Mon.-Sat., 8:30 A.M.-5 P.M.

Hawley Antique Center, 318 Main Avenue, Hawley, (570) 226-8990, Wed.-Fri., Sun., and Mon., 10 A.M.-5 P.M., Sat., 11 A.M.-6 P.M.

Hawley Antique Exchange, Route 6, Hawley, (570) 226-1711, Thur.-Tues., 10 A.M.-5 P.M.

Loft Antiques, Route 590 East, Hawley, (570) 685-4267, Fri.-Mon., 11 A.M.-5 P.M.

Northeast Flyfishers, 923 Main Street, (570) 253-9780, Mon.-Sat., 10 A.M.-6 P.M.

Northeast Sports, 107 8th Street, (570) 253-1145, Mon.-Thur., 9 A.M.-6 P.M., Fri., 9 A.M.-9 P.M., Sat., 9 A.M.-5 P.M., and Sun., 9 A.M.-1 P.M.

The Outpost, Routes 6 and 590, Hawley, (570) 226-6005, Mon.-Thur. and Sat., 9 A.M.-5 P.M., Fri., 9 A.M.-8 P.M., and Sun., 9 A.M.-3 P.M.

Player's Choice Golf & Country Crossroads, Weis Shopping Plaza, Route 590, (570) 689-5114, Mon.-Sat., 10 A.M.-8 P.M., Sun., noon-6 P.M.

Ros-Al Floral & Antiques, Route 6, Hawley, (570) 226-8650, Thur.-Tues., 10 A.M.-5 P.M.

Robert Williams Antiques, Route 191, Honesdale, Mon.-Fri., 10 A.M.-5 P.M., weekends by chance.

Annual Events:

Bike Tour of Lake Wallenpaupack, mid-May, (570) 586-1728.

Memorial Day Parade, Hawley.

Arts & Crafts Fair, mid-June, Hawley.

Hawley VFW Block Party, late June.

Stourbridge Line train trips, Easter through Christmas, (800) 433-9008.

Ritz Company Playhouse performances, July and August, Hawley, (570) 226-9752.

Wayne County Antiques Show, mid-July, Wayne Highlands Middle School, Route 191, Honesdale, (800) 433-9008.

Perkins Memorial 5K Run, third Saturday in July, Honesdale, (570) 253-1960.

Wildflower Music Festival, Dorflinger-Suydam Wildlife Sanctuary, White Mills, July and August, (570) 253-1185.

Wayne County Fair, Route 191, Honesdale, early August.

Arts & Crafts Fair, Hawley, third Saturday in September.

Hawley Harvest Hoedown, first Saturday in October, (570) 226-3191.

Honesdale Harvest Days, second weekend in October, (570) 253-1960.

The Active Life:

Many visits to Honesdale include some sort of activity. Strolling up and down Main Street will give you a good walk. Lake Wallenpaupack is busy with boaters and swimmers. The Lackawaxen River has rapids that are popular with rafters and tubers. Call **Scotty's White Water Raft Rides** in Hawley for information, (570) 226-3551. Bicyclists will find many miles of lightly traveled rural roads that have a few hills and beautiful scenery. Runners will find the **Perkins 5K Run** in July pleasantly flat with an interesting finish on a horse racing track.

A Great Place to Relax:

The town square in Honesdale, in front of the courthouse on Court Street, has a beautiful fountain, tall trees, and park benches. It's a good place to sit.

Covered Bridges:

There's one at the entrance to the Wayne County Fairgrounds on Route 191.

Tourist Information:

• (800) 433-9008

Where is it? Northeast corner, on U.S. 6.

Getaway Rating: 3

14

HUNTINGDON COUNTY . . . STREAMS AND STEAM

(H, N, R)

Visitors flock to this area of south central Pennsylvania to enjoy the activities and the inactivities available along and around **Raystown Lake.** With 118 miles of shoreline and 8,300 acres of water, Raystown Lake is the largest man-made lake within Pennsylvania.

Not far from the lake is the country's most authentic tourist railroad. The **East Broad Top Railroad** (EBT), operating in Orbisonia, is different from other tourist railroads because the EBT doesn't re-create an earlier era of railroading. Instead, the EBT simply maintains that earlier era.

Raystown Lake is newer than the EBT, and it's open every day. It's the biggest attraction in the area. Boating, fishing, jet skiing, and parasailing are some of the popular activities. For many, simply sitting and watching the water is the best possible inactivity. **Huntingdon,** with about 7,000 people, is the big city in the region. It's the county seat, and it's home to **Juniata College** and **Lincoln Caverns.**

The history of Huntingdon County is largely a history of coal mining. Large deposits of soft coal lie in the region, and many small mining towns grew up, especially in the Broad Top area. Today, coal mining activity is almost gone, and signs of mining

Harbor on Raystown Lake

operations are disappearing as forests reclaim the hillsides. The county is green, and in the valleys farming is flourishing. Many Amish families live in the area, and their buggies are common sights in some areas.

In Orbisonia, Saturdays and Sundays bring people and the sound of excitement to a quiet little town. The EBT holds a special place in the lives of railroad enthusiasts, and many of them regard a trip to Orbisonia as a sort of religious pilgrimage.

The EBT is a **National Historic Landmark** and the last remaining narrow gauge steam railroad east of the Rockies. The rails are only 36 inches apart, instead of the 56½ on standard gauge railroads, and the difference is noticeable whenever the train rounds a curve. Because of the narrow wheelbase, the cars lean much farther than the cars on a traditional train do.

The narrow gauge is one of several factors that make the EBT memorable. Even more important is that the EBT is still using its own original equipment. The locomotives arrived in the 1910s, and the passenger cars began running on these tracks back in the 1880s. Because the equipment is old, the railroad limits both the number of trips that it makes and the speed that it attains. The trains run only on weekends from June through

Columbus Day weekend in October, and their speed rarely tops 10 mph. Those limitations help preserve the equipment.

The EBT operates on steam power, and riders in one of the open passenger cars will quickly get a lesson in cinders. They pour out of the engine along with the black smoke, and they fall on the passengers, who don't seem to mind. For a railroad enthusiast, a shirt soiled by cinders from the EBT is a souvenir to be framed without ever going near a washing machine. If you don't like the idea of having cinders land on you, you can ride inside one of the old cars and experience the luxury of rail travel in the 1880s.

The EBT runs through the Aughwick Valley, beside Route 522. Photographers wait at every road crossing, and the train gives riders an opportunity to take along a lunch and enjoy it at a picnic grove. Riders on either of the first two trips may get off at Colgate Grove and catch a later train back to the station.

Adjacent to the EBT is the **Rockhill Trolley Museum,** which operates and restores trolleys. Visitors can take a short ride on a streetcar and visit the museum to see how streetcars moved millions of Americans around cities before the automobile came to dominate American life. The trolley schedule is staggered so visitors can ride both the trolley and the EBT.

In Huntingdon, auto lovers will enjoy a visit to the **Swigart Antique Auto Museum** on Route 22, east of the borough. Immaculately restored autos from the early days to the present are on a revolving display. The collection numbers in the hundreds, with as many as 50 on display at a time. Many were the ultimate in luxury in their days. Some are unique, such as the world's only 12-cylinder 1936 Duesenberg, and the authentic *Herbie,* the "Love Bug" of Disney fame. The museum also has an interesting collection of automobile toys, clothing, and lights, as well as the world's largest collection of license plates.

Northeast of Huntingdon, on Route 26, is **Shaver's Creek Environmental Center.** Operated by Penn State University, the center offers environmental educational programs such as natural history, summer camps for children and teens, and a Raptor Center with live falcons, hawks, owls, and eagles.

At **Lincoln Caverns** on Route 22, west of Huntingdon, you can journey to the center of the earth. Interpretive programs and trained guides lead tours into two crystal caverns where many bats live. Also on the grounds are picnic pavilions and nature trails.

Raystown Lake is a comparatively recent addition to the map of Pennsylvania. It opened in 1975 as a flood control project on the Raystown Branch of the Juniata River, and it's become a major recreational area, although most of the area is still unspoiled by any sort of development.

Visitors have many lodging options. Some simply find a little flat spot and pitch a tent. Others prefer the comfort of a motel, a bed and breakfast, or a houseboat on the lake. Houseboat rentals are available at **Seven Points Marina** in Hesston. The boats come equipped with cooking and eating utensils, furniture, bottled water, safety equipment, and much more.

If your preference is to sleep on land, **Lake Raystown Resort & Lodge** offers very affordable accommodations overlooking the lake. Also on the property are restaurants, cabins, a marina, swimming, mini-golf, a waterpark, and cruises on a paddle-wheeler called the *Proud Mary.*

Steam and streams make Huntingdon County an interesting place to get away from the fast pace of daily life.

Attractions:

East Broad Top Railroad, Route 994, Orbisonia, (814) 447-3011, Sat. and Sun., 11 A.M., 1 P.M., and 3 P.M., June through October.

Rockhill Trolley Museum, Route 994, Orbisonia, (814) 447-9756, Sat. and Sun., 11:30 A.M.-4:30 P.M., June through October.

Raystown Lake.

Swigart Antique Auto Museum, Route 22, Huntingdon, (814) 643-0885, open daily, Memorial Day through October, 9 A.M.-5 P.M.

Lake Raystown Resort, Route 994, Entriken, (814) 658-3500.

Cruise Boat on Raystown Lake

Shaver's Creek Environmental Center, Route 26, (814) 863-2000.

Seven Points Marina, Hesston, (814) 658-3074.

Lincoln Caverns, Route 22, west of Huntingdon, (814) 643-0268, opens daily at 10 A.M.

Broad Top Area Coal Miners Museum, Robertsdale, (814) 635-3807, Sat. and Sun., noon-5 P.M.

Dining:

Brothers Pizza, 22 West Shirley Street, Mount Union, (814) 542-4637, Mon.-Sat., 11 A.M.-11 P.M., Sun., 3 P.M.-11 P.M.

Donna's Family Restaurant, Route 22, Smithfield, (814) 643-6113, Sun.-Thur., 6 A.M.-10 P.M., Fri. and Sat., 24 hours a day.

Happy Hollow Restaurant, Route 26, Saxton, (814) 635-3900, open 9 A.M.-9 P.M. daily.

Hoss's, Route 22, Huntingdon, (814) 643-6939, open 11:30 A.M.-9:30 P.M. daily.

Main Street Café, Alexandria, (814) 669-4494, Mon.-Sat., 7 A.M.-8 P.M.

Midtown Pizza, 612 Washington Street, Huntingdon, (814) 641-9498, Mon.-Sat., 11:30 A.M.-11 P.M., Sun., 1 P.M.-11 P.M.

Miller's Diner, Route 22, east of Huntingdon, (814) 643-3418, Mon.-Sat., 5:30 A.M.-8 P.M., Sun., 7 A.M.-8 P.M.

Seven Points Eatery, Hesston, (814) 658-2955, open 7 A.M.-9 P.M. daily.

Sunny Ridge Restaurant, Route 522, Shade Gap, (814) 259-3868, open 7 A.M.-8 P.M. daily.

Vista Vu Restaurant, Route 22 East, Huntingdon, (814) 643-2544, open 7 A.M.-9 P.M. daily.

Lodging:

Aunt Susie's Bed & Breakfast, RD #1, Hesston, (888) 232-5253.

Days Inn, Route 22, Huntingdon, (814) 643-3934.

Edgewater Acres, RD #1, Alexandria, (814) 669-4144.

The Inn at Solvang, Route 26 North, Huntingdon, (814) 643-3035.

Lake Cottages, Raystown Lake, Hesston, (814) 658-3824.

The Lodge at Lake Raystown Resort, Route 994, Entriken, (814) 658-3500.

Seven Points Marina Houseboat Rentals, Hesston, (814) 658-3074.

Vista Vu Motel, Route 22 East, Huntingdon, (814) 643-2544.

Weaver's Ridge Bed & Breakfast, Saxton, (814) 635-3730.

Campgrounds at Lake Raystown Resort, Route 994, Entriken, (814) 658-3500.

Robinson's Hideaway Campground, Route 994, Entriken, (814) 658-3663.

Shopping:

Village Art Glass, 500 Washington Street, Huntingdon, (814) 643-0636, Mon.-Sat., 10 A.M.-5 P.M.

James Creek Outfitters, 1101 Church Street, Saxton, (814) 635-2828, Tues.-Sun., 10 A.M.-6 P.M.

Cloudminders Kite Shoppe, 515 Washington Street, Huntingdon, (814) 643-5121, Mon.-Sat., 10 A.M.-5 P.M.

Martin General Store, Route 22 West, Mount Union, (814) 542-2751, Mon.-Sat., 9 A.M.-8 P.M.

Annual Events:

Call (888) RAYSTOWN for information.

Huntingdon Quilt Show, May, Community Center.

Springfest, downtown Huntingdon, May.

Raystown Regatta, June.

Saxton Street Scene, August.

Huntingdon County Fair, August.

Broad Top Homecoming, Labor Day weekend.

Canal Era Day, Mount Union, October.

East Broad Top Fall Spectacular, second weekend in October.

Ghosts & Goblins Tours, Lincoln Caverns, October.

Festival of Trees, Huntingdon County Historical Society, December.

The Active Life:

   Raystown Lake is popular for all sorts of activities, such as boating, swimming, water skiing, and fishing. Hikers will enjoy "The Thousand Steps," a landmark at **Jack's Narrows,** where the Juniata River cuts a deep gorge through Jack's Mountain. The climb is only two miles, but the elevation change is 1,000 feet, so it's a strenuous climb. "The Thousand Steps" is two miles east of Mount Union on Route 22.

   Huntingdon County has some good sections for bicycling, but in many places only one road passes through a valley, leading to heavy traffic. For a 25-mile ride that's not terribly hilly, go west from Orbisonia on Route 994 to the town of Three Springs. There, go north on Route 747. At State Route 2016, turn right and follow that road back to Orbisonia.

A Great Place to Relax:

Raystown Lake provides miles of quiet places, and the train station at East Broad Top is a fine place to sit and enjoy the action.

Covered Bridges:

The last covered bridge in Huntingdon County lies beside Route 522, between the Pennsylvania Turnpike and the town of Orbisonia.

Tourist Information:

- (800) 269-4684

Where is it? South Central, on U.S. 422, U.S. 522 and the Pennsylvania Turnpike.

Getaway Rating: 4

Pleasure boat on Raystown Lake

15

JIM THORPE . . .
FROM BLEAK TO CHIC
(A, H, R, R&R)

Two decades ago, Jim Thorpe was a declining little town beside the Lehigh River in Carbon County. Today it's still a little town beside the river, but a revival has turned it into a vibrant vacation destination with something for almost everyone.

Coal made Jim Thorpe (originally Mauch Chunk) a prosperous place in the 19th century, and **The Molly Maguires** operated in Carbon and neighboring Schuylkill County.

The coal industry flourished for a century or more, but it has declined, and the people of Jim Thorpe have developed their other resources to make their town a destination that attracts antique shoppers and whitewater rafters.

A beautiful setting that draws comparisons to Switzerland, Victorian architecture, lots of history, and a location within easy driving range of Philadelphia and New York have made Jim Thorpe a popular place. Whether you like to relax in luxury or to challenge nature and your muscles, you'll find something to please you in Jim Thorpe.

The first thing that a visitor will notice is that flat space is scarce. On both sides of the river, the land rises steeply, and it was this setting that gave Jim Thorpe its reason for existence.

Train Station in Jim Thorpe

Carbon County takes its name from the anthracite coal in the region, and the Lehigh River was the best form of transportation before the railroads came.

In 1827, the second railroad in America began carrying coal from the Summit mines down to the river. The **Switchback Railroad** used gravity to take the coal down and mules to pull the empty cars back up. The mules rode down the slopes on sliding platforms, and legend says that they enjoyed their rides so much that they refused to walk downhill.

By 1870, railroads served the mines directly, and the Switchback Railroad found new life as a tourist attraction. It reached speeds of 65 mph and inspired the development of roller coasters. The Switchback went out of business in 1933, and the owners sold the tracks, but the right-of-way is still in use as a trail. Freight trains are still operating in the area and **Rail Excursions** takes passengers on scenic rides on weekends from Easter until the Christmas season.

·The man most responsible for Jim Thorpe's first era of prosperity was Asa Packer. In 1833, Packer arrived in Mauch Chunk to drive a canal boat, which he did for two years. Eventually he got into the railroad business and built the Lehigh Valley

Railroad into a large and profitable route. Today, the **Asa Packer Mansion** is one of Jim Thorpe's popular attractions.

The **Jim Thorpe Mausoleum** is a curious place for the great athlete (he was the star of the 1912 Olympics, and played professional baseball and football) to have found his final resting place. After his death in 1953, his widow couldn't find a city to give him a suitable memorial. In May of 1954, the citizens of Mauch Chunk and East Mauch Chunk voted to approve the merger of their boroughs into Jim Thorpe, with the stipulation that the new town would provide the man with a memorial. And that's how one of the country's most famous athletes found his final rest in a place that he had never visited. He had, however, attended school in Pennsylvania, at the Carlisle Indian School.

If you're looking for an active vacation, Jim Thorpe has the facilities. The **Lehigh Gorge Trail** begins at Jim Thorpe and goes north to White Haven. It's great for hiking and biking, and it's between 22 and 25 miles long. (The brochures say 25, but a bike odometer said 22.) At either distance, it's beautiful, passing waterfalls, rock formations, wildlife, and picnic areas. Mountain bikes are best, but road bikes are okay.

White Haven is 532 feet higher than Jim Thorpe, but the old railroad grade is almost flat. For its entire length, the trail has only one road crossing, and that's close to the northern end at White Haven. The trail runs beside a working railroad (Reading and Northern) for its first six miles. Then the tracks cross the river and run along the other side. Away from the trail, mountain biking is popular in the woods and on the **Switchback Trail.**

Another popular activity is **whitewater rafting.** When the water is high, the Lehigh is a fairly wild river. When the water is placid, it's good for leisurely floating. Spring is the prime whitewater season. In summer, the water is usually fairly low, but dam releases occasionally provide a day or two of action.

Mauch Chunk Lake in **Mauch Chunk Lake Park** provides boating, fishing, and swimming. The park offers camping and all the associated activities.

Downtown Jim Thorpe

A game that's relatively new and growing is Skirmish, more commonly known as **paintball.** It's a version of "Capture The Flag," and Jim Thorpe has a large and popular site.

Back in town, the atmosphere is calmer. Visitors stroll among the shops, historic sites, and restaurants. A good first stop is the restored Jersey Central railroad station that serves as the **Tourist Welcome Center.** Train rides depart from the station on weekends from mid-May through mid-October, with additional runs at Easter and Christmas.

A stroll around town provides a look at the beautiful Victorian homes. Built for the barons of rails, coal, and lumber, they're now both residences and businesses. Antique stores, galleries, and jewelry shops occupy many of them.

When you're hungry, you'll find plenty of choices, but no fast food franchises. The **Sunrise Diner,** on the square, is a fixture. It's an old-fashioned chrome diner with tables, counter seating, oldies on the jukebox, and a burger and fries menu. For a more elegant atmosphere, visit the restaurant and pub at **The Inn at Jim Thorpe.** You'll also find many other restaurants of all descriptions.

Jim Thorpe's major attractions include the **Old Jail Museum** and its mysterious hand print of a Molly Maguire. The Molly Maguires were a secret organization devoted to improving the lives of coal miners in Pennsylvania's anthracite fields. Sometimes they threatened and even killed mine owners, foremen, and law officers. In 1879, three Mollies were hanged, and all swore that they were innocent. One man, to prove his innocence, placed his hand on the wall of his cell and proclaimed that his handprint would remain forever as a sign of his innocence. The print is still on the wall of Cell 17.

The Asa Packer Mansion was the home of the railroad magnate. It's a stunning example of Italiante architecture that contains every opulence that a man of fabulous fortune could buy.

The **Mauch Chunk Museum and Cultural Center** displays artifacts and tells the story of Mauch Chunk and of Jim Thorpe the athlete. In the museum are working models of the Switchback Railroad and a canal lock.

Major events are the **Laurel Festival** in June, the **Fall Foliage Festival** in October, and **Olde Time Christmas** in December.

For overnight stays, Jim Thorpe offers a nice selection of bed and breakfasts and inns, but no chain motels. The Inn at Jim Thorpe is a restored Victorian hotel with fireplaces, whirlpools, and a relaxing balcony.

One of Jim Thorpe's attractions is that it's very compact. You can park the car when you arrive and easily walk to many of the town's attractions.

Jim Thorpe has undergone a positive transformation, and the result is a beautiful little town that's an ideal getaway destination.

Attractions:

Downtown Shopping District.

Rail Tours train rides, train station, downtown, (570) 325-4606, Sat. and Sun., noon, 1 P.M., 2 P.M., and 3 P.M.

Mountain biking and river rafting.

Lehigh Gorge rail trail.

Jim Thorpe Memorial

Mauch Chunk Lake Park, Lentz Trail, (570) 325-3669.

Asa Packer Mansion, downtown, (570) 325-3229, open 11 A.M.-5 P.M. in season.

Mauch Chunk Opera House, Broadway, (570) 325-4439.

Millionaires' Row, Broadway.

Mauch Chunk Museum, 41 West Broadway, (570) 325-9190, open 11 A.M.-5 P.M., weekends in April and May, and Thur.-Sun. in May through October.

The Old Jail Museum, 128 West Broadway, (570) 325-5259, Thur.-Tues., noon-4:30 P.M.

Dining:

Black Bread Café, 45-47 Race Street, (570) 325-8957, lunch and dinner daily.

The Emerald Restaurant & Molly Maguire's Pub, 24 Broadway, (570) 325-8995, opens at 11:30 A.M. daily.

Gerber's Café, 501 North Street, (570) 325-8103, Tues., 4 P.M.-8 P.M., Wed. and Thur., 4 P.M.-10 P.M., and Fri. and Sat., 5 P.M.-10 P.M.

The Inn at Jim Thorpe, 24 Broadway, (800) 329-2599, dinner daily.

JT's All American Steak & Ale House, 5 Hazard Square, (570) 325-4563.

Sequoyah House, 68 Broadway, (570) 325-8824, Mon.-Thur., 11:30 A.M.-5 P.M., Fri.-Sun., 11:30 A.M.-9 P.M.

Sunrise Diner, 3 Hazard Square, (570) 325-4093, open 5 A.M.-8 P.M. daily.

Lodging:

The Inn at Jim Thorpe, 24 Broadway, (800) 329-2599.

A Suite on Broadway, 97 Broadway, (570) 325-3540.

Victoria Ann's, 68 Broadway, (570) 325-8107.

Hotel Switzerland, 5 Hazard Square, (570) 325-4563.

The Diminick House, 110 Broadway, (570) 325-4368.

Cozy Corner Bed & Breakfast, 504 North Street, (570) 325-2961.

The Harry Packer Mansion Bed & Breakfast, downtown historic district, (570) 325-8566.

Tiffany's Grand Victoria Bed & Breakfast, 218 Center Street, (888) 541-2206.

Shopping:

Anne's Early Attic, 23 Broadway, (570) 325-2299, open noon-5 P.M. daily.

Dugan's Store, 60 Broadway, (570) 325-4600, Mon.-Sat., 9 A.M.-5:30 P.M., Sun., noon-5 P.M.

Earth Tribe, 12 Hill Road, (570) 325-5217, Tues.-Sun., 11 A.M.-5 P.M.

Emporium of Curious Goods, 15 Broadway, (570) 325-4038, Mon.-Sat., 11 A.M.-5 P.M., Sun., noon-5 P.M.

Everything Nice Shop, adjacent to railroad station, (570) 325-2248, open 10 A.M.-5 P.M. daily.

Maria Feliz Gallery & Sculpture Garden, 60 West Broadway, (570) 325-8969, opens Sat. and Sun. at noon

1st Class Stained Glass, 221 High Street, (570) 325-4381, Wed.-Mon., 11 A.M.-6 P.M.

The Gem Shop, 37 Broadway, (570) 325-3007, open daily.

Heart's Delights, 37 Race Street, (570) 325-4374, open noon-5 P.M. daily, June through December.

Mauch Chunk 5 & 10, 9 Broadway, Mon.-Thur., 9 A.M.-5 P.M., Fri., 9 A.M.-6 P.M., Sat., 9 A.M.-5 P.M., and Sun., noon-5 P.M.

J.E. Morgan Outlet, Race Street, (570) 325-3005, Mon.-Sat., 10 A.M.-6 P.M., Sun., noon-5 P.M.

Mystique, 111 Broadway, (570) 325-2354, flexible hours, open daily.

Natural Impressions, 92 Broadway, (570) 325-8371, Wed.-Mon., 11 A.M.-5 P.M.

Stone Row Gallery, 31 West Broadway, (570) 325-4568, open 10 A.M.-5 P.M. daily.

TSS Antiques, 14 Race Street, (570) 325-4776, open 10 A.M.-5 P.M. daily, May through December.

Annual Events:

Spring whitewater season, March and April.

Train rides, mid-May through mid-October.

Jim Thorpe Birthday Celebration, mid-May.

Festival of the Arts, last three weekends in May.

Rotary/CC Art Show, first weekend in June.

Laurel Blossom Festival, mid-June.

Fall Foliage Festival, second weekend in October.

Old Time Christmas, first two weekends in December.

The Active Life:

Whitewater rafting is a popular activity here. In spring, when the snow melts, the Lehigh River is high and wild, with Class 2 and Class 3 rapids. In summer, the river is calmer but still busy.

Mauch Chunk Lake

In late afternoon on a summer Saturday, school buses full of the adventurous roll steadily through the town. Two different companies offer escorted river tours. Call **Jim Thorpe River Adventures** at (570) 325-2570 or **Pocono Whitewater Rafting** at (800) 944-8392.

Road biking isn't good in the area because the mountains are steep and the roads are few. Mountain biking, however, is extremely popular, and visitors can rent bikes from **Jim Thorpe River Adventures** (see number above) and **Blue Mountain Sports,** which is on Route 209 in the center of town. Call (800) 599-4421 for information.

The surrounding mountains are full of trails, and *Outside* magazine has called Jim Thorpe Pennsylvania's best mountain biking. That magazine has also spoken highly of the Lehigh Gorge rail trail. Mountain bikes are best for the trail, but you can ride it on a road bike.

Mauch Chunk Lake State Park on Lentz Trail has 350 acres for swimming, boating, and fishing. Hiking trails circle the water, and the Switchback Trail starts in the park. The park has boat rentals and cross-country ski rentals. Call (570) 325-3669 for information.

After the Activities:

A massage is an excellent way to end a day of hiking, biking, or rafting, and Jim Thorpe has several places where you can receive a massage and other healing help. **The Healing Place** at 114 Hill Road offers Shiatsu, acupressure, homeopathy, and other methods. Call (570) 325-2800 for information. **The Therapy Option** at 616 Center Street provides neuromuscular therapy, foot reflexology, and deep muscle massage. Call (570) 325-9477. **Sequoyah House** at 68 Broadway offers organic, vegetarian dining, as well as acupuncture and massage. Call (570) 325-8824 for details.

A Great Place to Relax:

Grab a drink and a sandwich and take a seat under the big tree right on the square. Or, sit by the water in Mauch Chunk Lake State Park.

Covered Bridges:

In Beltzville State Park, about 10 miles north along Route 209.

Tourist Information:

• (888) JIM-THORPE

Where is it? Northeast quadrant, on U.S. 209.

Getaway Rating: 4

16

LANCASTER
(LANK' ISS TUR) . . .
LIVING HISTORY
(A, R, R&R)

Lancaster's history is long and important to the growth of the United States, and Lancaster's present is prosperous. In 1728, Lancaster was a hamlet of 200 people, but by 1800 it had the distinction of being the largest inland city in the United States, with a population of 3,405. By then, it had become the western terminus of America's first turnpike, which opened in 1794 and extended from Philadelphia to Lancaster.

Lancaster played a large role in building the new nation. The Conestoga wagons that carried settlers across the country originated in Conestoga, just south of Lancaster, in the 18th century. In May of 1775, a fiery declaration from Lancaster sparked the resistance of the "back country" to British rule. The resolution called the edicts of the British Parliament "unjust, tyrannical, and cruel." The people vowed that they would not "become easy prey or tamely submit and bend our necks to the yoke prepared for us."

At the height of the Revolutionary War, Lancaster provided a haven for refugees from Philadelphia and Washington while British troops occupied those cities. On its flight west from Philadelphia, The Continental Congress stopped in Lancaster long enough to hold one session. During the war, Lancaster

Central Market

provided food, uniforms, shoes, blankets, and the deadly Pennsylvania Rifle.

After the war, Lancaster prospered and grew. The city was the center of a fertile agricultural region and an important manufacturing center, a description that still applies. Lancaster's biggest manufacturer is **Armstrong World Industries,** the world's largest maker of vinyl flooring products.

Pennsylvania's only "native" president, **James Buchanan,** lived at **Wheatland** on Marietta Avenue. **Central Market,** the oldest continuously operating public market house in the country, opened in the 1740s and first occupied its present building in 1889.

Today, Lancaster is a busy place with a diverse economy. Visitors come for history, shopping, business, food, and even music. In the years before **Live** gained national fame, the rock band performed frequently at the **Chameleon Club** on North Water Street, and the band now has its headquarters in Lancaster. The Chameleon Club is a popular night spot where many aspiring bands get valuable stage time, and Live occasionally plays there.

Fulton Opera House

Just down the street from the Chameleon are some of Lancaster's most important historic sites. The **Fulton Opera House** opened in the 1850s and recently underwent an extensive renovation. The Fulton hosts a busy schedule of stage productions and concerts throughout the year. Half a block away is Central Market. On Tuesdays, Fridays, and Saturdays, shoppers come to market in a tradition almost as old as Lancaster itself.

In its earlier days, almost everything sold at market came from the rich soils of Lancaster County. Farmers would load their wagons and haul their goods to the city. In the past decades, the market's character has changed somewhat and expanded. Fresh Lancaster County produce and meat are still abundant, and so are many other types of food. Central Market has become an international food bazaar, with offerings from the Middle East, Europe, and Latin America, and with much more diverse offerings than were available even 30 years ago. Shoppers will find spices, coffees, potato chips, and **Long's Horseradish,** a staple among Lancastrians for decades.

For Lancastrians, a visit to market is both a shopping and a social experience. Friends pause to talk, and a shopping trip to market usually lasts much longer than a trip to a suburban supermarket.

Wheatland

Beside Central Market on **Penn Square** is **The Heritage Center Museum,** which has free admission. The museum has displays of Lancaster County history and arts, with changing exhibitions and interpretive programs. For a quick look at Lancaster's history, take a walk down the first block of South Queen Street. There, the **Lancaster Newspaper's Newseum** shows Lancaster's history through 200 years of newspaper headlines. The Newseum is a glass-enclosed structure on the side of a building, and you can see it from the sidewalk. At the bottom of the hill is the **Downtown Visitors Information Center,** where you can pick up brochures and get suggestions and directions from people who know the area well.

On the western side of the city are three places of interest. Wheatland, James Buchanan's home, offers glimpses into the life of the president who held office just before the Civil War. The home is an expansive example of federal architecture, where the nation's only bachelor president lived. His "First Lady" was Harriet Lane, a niece. She frequently played the piano at family gatherings. In the library, Buchanan wrote his Inaugural Address, and, after his term, authored his only book, *Mr. Buchanan's Administration on the Eve of the Rebellion.*

Adjacent to Wheatland is the **Lancaster County Historical Society,** which houses a large collection of exhibits, books and archives. The library and the archives are available to the public for historical and genealogical research.

Three blocks away is the **North Museum of Natural History and Science.** The North Museum has a planetarium, and displays on Pennsylvania mammals, electricity, geology, people of the Susquehanna, birds, and oceans. Beside the North Museum are **Franklin & Marshall College** and **Buchanan Park.** Franklin & Marsahll is a small, private liberal arts college that takes part of its name from Benjamin Franklin. Buchanan Park is a large green area with attractive rose gardens.

North of Lancaster on Route 272 are **Landis Valley Farm Museum** and the **Hands-on-House.** Landis Valley collects, conserves, and exhibits Pennsylvania German culture and history from the 1750s to the 1940s. A unique aspect of the museum is the **Heirloom Seed Program.** This program preserves many varieties of plants grown by early German settlers in the area, and seeds for many heirloom varieties are on sale at the museum. Landis Valley was used for filming part of the movie *Beloved.*

Across the street, **Hands-on-House, The Children's Museum of Lancaster** makes playing the key to learning. The center has eight interactive exhibit areas where children paint their faces, design their own towns, and work in a corner grocery. Exhibits are best for children from 2 through 10.

As the center of the nation's most productive non-irrigated agricultural county, Lancaster is home to many food businesses, and some of them are interesting places to visit. **Hammond's Pretzels,** at 716 South West End Avenue, is a very small bakery with a very loyal following. Everybody in Lancaster seems to know a story of a Lancaster native who took a bag or a can of Hammond's to college or to a new home and "turned on" people there to these hard, salty pretzels.

A considerably bigger pretzel bakery is **Anderson's,** on the Old Philadelphia Pike, Route 340, just east of the city limits. Anderson's says that it's the world's largest pretzel bakery, and it makes many varieties, most of which don't carry the

Anderson label. For instance, if you buy Richard Simmons' pretzels, you'll have bought pretzels from Anderson's. The plant offers a self-guided tour through its facilities and free samples.

Lancaster County is part of a region that can claim to be the salty snack capital of the world. Pretzels and potato chips are favorite foods and large economic forces in **Pennsylvania Dutch Country.** If you want to stock up on chips and pretzels, stop in a supermarket around Lancaster. You'll find many varieties of regionally-made snacks.

The traditional Lancaster County cuisine is Pennsylvania Dutch, which is hearty, heavy, and rarely spicy. The best known eating establishment is the **smorgasbord,** an all-you-can-eat buffet that's long been popular with Lancaster residents. The traditional Lancaster smorgasbord is **Miller's,** on Route 30 East.

Over the last three decades, Lancaster's restaurant scene has expanded and diversified greatly. Not too long ago, Lancaster had Pennsylvania Dutch, German, Italian, and American restaurants. Now diners can also enjoy Chinese, Thai, Vietnamese, Italian, Mediterranean, Cajun, and Indian flavors. The offerings have grown, but the traditional favorites are still easy to find.

When they're not eating, Lancastrians are usually working or playing hard, and the region has plenty of recreational possibilities. One lightly used facility is **Lancaster County Central Park,** a 560-acre plot that's partially within the city limits. A mile from the center of the city, park visitors are likely to see deer grazing beside a placid stream. A system of trails in the park provides many miles of hiking where visitors are likely to spot deer and great blue herons along the Conestoga River or Mill Creek. The park is also popular with trail runners who can enjoy a long, hard run without having to travel to the mountains. The pool in the park is open to the public from Memorial Day to Labor Day.

In the past decade, Lancaster has become a major shopping destination. Tourists by the busload arrive at outlet centers along Route 30 east of the city. **Tanger Outlet Center** and **Rockvale Square Outlets** are on Route 30 near Route 896.

Route 30 East is Lancaster's biggest tourist strip. It's full of motels, restaurants, and attractions focused on the Amish. If you like crowds, it's a good place to visit, but if you want to get away from that sort of place, you'll do well to avoid Route 30.

For a completely different type of shopping experience, head to **Root's Country Market,** about five miles north of the city, just off Route 72. Root's is a place where you can buy almost anything. Fresh produce is the most common offering, and everything from antiques to clothing is also available. If you want to shop at Root's, you'll have to plan your getaway for a Tuesday, because that's the only day when Root's is open.

Lancaster's biggest amusement parks are on Route 30. **Dutch Wonderland** has 25 rides on 48 acres, as well as botanical gardens, exhibits, and the **Great American High Diving Show. Eagle Falls Adventure Park** has water slides, go-kart rides, miniature golf, and kid's bumper boats.

On Route 30 East is the **American Music Theatre,** a modern theater that presents musicals and stage productions, such as *Branson to Broadway,* a show that focuses on the American experience. **The Rainbow Dinner Theatre** on Route 30 East in Paradise presents stage productions with an "all-you-can-eat" meal. The **Dutch Apple Dinner Theatre,** at the Centerville Road exit of Route 30 West, combines Broadway-style shows with fine dining.

In Lancaster you'll find generous helping of food, fun, history, and shopping.

Attractions:

Central Market, on Penn Square, open Tues., Fri., and Sat., 6 A.M.-3 P.M.

Wheatland, home of President James Buchanan, 1120 Marietta Avenue, (717) 392-8721, open 10 A.M.-4 P.M. daily, April through November.

Fulton Opera House, 12 North Prince Street, (717) 397-7425, hours vary according to show times.

Landis Valley Farm Museum, Route 272 North, (717) 569-0401, Mon.-Sat., 9 A.M.-5 P.M., Sun., noon-5 P.M.

Heritage Center Museum, Penn Square, (717) 299-6440, Tues.-Sat., 10 A.M.-5 P.M.

Lancaster Walking Tour, Queen and Vine Streets, (717) 392-1776, Mon., Wed., Thur., and Sun., tour is at 1 P.M., Tues., Fri., and Sat., tours are at 10 A.M. and 1 P.M.

Anderson Pretzel Bakery, 2060 Old Philadelphia Pike, (717) 299-1616, Mon.-Fri., 9 A.M.-5 P.M.

North Museum, College and Buchanan Avenues, (717) 291-3941, Tues.-Sat., 9 A.M.-5 P.M., Sun., 1:30 P.M.-5 P.M.

Watch & Clock Museum, 514 Poplar Street, Columbia, (717) 684-8261, Tues.-Sat., 9 A.M.-4 P.M.

Demuth House, 114 East King Street, (717) 299-9940, Tues.-Sat., 10 A.M.-4 P.M., Sun., 1 P.M.-4 P.M.

Rock Ford Plantation, Lancaster County Central Park, (717) 392-7223, Tues.-Fri., 10 A.M.-4 P.M., Sun., noon-4 P.M.

Dining:

Lancaster's restaurant scene has diversified greatly in the past decade. Once, the only flavors available were American and Pennsylvania Dutch. Now tastes from many parts of the world are easy to find, as are many national chain restaurants.

Avenues, 10 South Prince Street, (717) 299-3456, opens at 4 P.M. daily.

Barn Door, 14 Blue Rock Road, Millersville, (717) 872-9943, open 11 A.M.-midnight, daily

Bonafiglio Pasta Company, 1575 Manheim Pike, (717) 560-4700, Mon.-Fri., 10 A.M.-7 P.M., Sat., 10 A.M.-4 P.M.

Brunswick Hotel, North Queen and Chestnut Streets, (717) 397-4801, breakfast, lunch, and dinner seven days a week.

Carlos & Charlie's, 919 North Plum Street, (717) 293-8704, Sun.-Thur., 11 A.M.-midnight, Fri. and Sat., 11 A.M.-2 A.M.

Bube's Brewery & Catacombs, 102 North Market Street, Mount Joy, (717) 653-2056, 11 A.M.-2 A.M., seven days a week.

Dutch Apple Dinner Theatre, 510 Centerville Road, (717) 898-1700, Tues.-Sun, lunch and dinner shows.

East of Eden, 680 Millcross Road, (717) 299-0159, Mon.-Fri., opens at 11 A.M., Sat. and Sun., opens at 4 P.M.

Fulton Bar & Restaurant, 637 North Plum Street, (717) 291-1098, open 11 A.M.-2 A.M., seven days a week.

Greenfield Inn, 595 Greenfield Road, (717) 393-0668, lunch and dinner seven days a week, breakfast and brunch on Saturday and Sunday.

Harmony Inn, 402 North Queen Street, (717) 394-2422, Mon.-Sat., 11 A.M-2 a.m.

Isaac's Deli, 44 North Queen Street, (717) 394-5544, open 11 A.M.-9 P.M. daily.

Kegel's Seafood, 551 West King Street, (717) 397-2832, open daily from 11:30 A.M.

Lancaster Malt Brewing Company, 302 North Plum Street, (717) 391-6258, lunch and dinner daily.

Lanvina's Vietnamese Restaurant, 1762 Columbia Avenue, (717) 393-7748, open 11 A.M.-2 P.M. and 4:30 P.M.-9 P.M. daily.

Lemon Grass Thai Restaurant, 2481 Lincoln Highway East, (717) 295-1621, open 11 A.M.-9 P.M. daily.

Lombardo's, 216 Harrisburg Avenue, (717) 394-3749, Mon.-Thur., 11 A.M.-10 P.M., Fri. and Sat., 11 A.M.-1 A.M.

Loreto's Ristorante, 173 South 4th Street, Columbia, (717) 684-4326, opens at 11 A.M. Tues.-Fri., and 4 P.M. on Sat. and Sun.

Market Fare, 50 West Grant Street, (717) 299-7090, open 11 A.M.-2:30 P.M. and 5 P.M.-9 P.M. daily.

Miller's Smorgasbord, 2811 Lincoln Highway East, Ronks, (717) 687-6621, breakfast, lunch, and dinner daily.

Mr. Z's Pizza, 701 South Prince Street, (717) 397-0212, Mon.-Sat., 11 A.M.-midnight, Sun., 1 P.M.-midnight.

Neptune Diner, 924 North Prince Street, (717) 399-8358, Mon.-Thur., 5:30 P.M.-10 P.M., Fri. and Sat., 24 hours a day, close at 3:30 P.M. on Sundays.

O'Halloran's Irish Pub, High Street and Fairview Avenue, (717) 393-3051, Mon.-Sat., 7 A.M.-2 A.M., Sun., 11 A.M.-midnight.

Onion's Café, 340 North Queen Street, (717) 396-8777, opens at 7 A.M., Mon.-Sat.

The Pressroom, 26 West King Street, (717) 399-5400, Mon.-Sat., 11 A.M.-9:30 P.M.

Quips Pub, 457 New Holland Avenue (717) 397-3903, open 11:30 A.M.-till daily.

Roseville Tavern, 1860 Oregon Pike, (717) 569-1531, Mon.-Sat., 11 A.M.-2 A.M.

Strawberry Hill, 128 West Strawberry Street, (717) 393-5544, open 5 P.M.-midnight daily.

Symposium, 125 South Centerville Road, (717) 391-7656, open 11:30 A.M.-9 P.M. daily.

Taj Mahal Indian Restaurant, 2080 Bennett Avenue, (717) 295-1434, Mon.-Sat., 11:30 A.M.-2:30 P.M. and 5 P.M.-10 P.M., Sun., noon-9 P.M.

Valentino's Café, 132 Rider Avenue, (717) 392-9564, Mon.-Sat., 7 A.M.-2 A.M.

Zimmerman's Family Restaurant, 66 North Queen Street, (717) 394-6977, opens at 6 A.M., Mon.-Sat.

Lodging:

Lancaster has an abundance of hotel and motel rooms. As a result, they're comparatively inexpensive, especially in the off-season, but don't let that fact lull you into believing that you can always find a room when you come. The "No Vacancy" signs shine brightly on many weekends, so call ahead to be sure of the lodging that you want.

Best Western Eden Resort, 222 Eden Road, (717) 569-6444.

Best Western Inn at Millersville, 101 Shenks Lane, (717) 872-4600.

Classic Inn, 2302 Lincoln Highway East, (717) 291-4576.

Continental Inn, 2285 Lincoln Highway East, (717) 299-0421.

Country Living Inn, 2406 Old Philadelphia Pike, (717) 295-7295.

Comfort Inn, Centerville Road and Route 30 West, (800) 223-8963.

Days inn Lancaster, 30 Keller Avenue, (717) 299-5700.

Econo Lodge, 2165 Lincoln Highway East, (717) 299-6900.

Fairfield Inn, 150 Granite Run Drive, (717) 581-1800.

Fulton Steamboat Inn, Route 30 and Route 896, (717) 299-9999.

Garden Spot Motel, 2291 Lincoln Highway East, (717) 394-4736.

Hampton Inn, Route 30 and Greenfield Road, (717) 299-1200.

Holiday Inn, 1492 Lititz Pike, (717) 393-0771.

Howard Johnson, 2100 Lincoln Highway East, (717) 397-7781.

Hotel Brunswick, Queen and Chestnut Streets, (717) 397-4801.

McIntosh Inn, Lincoln Highway East, (717) 299-9700.

Rodeway Inn, 2231 Lincoln Highway East, (717) 397-4973.

Rockvale Village Inn, 24 South Willowdale Drive, (717) 293-9500.

Travelodge, 2101 Columbia Avenue, (717) 397-4201.

Westfield Inn, 2929 Hempland Road, (717) 397-9300.

Gardens of Eden Bed & Breakfast, 1894 Eden Road, (717) 393-7722.

King's Cottage Bed & Breakfast, 1049 East King Street, (717) 397-1017.

Lincoln Haus Inn Bed & Breakfast, 1687 Lincoln Highway East, (717) 392-9412.

Maison Rouge Bed & Breakfast, 2236 Marietta Avenue, (717) 399-3033.

Meadowview Guest House, 2169 New Holland Pike, (717) 299-4017.

Nissly's, 624 West Chestnut Street, (717) 392-2311.

Merchant at Central Market

O'Flaherty's Dingeldein House Bed & Breakfast, 1105 East King Street, (800) 779-7765.

Witmer's Tavern, 2014 Old Philadelphia Pike, (717) 299-5305.

Shopping:

Along major highways, shopping centers have become a cash crop. Downtown Lancaster has a more interesting shopping atmosphere, and the result is that you can buy just about everything here.

For a touch of the unusual, visit the **300 block of North Queen Street** in downtown Lancaster. It's home to antiques shops, a vintage clothing store, a magic shop, and other interesting stores.

Park City Center, Route 30 and Harrisburg Pike, (717) 393-3851, Mon.-Sat., 9:30 A.M.-9 P.M., Sun., noon-5 P.M.

Quality Centers, 2495 Lincoln Highway East, (717) 299-1949, Mon.-Sat., 9:30 A.M.-9 P.M., Sun., noon-6 P.M.

Rockvale Square Outlets, Route 30 and Route 896, (717) 293-9595, Mon.-Sat., 9:30 A.M.-9 P.M., Sun., noon-6 P.M.

Tanger Outlet Center, Lincoln Highway East, (717) 392-7260, Mon.-Sat., 9 A.M.-9 P.M., Sun., 11 P.M.-6 P.M.

Approachable Art, 47 North Prince Street, (717) 394-1227, Mon.-Sat., 11 A.M.-5 P.M.

Central Market Art Company, 15 West King Street, (717) 392-4466, Mon.-Sat., 10 A.M.-5 P.M.

Hermansader's Gallery, 847 Park City Center, (717) 393-7773, Mon.-Sat., 9:30 A.M.-9 P.M., Sun., noon-5 P.M.

Cherry Hill Orchards, Long Lane, New Danville, (717) 872-9311, Mon.-Sat., 8 A.M.-6 P.M.

Cycle Circle, 310 North Queen Street, (717) 295-3193, Tues.-Sat., 10 A.M.-6 P.M.

Here to Timbuktu, 46 North Prince Street, (717) 293-8595, Mon.-Sat., 10 A.M.-5 P.M.

Miese's Candies, 60 North Queen Street, (717) 397-9415, Mon.-Sat., 9:30 A.M.-5 P.M.

Puff 'n Stuff, 307 North Queen Street, (717) 383-9772, Mon.-Sat., 11 A.M.-6 P.M.

Secret Sneaker, 409 Granite Run Drive, (717) 669-6101, Mon.-Sat., 9 A.M.-8 P.M., Sun., noon-4 P.M.

Stan's Record Bar, 48 North Prince Street, (717) 397-5200, Mon.-Sat., 9:30 A.M.-5 P.M.

Sun Earth Moon, 314 North Queen Street, (717) 291-6666, Mon.-Sat., 11 A.M.-6 P.M.

The Comic Store, 28 McGovern Avenue, (717) 397-8737, Mon.-Sat., 11 A.M.-7 P.M.

Zanzibar, 45 North Market Street, (717) 390-2868, Mon.-Sat., 11 A.M.-5 P.M.

Zap & Company, 320 North Queen Street, (717) 397-7405, Mon.-Sat., 11 A.M.-6 P.M.

Annual Events:

The calendar is busy. Something is happening just about every weekend. One major center of activity is **Long's Park** on Harrisburg Pike. Even when nothing is happening, it's a quiet oasis in the midst of a busy suburban area.

Greater Lancaster Antiques Show, March, F&M College, (717) 299-6440.

Quilter's Heritage Celebration, April, Lancaster Host Resort, (800) 233-0121.

Mrs. Smith's Challenge 5-mile Run, Lancaster County Central Park, Saturday before Mother's Day, (717) 394-7812.

Red Rose 5-Mile Race, Saturday after Memorial Day, downtown Lancaster, (717) 291-4711.

First Union professional bike race, first Tuesday in June, downtown, (717) 291-4711.

German Summerfest, June, Lancaster Liederkranz, (717) 898-8451.

Pedal To Preserve Bike Tour, June, (800) 324-1518.

Smith's Challenge 10K Run, Lancaster County Central Park, Father's Day, (717) 394-7812.

Old Fashioned Ice Cream Festival, downtown, July, (717) 399-7977.

Fireworks, downtown, July 3, (717) 399-7977.

LancasterFest, downtown, August, (717) 399-7977.

Long's Park Arts & Crafts Festival, Labor Day weekend, (717) 295-7054.

Conestoga Trail Run, 10 miles, September, (717) 394-7812.

Harvest Days, Landis Valley Farm Museum, second weekend in October, (717) 569-0401.

Victorian Christmas, December, Wheatland, (717) 392-8721.

The Active Life:

   Lancaster County has never established itself as a destination for active vacations, although it has the ingredients to be one of the great recreational bicycling destinations in the world. Thousands of miles of lightly traveled country roads, the second highest number of covered bridges of any county in the country, and a vast network of bed & breakfast inns give bikers good reasons to spend a weekend or a week here.

A **45.9-mile bike** tour begins at the Landis Valley Farm Museum and takes riders to the Ephrata Cloister and the Railroad Museum of Pennsylvania in Strasburg. Direction sheets are available at all three museums.

Lancaster County has many golf courses. Visitors who want to play a good public course can head just north of the city to **Overlook** on Lititz Pike, Route 501.

A favorite local activity is floating down the Pequea (Peck' way) Creek in large inner tubes. Tube rentals are available at **Sickman's Mill** in Pequea, (717) 872-5951.

A Great Place to Relax:

Long's Park, on Harrisburg Pike, west of the city. The park has lots of shade and a lake where people come to feed the ducks.

Covered Bridges:

Lancaster County has 30, and two are close to the city of Lancaster. **Landis Mill Bridge** is close to Park City shopping center. From Lancaster, go west on Harrisburg Pike. Turn right at the light at Plaza Boulevard. Then make a left at the entrance to Ollie's store. The bridge is straight ahead.

Kurtz's Mill Bridge is in Lancaster County Central Park. From the center of the city, go south on South Duke Street, then right on Eshelman Mill Road, right on Golf Road, and left on Kiwanis Road.

Tourist Information:
• (800) PA-DUTCH

Where is it? Southeast quadrant, on U.S. 30 and U.S. 222.

Getaway Rating: 2

Professional Bike Race in Lancaster County Central Park

17

THE LEHIGH VALLEY . . . STEEL, GOOD HEALTH, AND CRAYONS

(H, R)

The quiet of a country road crossed by a covered bridge and the screams of terrified riders on the longest, tallest, fastest roller coaster in the east are equally important parts of the **Lehigh Valley.** Located about 60 miles north of Philadelphia, the valley takes its name from the Lehigh River, which flows through **Allentown** and **Bethlehem** and empties into the Delaware River at **Easton.**

Allentown is a busy industrial city and the seat of Lehigh County. It's home to many manufacturers, including **Mack Truck** and many high-tech companies. On the south side of Allentown is **Dorney Park** and **Wildwater Kingdom,** a summer playground that cools and scares visitors.

Bethlehem Steel Corporation produced much of the metal that helped build America, and the corporation's headquarters are still in the city, although its manufacturing presence has diminished greatly. Bethlehem is also the site where the **Moravian Church** began its operations in North America in 1741, and the city is home to **Moravian College** and **Lehigh University.** During the Christmas season, Bethlehem's celebrations are major tourist attractions that feature Moravian music and special displays, including an enormous lighted **Star of Bethlehem** on a nearby mountaintop.

Crayola Store in Easton

Easton produces something that has colored the world of just about every child in the United States for many generations. **Crayola** crayons come from Easton, and rare is the child who hasn't used them.

The countryside surrounding the three cities is a rich agricultural region with hundreds of miles of quiet country roads, and seven covered bridges combined in a guided tour that you can follow in a car or on a bike.

The Lehigh Valley offers ample doses of modern excitement and history. For modern excitement, the Lehigh Valley's biggest attraction is Dorney Park. This large amusement park will keep you cool with its assortment of water rides and its latest bit of vertical terror—**Steel Force,** advertised as the longest, tallest, fastest coaster in the east. For coaster lovers, Steel Force is pure joy. For those of a more timid nature, it's something enjoyable to watch.

Fortunately, Dorney Park has many other rides, and everyone will find something enjoyable to do in this park, even if it's just watching others endure the thrill of dropping almost straight down on Steel Force. For instance, you can ride the **Dentzel Carousel,** built in 1921 and equipped with a **Wurlitzer Band Organ.**

A smaller amusement park is **Bushkill Park** at 2100 Bushkill Park Drive in Easton, which features nine children's rides and eight rides for older people. Call (610) 258-6941 for information.

For a considerably more relaxing day, pay a visit to the **Rodale Institute Experimental Farm.** The Rodale family operates many enterprises that focus on health and fitness, and most are in the Lehigh Valley. In Emmaus, Rodale publishes magazines such as *Runner's World, Bicycling,* and *Prevention.* On this farm, dedicated workers practice organic farming and regenerative agriculture. Visitors can wander around the farm or take guided tours.

The farm is a tranquil place where it's pleasant to sit and watch the crops grow. The place is meticulous, and butterflies love it. At the bookstore/restaurant, you can enjoy light, healthful meals, and during the growing season you can purchase the farm's organic produce. Whether you want to learn more about food production or just get away from noise and congestion, the Rodale Institute Experimental Farm is an excellent place to spend a few hours or a day. The address is 611 Siegfredale Road, Kutztown. To get there, follow Route 222 south of Allentown and look for signs. The farm is west of 222. Call (610) 683-1400 for information.

A few miles north, along route 222 in Trexlertown, is the **Lehigh County Velodrome,** where exciting bicycle races take place during the summer months, usually on Friday nights. Bike racing at a velodrome is considerably different from road racing. The bikes on the track have only one gear and no brakes. Strategy is crucial as riders battle for position, especially on the last lap, and the racers go very fast. This facility has hosted many important national and international events, and the top pros race here regularly.

When the pros aren't racing and when nobody's using the velodrome to practice, anyone may use it. Although it looks as though bikes will slide down the track, the tires grip the surface quite well. So, if you have a bike handy, go for a spin. There are only 20 similar facilities in the country, so you won't get this opportunity everywhere. Call (610) 967-7587 for information and schedules. And bring your rollerblades. Adjacent to the velodrome is a park with trails for rollerbladers.

For one week a year, the week before Labor Day, **The Great Allentown Fair** brings the farm into the city. Food, rides, games, exhibits, and music turn the fairgrounds into one big party. Call (610) 435-7541 for details.

Throughout the Lehigh Valley, museums tell the stories of everything from trucks to organs to The Liberty Bell, which spent some time here. In 1777, the Americans hid the **Liberty Bell** from the British in Allentown. The **Liberty Bell Shrine Museum,** at **Zion's Reformed Church,** 622 Hamilton Mall, tells the story. The museum is generally open Monday through Saturday from 12 P.M. to 4 P.M. and Sundays by appointment, but call (610) 868-6868 for exact times.

The **Mack Truck Historical Museum** at 997 Postal Road in Allentown documents the history of one of the world's most important truck builders and innovators. Old trucks are on display and visitors can learn how truck technology has advanced since the early days of the 20th century. For reservations (required), call (610) 266-6767.

The **Allentown Art Museum** has permanent exhibitions of European masters, as well as exhibits of American painting and sculptures, with a special emphasis placed on works of eastern Pennsylvania. The museum is at Fifth and Court streets. Call (610) 432-4333 for information on current shows.

The **Moravian Museum of Bethlehem** shows the lives of Bethlehem's early Moravian settlers. Part of the exhibit is the 1741 **Gemeinhaus,** the oldest building in Bethlehem. The Christmas season is the best time to visit this museum. Then, you can take a walking tour or a lantern tour and then stop by the nearby **Sun Inn** to warm yourself by a fire and to enjoy refreshments. The Moravian Museum is at 66 West Church Street. Call (610) 867-0173 for information.

The Sun Inn, built in 1758, is still operating as a restaurant and museum at 564 Main Street. Call (610) 866-1758 for further information.

Rodale Experimental Farm

The most colorful place in the valley is definitely the **Crayola Factory** on the square in downtown Easton. Children of all ages love this place, where they can see how crayons come to life and where they can color on giant glass walls. In addition, you can buy all sorts of crayons and souvenirs.

On the same property is the **National Canal Museum,** which shows what America was like before computers, planes, cars, and even trains. It has exhibits on the history and technology of America's 19th-century canals. Interactive exhibits let visitors operate an incline plane and pilot a boat. The exhibits are at 30 Center Square in Easton. Call (610) 515-8000 for information.

One pleasant aspect of downtown Easton is that the city has banned cars from the area around the square, making it much quieter than other downtown areas. Just a couple of blocks from the square is the confluence of the Lehigh and Delaware rivers, a nice place to sit and watch the water flow. Just down the river is **Hugh Moore Park,** where visitors can take a ride on a mule-drawn canal boat. The rides operate Tuesday through Sunday from May through September. Call (610) 515-8000 for information. They have a variety of hours: they are open Tues.-Fri., 9:30 A.M.-3 P.M., Sat. and Sun., 12:50 P.M.-3:50 P.M., May

through early June; Mon.-Sat., 10:30 A.M.-5 P.M., Sun., 12:45
P.M.-5 P.M., early June through Labor day; and Sat. and Sun.,
1:20 P.M.-3:50 P.M. in September (after labor day).

You can watch the animals at **The Game Preserve** at 5150 Game
Preserve Road in Schnecksville. Call (610) 799-4171 for information (open 10 A.M.-5 P.M. daily, from the last weekend in April
through October 31). Native and exotic animals live on this 1,200-
acre preserve, which features a petting zoo and hiking trails.

At the **Highland Farm,** horseback riding is a featured activity, but it's not all roughing it. Guests can stay in a restored
1790 stone farmhouse and enjoy the indoor pool and jacuzzi.
The farm is at 2514 Brunner Road in Emmaus. Call (610) 965-
3843 for additional information.

Auto racing fans descend on **Nazareth Speedway** for three
weekends each year, one each in April, May, and July. The track
is on Route 191 in Nazareth, north of Bethlehem. Call (800)
629-RACE for tickets.

Winter brings snow, either natural or man-made, to **Doe
Mountain** in Macungie, south of Allentown. Downhill skiers
can call (800) ISKI-DOE for skiing conditions. The ski area is
at 101 Doe Mountain Lane.

Golfers will find a variety of public courses, including municipal
courses in Allentown and Bethlehem. Together with the Pocono
Mountain Region, the Lehigh Valley has introduced a package of
golf vacations called **Stay 'N Play,** with overnight packages starting
at just $68.00. For the brochure, call (888) 246-5337.

The Lehigh Valley offers activities, shopping, history, and
quiet getaways. It's a diverse destination that's easy to reach.

You Can Go Downtown

All three of these cities have pleasant downtowns filled with
historic sites, interesting shopping, and good restaurants. Park
the car, take a stroll, and you'll find stores, museums, and
places to relax.

Attractions:

Crayola Factory, 30 Center Square, Easton, (610) 515-8000,
Tues.-Sat., 9:30 A.M.-5 P.M., Sun., noon-5 P.M.

Canal Boat, Easton

Christmas in Bethlehem.

Discovery Center for Science & Technology, 511 East 3rd Street, Bethlehem, (610) 865-5010, Tues.-Sat., noon-5 P.M.

Dorney Park & Wildwater Kingdom, 3830 Dorney Park Road, Allentown, (800) FUN-TIME, opens at 10 A.M. in summer (closings vary).

National Canal Museum, Centre Square, Easton, (610) 515-8000, Tues.-Sat., 9:30 A.M.-5 P.M., Sun., noon-5 P.M.

Lehigh Valley Velodrome, Routes 222 and 100, Trexlertown, (610) 967-7587, races Friday nights in summer, open for riders at various times.

Lost River Caverns, Durham Street, Hellertown, (610) 838-8767, open 9 A.M.-5 P.M. daily, except for 9 A.M.-6 P.M. Memorial Day through Labor Day.

Mack Truck Museum, 7000 Alburtis Road, Macungie, (610) 709-3566, call for appointment.

Off Track Betting—The Downs at Lehigh Valley, Airport Road just south of Route 22, Allentown, (610) 266-6559, opens at 11:30 A.M. daily.

Rodale Institute Experimental Farm, 611 Siegfredale Road, Kutztown, (610) 683-1400, Mon.-Fri., 9 A.M.-5 P.M., Sun., noon-5 P.M.

Trains 'N More, 1901 South Twelfth Street, Allentown, (610) 791-9397, Fri., 4 P.M.-9 P.M., Sat., 10 A.M.-7 P.M., and Sun., 10 A.M.- 5 P.M.

Dining:

Al Dente Italian Restaurant, 1901 Hamilton Street, Allentown, (610) 782-0900, Mon.-Sat., 4 P.M.-2 A.M.

Aladdin, 651 Union Blvd, Allentown, (610) 437-4023, Tues.- Sun., opens at 5 P.M.

All Star Sports Bar, 117 East Third Street, Bethlehem, Mon.- Sat., 11 A.M.-2 A.M.

Bruno Sciponi's, 4034 Easton Avenue, Bethlehem, (610) 867-9040, Mon.-Sat., 11 A.M.-11 P.M., Sun., 11 A.M.-9 P.M.

Briggs Tavern, 665 Northampton Street, Easton, (610) 252-6692, Mon.-Thur., 11 A.M.-midnight, Fri. and Sat., 11 A.M.-2 A.M., and Sun., 1 P.M.-9 P.M.

College Grill Tavern, 420 Cattell Street, Easton, (610) 252-9456, Mon.-Sat., 11 A.M.-11 P.M.

Confetti Café, 462 Main Street, Bethlehem, (610) 861-7484, Mon.-Sat., 11 A.M.-10 P.M., Sun., noon-5 P.M.

G's Steaks & Subs, 29 West 4th Street, Bethlehem, (610) 866-7016, Mon.-Thur., 11 A.M.-9 P.M., Fri. and Sat., 11 A.M.-10 P.M.

King George Inn, Cedar Crest and Hamilton Boulevards, Allentown, (610) 435-1723, lunch and dinner daily.

Louie's, 1207 Chew Street, Allentown, (610) 434-2340, Mon.- Fri., 11 A.M.-10 P.M., Sat., 4:30 P.M.-10 P.M., and Sun., 4 P.M.-9 P.M.

Lehigh Pizza, 13 West Third Street, Bethlehem, (610) 866-1088, Mon.-Thur., 10:30 A.M.-midnight, Fri. and Sat., 10:30 A.M.-1 A.M., and Sun. 11 A.M.-midnight.

Pino's Italian Restaurant, 200 Cattell Street, Easton, (610) 253-5533, Mon.-Thur., 11 A.M.-10 P.M., Fri. and Sat., 11 A.M.-11 P.M.

Rolata Sushi Bar, 37 South Ninth Street, Allentown, (610) 821-6900, opens Tues.-Sun. at 5 P.M.

The 1758 Sun Inn, 554 Historic Main Street, Bethlehem, (610) 974-9451, Mon., 11 A.M.-4 P.M., Tues.-Thur., 5 P.M.-9 P.M., Fri. and Sat., 5 P.M.-10 P.M., and Sun., 4:40 P.M.-9 P.M.

Stefano's Italian Restaurant, 2970 Linden Street, Bethlehem, (610) 866-8886, Mon.-Sat., 11 A.M.-11 P.M., Sun., 11 A.M.-10 P.M.

Lodging:

Allentown Comfort Inn, I-78 and Route 100, (610) 391-0344.

Allentown Comfort Suites, 3712 Hamilton Boulevard, Routes 222 and I-78 at Dorney Park, (610) 437-9100.

Allentown Hilton, 904 Hamilton Mall, (610) 433-2221.

Allenwood Motel, 1058 Hausman Road, Allentown, (610) 395-3707.

Best Western Easton Inn, 185 South 3rd Street and Larry Holmes Drive, Easton, (800) 883-0113.

Black Horse Inn, 825 South Delaware Drive (Route 611), Easton, (888) 272-1782.

Blue Mountain Sumit Inn, Route 309, Andreas, (570) 386-2003.

Blue Ridge Inn, 6799 Madison Street, New Tripoli, (610) 298-2777.

Classic Victorian Bed & Breakfast, 35 North New Street, Nazareth, (610) 759-8276.

Comfort Inn-Bethlehem, U.S. 22 and PA 191, Bethlehem, (610) 865-6300.

Comfort Suites Bethlehem, 120 West 3rd Street, (610) 882-9700.

Days Inn, Route 22 and Route 309, Allentown, (888) 395-5200.

Days Inn, 2622 Lehigh Street, Bethlehem, (610) 797-1234.

Fairfield Inn, 2140 Motel Drive, Bethlehem, (610) 867-8681.

Hampton Inn, Route 100 at I-78, Allentown, (610) 392-1500.

Hampton Inn, Route 22 and Route 512, Bethlehem, (610) 868-2442.

Holiday Inn, Route 22 and Route 512, Bethlehem, (610) 866-5800.

Holiday Inn Express, 1715 Plaza Lane, Allentown, (610) 435-7880.

Inn at Heyers' Mill, 568 Heyer Mill Road, Nazareth, (610) 759-6226.

Lafayette Inn, 525 West Monroe Street, Easton, (610) 253-4500.

McIntosh Inn, Route 22 and Airport Road, Allentown, (610) 264-7531.

Park Manor Motel, 731 Hausman Road, Allentown, (610) 395-3377.

Sayre Mansion Inn, 250 Wyandotte Street, Bethlehem, (610) 882-2100.

Wydnor Hall Inn, 3612 Old Philadelphia Pike, Bethlehem, (800) 839-0020.

Hawk Mountain Inn Bed & Breakfast, 221 Stony Run Valley Road, Kempton, (610) 756-4224.

Highland Farm Bed & Breakfast, 2514 Brunner Road, Emmaus, (610) 965-3843.

Allentown/Lehigh Valley KOA Campground, 6750 KOA Drive, New Tripoli, (610) 298-2160.

Shopping:

Banana Factory, 211 Plymouth Street, Bethlehem, (610) 332-1305, Mon.-Fri., 10 A.M.-7 P.M., Sat., 10 A.M.-5 P.M.

Country Caper, 508 Main Street, Bethlehem, (610) 865-2336, Mon.-Sat., 10 A.M.-5 P.M., Sun., 1 P.M.-4 P.M.

Donegal Square, 544 Main Street, Bethlehem, (610) 866-3244, open daily.

Downtown Bethlehem Association, 10 East Church Street, (610) 865-7214.

Downtown Easton Shopping, (610) 253-4211, hours vary by store (but, mostly, Mon.-Sat., 10 A.M.-5 P.M.).

Eagles Nest Antiques, 1717 Butler Street, Easton, (610) 258-4092, Tues.-Sat., 10 A.M.-5 P.M.

Emmaus Main Street Program, (610) 965-6279, hours vary by store (but, mostly, Mon.-Sat., 10 A.M.-5 P.M.).

Geiser's Furniture, 526 Main Street, Bethlehem, (610) 694-9788, Mon.-Sat., 10 A.M.-5 P.M., Sun., noon-4 P.M.

Homespun Weavers, 55 South 7th Street, Emmaus, (610) 967-4550, Mon.-Sat., 10 A.M.-4 P.M.

Legends, Traditions, & Friends, 11 East Third Street, Bethlehem, (610) 865-4755, Tues. and Wed., 11 A.M.-6 P.M., Thur. and Fri., 11 A.M.-8 P.M., and Sat., 11 A.M.-5 P.M.

Lehigh Valley Mall, Route 22 and Route 145 North, Whitehall, (610) 264-5511, Mon.-Sat., 10 A.M.-9:30 P.M., Sun., 11 A.M.-6 P.M.

The London Shop, 339 Northampton Street, Easton, open 9:30 A.M.-5 P.M. daily, and till 8 P.M. on Tuesday and Friday.

Moravian Book Shop, 428 Main Street, Bethlehem, (610) 866-5481, Mon.-Fri., 10 A.M.-6 P.M., Sat., 10 A.M.-5 P.M.

Mary Beth Gallery, 446 Main Street, Bethlehem, (610) 868-8588, Mon.-Fri., 10 A.M.-5:30 P.M., Sat., 10 A.M.-5 P.M.

Sign of the Carpenter, 243 Northampton Street, Easton, (610) 250-0875, Mon.-Sat., 10 A.M.-5 P.M.

Spring Garden Gallery, 208 Spring Garden Street, Easton, (610) 250-0118, Mon.-Sat., 10 A.M.-5 P.M.

Tail Waggers & Treasure Alley, 228 Northampton Street, Easton, (610) 252-8434, Mon.-Fri., 10 A.M.-5:30 P.M., Sat. and Sun., 10:30 A.M.-5:30 P.M.

The Thought O' You, 260 East Broad Street, Bethlehem, (610) 861-7751, Mon.-Fri., 10 A.M.-9 P.M., Sat., 10 A.M.-5 P.M., and Sun., noon-5 P.M.

Annual Events:

One of the oldest annual events is the football game between Lafayette in Easton and Lehigh in Bethlehem. Held on a

Saturday in late November, it's one of college football oldest rivalries and an event filled with great traditions.

A Look BACH at the Wolle Family, May to July, Moravian Museum, Bethlehem, (610) 867-0173.

Great Allentown Fair, week before Labor Day, (610) 433-7541.

Celtic Classic Highland Games & Festival, 65 East Elizabeth Avenue, Bethlehem, (610) 868-9599.

Christkindlmarkt Bethlehem, Christmas season, Main and Spring Streets, Bethlehem, (610) 861-0678.

Christmas in Bethlehem, late November to early January, (610) 868-1513.

Das Awkscht Fescht, Macungie Memorial Park, first weekend in August (large antique car show and festival), (610) 967-2317.

Mayfair Festival of the Arts, Memorial Day weekend, parks in Allentown, (610) 437-6900.

Musikfest, historic district of Bethlehem, mid-August, hundreds of free performances, (800) 360-3378.

The Active Life:

Bring your bike. The **Lehigh County Velodrome** hosts championship bike races on Friday nights and at different times on Saturdays and Sundays, but when the racers aren't using the track, it's open to the public. If you've ever wondered what's it's like to ride on a banked track, here's your chance to find out. (Hint: It feels weird at first, but it's actually safe and pretty exciting. If the track is wet, however, stay off.) On Route 100 and Route 222, Trexlertown (south of Allentown). Call (610) 967-7587 for information.

Dorney Park and Wildwater Kingdom is a big amusement park with lots of water rides, roller coasters, and live entertainment. Located at 3700 Hamilton Boulevard, Allentown, (610) 395-3724.

A Great Place to Relax:

The **Rodale Institute Experimental Farm** off Route 222,

south of Allentown, is a tranquil place. Stroll among the gardens, and take a seat in the little pavilion.

Covered Bridges:

The valley has seven, and a detailed tour will take you to all of them. Five are close together and cross Jordan Creek northwest of Allentown. The easiest bridge to find is **Bogert's Bridge** in **Little Lehigh Park** in Allentown. It crosses the Little Lehigh River between Hamilton Boulevard and Lehigh Street in the city. For a copy of the tour, call the visitors' bureau at (800) 747-0561.

Tourist Information:

- (800) 747-0561.

Where is it? Southeast, on U.S. 22, U.S. 222, I-78, and the Northeast Extension of the Pennsylvania Turnpike.

Getaway Rating: 2

Lehigh Valley Velodrome

18

LEWISBURG . . .
THE SUSQUEHANNA VALLEY
(A, R, R&R)

Lewisburg is a pretty Victorian town beside the Susquehanna River, right in the middle of the state. It's also near the center of the region called The Susquehanna Valley, which extends roughly from Williamsport to Millersburg on both sides of the river.

Bucknell University gives Lewisburg a college atmosphere, and the surrounding countryside is a rich agricultural area. You can spend a weekend strolling the streets, eating at an outdoor café, and shopping, or you can explore the county's covered bridges on a bike. The valleys of the Susquehanna are a pleasant place to get away and slow down.

Scotch-Irish and English settlers arrived in the valley in the mid-1700s, and German immigrants came after the Revolutionary War. In the early 1800s, the Susquehanna Valley boomed with development as the **Pennsylvania Canal** came to the area. The Susquehanna is a wide river, but it's shallow and rocky and very poor for transportation. Thus, the canal came to the region to move goods and farm products. The Susquehanna had long been a highway for Indians, and the canal opened it up for commerce. The valley prospered, and merchants built beautiful homes in Federal and Victorian styles.

Hufnagle Bridge

Historic homes and stately hotels line **Market Street** in Lewisburg, and the river is at the end of the street. In the center of town is **Gordon Hufnagle Memorial Park,** home to an interesting little covered bridge that's open only to pedestrians. The park is a good place to relax after a good walk around town and across the river.

At 15 North Water Street is the **Packwood House Museum,** a log structure that dates back to 1796. The building has grown to three stories with 27 rooms that contain a collection of American artifacts, especially local pieces. The **Silfer House Museum** on Route 15 North dates back to 1860 and is one of many beautiful Victorian homes in the town. The museum contains displays of Victorian furnishings and decorative arts.

The green valley between Lewisburg and Mifflinburg along Route 45 is a fertile agricultural region, and you may see Amish buggies in the valley. In Mifflinburg, 10 miles west of Lewisburg, buggies were once the main business, and the **Mifflinburg Buggy Museum** recalls an era when the town was one of the biggest buggy builders in the nation. As many as 50 buggy makers once plied their trade here, producing more than 6,000 vehicles a year.

One buggy shop was the William A. Heiss Coach Works at 523 Green Street. One day, in 1922, he just shut the doors and walked away, leaving everything, including a buggy in progress, just as it was. When the Museum Association organized in 1978, someone opened the doors and found the makings of a museum. A restoration has returned the complex to its 1800s feel, and it's now the Mifflinburg Buggy Museum.

Down on Chestnut Street, the houses and stores are old and attractive. One frequently busy store is **Mary Koons** at 408 Chestnut Street. The store sells Amish quilts, as well as yarn, needlework, and apparel (open Mon.-Sat., 9 A.M.-5:30 P.M.). The **Thymless Treasure Shoppe** at 340 Chestnut Street sells crafts, baskets, afghans, and candles (open Mon.-Sat., 10 A.M.-6 P.M.). The **Lilac Moon** at 347 Chestnut is a bed and breakfast with a restaurant that serves lunches and dinners in a bistro atmosphere.

On North 4th Street, right beside the **Hassenplug Covered Bridge** is the **Koons Trail,** a series of paths that traverse a fertile area of wildflowers, migratory birds, insects, amphibians, and reptiles. With good timing you may spot a great blue heron, an indigo bunting, or a scarlet tanager. The walk is short, easy, and pleasant.

In Penn's Creek, south of Mifflinburg on Route 104, the modern concept of organic farming had its beginnings in 1946. Paul Keene questioned the wisdom of spraying food with pesticides and herbicides, and he decided to grow fruits and vegetables without chemicals. The result was **Walnut Acres Farm,** which today is a flourishing natural foods business and an interesting place to visit, especially if you happen to stop by on a day when they're roasting peanuts for peanut butter. Your mouth and your nose will be glad you came (open Mon.-Sat., 9 A.M.-5 P.M., Sun., noon-5 P.M.).

Walnut Acres grows organic produce on the farm and sells it in the store, along with its own items and other natural foods. The store has a small restaurant, and tours of the bakery, cannery, and mill are available on weekdays. The store is open every day, however. Walnut Acres is also an excellent place to

Downtown Mifflinburg

take a bike ride. The valley is green, and the farm roads carry little traffic.

Farther south, along Route 15, is the western landing for the **Millersburg Ferry.** No bridge crosses the river between Sunbury and Duncannon, about 50 miles, and the ferry still carries cars, bikes, and passengers across this normally shallow section of river. This is the last ferry on the Susquehanna, and the two boats, the *Falcon* and *Roaring Bull,* are wooden double stern-wheel paddle boats believed to be the last of their type operating in the country.

The ferry operates from May until October between **Millersburg** on Route 147 and **Ferryboat Campsites** on Route 15 north of Liverpool.

Millersburg is a small town still untouched by suburban shopping malls. Downtown is a major shopping and dining destination, and **Leppert's ¢10 to $1 Store** is an old variety store with wooden floors. Some prices do top $1.00, but the feel is certainly different from more modern stores.

Millersburg has a large art consciousness for a small town. The **Ned Smith Center for Nature and Art** honors a man who was a self-trained naturalist and artist. The center covers hundreds of

Site of Little League World Series, South Williamsport

acres of meadows and forests that stretch from the Wiconisco Creek to the top of Berry Mountain. The area is home to abundant wildlife, and it serves as an educational center. Every year in July it hosts the **Ned Smith Wildlife Festival,** which features events ranging from art displays to programs on finding wild edibles.

In the valley east of Millersburg, the Amish have established a community, and their presence keeps automobile traffic low, making the region ideal for leisurely bike rides.

North of Lewisburg on Route 15 is a small town that becomes one of the focuses of the sports world during the last week in August. South Williamsport is the home of **Little League Baseball,** and the **Little League World Series** takes place at the headquarters every year.

To the east along the river is Bloomsburg, home of Bloomsburg University and the huge **Bloomsburg Fair.** Main Street in Bloomsburg is a pretty street with interesting restaurants and stores, and it's an easy walk down to the river. In neighboring Montour County, the **Montour Preserve** has a 165-acre lake and 15 miles of hiking trails.

The farmlands around the preserve are home to many Amish families, and the roads are ideal for bicycling. In Milton, Broadway shows take center stage all year at **Rockwell Center.**

Pleasant small towns line the Susquehanna in central Pennsylvania. Visit Lewisburg, Mifflinburg, or Millersburg, and you'll find a nice place to walk the downtown streets and do a little shopping.

Attractions:

Victorian Lewisburg.

Victorian Mifflinburg.

Walnut Acres Organic Farm, Route 104, (570) 837-5095, Mon.-Sat., 9 A.M.-5:30 P.M., Sun., noon-5 P.M.

Mifflinburg Buggy Museum, 523 Green Street, (570) 966-1355, Thur.-Sun., 1 P.M.-4 P.M., May through September, Sat. and Sun., 1 P.M.-4 P.M, October.

Little League Museum, Route 15, South Williamsport (570) 326-3607, open 10 A.M.-5 P.M. daily.

PP&L Montour Preserve, Washingtonville, (570) 437-3131.

Rockwell Center, 32 South Turbot Avenue, Milton, (800) 355-3099, hours vary by show times.

Millersburg Ferry, (570) 692-2442, operates in summer, call for information.

Dining:

Carriage Corner Restaurant, 257 East Chestnut Street, Mifflinburg, (570) 966-3666, lunch and dinner daily.

Country Cupboard, Route 15, Lewisburg, (570) 523-3211, open 7 A.M.-9 P.M. daily.

The Crafty Lady, 342 Arch Street, Sunbury, (570) 988-0527, lunch and dinner daily.

Front Street Station, 2 Front Street, Northumberland, (570) 473-3626, open 11 A.M.-midnight daily.

Harry's Grille, 20 West Main Street, Bloomsburg, (570) 784-3500, breakfast, lunch, and dinner daily.

The Inn at Olde New Berlin, 321 Market Street, New Berlin, (570) 966-0321, open noon-10 P.M. daily.

The Lewisburg Hotel, 136 Market Street, Lewisburg, (570) 523-7800, open 6 A.M.-10 P.M. daily.

The Lilac Moon, 347 Chestnut Street, Mifflinburg, (570) 966-4505, lunch and dinner daily.

Old Hardware Restaurant, 336 Mill Street, Danville, (570) 275-6615, lunch and dinner daily.

Russell's Restaurant, 117 West Main Street, Bloomsburg, (570) 387-1332, open 10 A.M.-2 A.M. daily.

Rusty's, Market and Sixth Streets, Lewisburg, (570) 523-6000, lunch and dinner daily.

Tedd's Landing, Route 11 and Route 15, Shamokin Dam, (570) 743-1591, Mon.-Fri., 11 A.M.-10 P.M., Sat. and Sun., 4 P.M.-9 P.M.

The Victorian Lady, 115 Old Turnpike Road, Lewisburg, (570) 568-6685, lunch and dinner daily.

Watson Inn, 100 Main Street, Watsontown, (570) 538-1832, lunch and dinner daily.

Lodging:

Comfort Inn, Route 11 and Route 15, Selinsgrove, (570) 374-8880.

Country Cupboard Inn, Route 15 North, Lewisburg, (717) 524-5500.

Days Inn, Route 15, Lewisburg, (570) 523-1171.

Golden Arrow Motel, Route 11 and Route 15, Selinsgrove, (570) 743-1611.

Hampton Inn, 3 Stettler Avenue, Selinsgrove, (570) 743-2223.

The Lewisburg Hotel, 136 Market Street, Lewisburg, (570) 523-7800.

Phillips Motel, Route 11 and Route 15, Shamokin Dam, (570) 743-3100.

Stone Castle Motel, 560 Montour Boulevard, Bloomsburg, (570) 784-6560.

Watson Inn, 100 Main Street, Watsontown, (570) 538-1832.

Ann's Inns & Outings, 302 North Third Street, Lewisburg, (570) 523-7163.

Brookpark Farm Bed & Breakfast, 100 Reitz Blvd., Lewisburg, (570) 523-0220.

The Inn at Olde New Berlin, 321 Market Street, New Berlin, (570) 966-0321.

The Lilac Moon, 347 Chestnut Street, Mifflinburg, (570) 966-4505.

Victorian Manor Bed & Breakfast, 312 Market Street, Millersburg, (570) 692-3511.

Ferryboat Campsites, Route 15, Liverpool, (570) 444-3200.

Hidden Valley Campground, Route 192, Mifflinburg, (570) 966-1330.

Little Mexico Campground, Route 304, Winfield, (570) 374-9742.

Shopping:

Brookpark Farm Antique Center, 100 Reitz Blvd., Lewisburg, (570) 523-6555, open 10 A.M.-5 P.M. daily.

Roller Mills, 517 St. Mary Street, Lewisburg, (570) 524-5733, Mon.-Sat., 10 A.M.-5 P.M.

Classic Thymes, 130 Buffalo Road, Lewisburg, (570) 523-3080, Mon.-Sat., 10 A.M.-5 P.M.

Colonial Candlecrafters, Route 15 South, Lewisburg, (570) 524-4556, open 9:30 A.M.-5 P.M. daily.

Cooley's Furniture, 1 Cedar Green Center, Mifflinburg, (570) 966-6111, Mon. and Fri., 9:30 A.M.-8 P.M., Tues.-Thur., 9:30 A.M.-5:30 P.M., and Sat., 9:30 A.M.-5 P.M.

Lewisburg Hotel

Lucinda's Country Crafts, Route 15 North, Lewisburg, (570) 568-1800, Wed.-Sat., 10 A.M.-5 P.M., Sun., 10 A.M.-3 P.M.

Mary Koons Quilt Shop, 408 Chestnut Street, Mifflinburg, (570) 966-0341, Mon.-Sat., 9 A.M.-5:30 P.M.

Nanalee's Doll's & Gifts, Route 15 North, Lewisburg, (570) 524-2080, Mon.-Sat., 10 A.M.-5 P.M.

Olde Barn Centre, (570) 546-7493, one mile east of I-180 on U.S. 220, Pennsdale, open 10 A.M.-5 P.M. daily.

The Bradley Shoemaker Gallery, 202 Market Street, Lewisburg, (570) 524-0423, Tues.-Sat., 10 A.M.-5:30 P.M.

Lewisburg Studio, 425 Market Street, (570) 523-7999, Mon.-Sat., 10 A.M.-5 P.M.

Penn's Creek Pottery, Route 104, Mifflinburg, (570) 837-3809, Mon.-Sat., 9:30 A.M.-5 P.M.

Route 15 Flea Market Center, Route 15 North, Lewisburg, (570) 568-8080, Sun., 8 A.M.-5 P.M.

Columbia Mall, I-80, Exit 34, Bloomsburg, (570) 784-9000, Mon.-Sat., 10 A.M.-9 P.M., Sun., noon-5 P.M.

Rising Sun Antiques, 6 Mill Street, Danville, (570) 275-1776, Mon.-Sat., 10 A.M.-6 P.M.

Amelia's Attic Treasures, 334 Mill Street, Danville, (570) 275-6870, Mon.-Sat., 10 A.M.-5 P.M.

Annual Events:

Lewisburg Market Street Arts Festival, April, (570) 523-0686.

Mifflinburg Buggy Days, late May, (570) 966-1355.

Strawberry Festival, June, Warrior Run Church, Watsontown, (570) 538-1928.

Union County West End Fair, August, Laurelton, (570) 966-0637.

New Berlin Heritage Day, August, (570) 966-0092.

Milton Harvest Festival, September, (570) 742-7341.

Lewisburg Craftfest, September, (570) 524-9240.

Bloomsburg Fair, late September, (570) 784-4949.

Warrior Run Heritage Days, October, (570) 546-9666.

Covered Bridge and Arts Festival, Bloomsburg, October, (570) 784-8279.

Lewisburg Antique Festival, October, (570) 523-3614.

Fall Festival, Lewisburg, October, (570) 524-9820.

Mifflinburg Christkindl Market, December, (570) 966-1666.

The Active Life:

Small towns such as Lewisburg and Mifflinburg are ideal for strolling and shopping. Golfers can swing away at **White Deer Golf Course** on Route 15 in Montgomery, (570) 547-2186. The valleys are superb for bicycling. The hills are modest, the scenery is excellent, and the traffic is light. **Milton State Park** borders the river and is a convenient place for walks and picnics.

A Great Place to Relax:

Gordon Hufnagle Park in the center of Lewisburg has a fitness trail, a covered bridge, and good places to sit, all in the center of town.

Covered Bridges:

The region has a decent number. The easiest to find is the **Hassenplug Bridge** in Mifflinburg. It crosses Buffalo Creek on Fourth Street, right beside a little nature preserve and athletic fields.

Tourist Information:

- (800) 458-4748

Where is it? Central, on U.S. 15 and Susquehanna River.

Getaway Rating: 3

Delta Place Station

19

LITITZ . . .
PRETZEL LOGIC
(A, R, R&R)

Lititz is a place where you can enjoy lazy days or active ones, and if you want to avoid driving for a few days, Lititz is ideal because you can spend an entire weekend without ever venturing more than a block from **Main Street.** Everything that you need for a couple of busy or thoroughly relaxing days is within a few blocks of the center of town.

Lititz is a picturesque town that's home to much history. On Main Street is the **Sturgis Pretzel Bakery,** the oldest in America. In 1861, Julius Sturgis established the business in an established bakery. In the bakery, visitors can learn how to twist their own pretzels, taste pretzels hot from the 200 year old ovens, and stock up for the long drive home.

Across the street from the bakery are two other historic sites. **Linden Hall,** established in 1746 by the Moravians, is the oldest girls residence school in the United States. It's still a private boarding school, just for girls.

In 1756, the Moravians dedicated Lititz as a Moravian community, and named it after the place in Bohemia where the **Moravian Church** began in 1456. For many years, only Moravians could live in Lititz.

Next to Linden Hall is the **Lititz Moravian Archives and Museum,** a small museum that documents the history of the

Sturgis Pretzel Bakery

Moravians in Lititz. Also on the grounds is a Moravian church that has regular Sunday services.

On the north side of Main Street is the **Johannes Mueller House**. Built in 1792, it consists of a stone house and an adjoining log structure. The stone house features period furnishings, and a museum next to the house contains early Lititz artifacts and paintings.

Tall trees line and shade Main Street, and the first block is home to many antique and craft shops. The **Herb Shop** smells good and sells items such as herbs, spices, and teas. The **Turquoise Shoppe** sells American Indian pottery, lamps, and jewelry. The **General Sutter Inn** is a hotel and restaurant on the square.

The smell of Lititz is sweet, as in chocolate. **Wilbur Chocolate** operates in the center of town, right beside the railroad tracks, and the delightful aroma frequently wafts through the air. The Wilbur Chocolate Company began in Philadelphia in 1884 and has been operating in Lititz since 1930. Most of the chocolate that Wilbur produces goes to other candy manufacturers such

Wilbur Chocolate Company

as Russell Stover, but Wilbur does make some products under its own name, and the favorite among them is **Wilbur Buds,** bite-sized chunks of chocolate.

At Wilbur is the **Candy America Museum,** where a video shows how raw ingredients become chocolate bars. Also at the museum are displays of antique candy-making machinery, cocoa tins, advertisements, and other candy items. At the factory store, you can buy Wilbur products.

Beside Wilbur is **Lititz Springs Park,** a popular, shaded little park that's an ideal place to relax and feed the ducks on a warm day. The park is host to a huge celebration on the Fourth of July, and on the last Saturday in July the **Lititz Outdoor Art Show** draws thousands of visitors to the park.

The **Heritage Map Museum** at 55 North Water Street houses hundreds of maps for viewing and purchase. The museum houses beautifully preserved maps from the 15th to the 19th century, and their accuracy is often amazing.

North of Lititz is the **Middle Creek Wildlife Management Area,** a lake created by the impoundment of a small creek. The area is now a major home for waterfowl such as Canada geese and snow geese. The Canada geese live there all year and the

Ephrata Cloister

snow geese pass through on their migrations. In March, the concentrations of snow geese are so heavy that from a distance they make hillsides appear to be snow-covered. The area is a favorite place for bird watchers and hikers who enjoy the section of the **Horseshoe Trail** that passes through the project. A visitor's center has displays of the wildlife in the area, and it provides a beautiful view of the lake.

Northeast of Lititz is Ephrata, home of the **Ephrata Cloister,** one of the oldest communal living societies in the United States. A group called the Seventh-Day German Baptists built the complex in the 1730s, and the community of religious celibates wrote music, printed books, and produced traditional German artworks called *frakturs*. It is now a museum.

Just north of Ephrata on State Street is the **Green Dragon Market,** which operates only on Fridays. The Green Dragon is a farmer's market, a flea market, and a place to buy just about anything you can imagine. Food, clothing, tools, and food are the biggest sellers. Farmers sell produce fresh from their fields, and such local delicacies as french fries and pretzels are easy to find.

Also in Ephrata is **Donecker's,** a complex that's home to a fashion store, a restaurant, The Artworks, a farmer's market, and a group of inns. The fashion store houses the finest for men and women. The restaurant offers classic French cuisine, which is a decidedly different touch in the very heart of Pennsylvania Dutch Country. The inns consist of four different older buildings, each of which has an elegant touch and charm. **The Artworks** is a four-story brick factory converted to a showplace for art, crafts, and quilts. The Farmer's Market sells fresh produce, meats, seafood, pies, cakes, and other taste treats from Lancaster County.

On Main Street in Ephrata is **The ReUzit Shop,** a small store run by Mennonites to raise money for their missions. The ReUzit Shop sells used goods and items made by people around the world, such as jewelry from Africa. You never know what you'll find here, but many of the items are intriguing, and you may come up with a great bargain.

On Route 272 North are **Ten Thousand Villages** and **Nav Jiwan International Tea Room,** which, combined, are something of an international shopping and dining bazaar. Operated by the Mennonite Church, the shop features crafts from 35 developing countries, and every week the tea room features the foods of a different country. If you can't get to Kenya to pick up that carved wooden elephant, you may be able to find it here.

At the intersection of Routes 501 and 322 is the village of Brickerville, home of the **Brickerville House** and shops, a collection of a restaurant and courtyard shops. The restaurant is in an 18th-century inn, and the shops sell antiques, crafts, and cross-stitch necessities.

Take a stroll down Main Street in Lititz and you'll find antiques and history. Drive over to Ephrata and you'll find more history and some interesting shopping.

Attractions:

Heritage Map Museum, 55 North Water Street, (717) 626-5002, Mon.-Sat., 10 A.M.-5 P.M.

Lititz Historical Foundation, 145 East Main Street, (717) 627-4636, Mon.-Sat., 10 A.M.-4 P.M., May through November.

Middle Creek Wildlife Management Area, Kleinfeltersville Road, (717) 733-1512, always open.

Moravian Museum, Church Square, East Main Street, (717) 626-8515, open Saturdays in summer and by appointment.

Sturgis Pretzel House, 219 East Main Street, (717) 626-4354, Mon.-Sat., 10 A.M.-5 P.M.

Wilbur Candy Store/Museum, 48 North Broad Street, (717) 626-3249, , Mon.-Sat., 10 A.M.-5 P.M.

Ephrata Cloister, 632 West Main Street, Ephrata, (717) 733-6600, Mon.-Sat., 9 A.M.-5 P.M., Sun., noon-5 P.M.

Dining:

The Brickerville House, Route 501 and Route 322, (717) 626-0377, open 11 A.M.-3 P.M. daily.

Chimney Corner Restaurant, Route 772 East, (717) 626-4707, breakfast, lunch, and dinner daily.

Dosie Dough Bakery, 45 South Broad Street, (717) 626-2266, open daily.

Edel's Main Street Deli, 53 East Main Street, (717) 627-4411, Mon.-Sat., 10 A.M.-6 P.M.

General Sutter Inn, 14 East Main Street, (717) 626-2115, opens daily at 11:30 A.M.

It's Only Natural Health Foods Café, 10 East Front Street, (717) 627-1174, , Mon.-Sat., 10 A.M.-5 P.M.

Roma Pizza, 54 East Main Street, (717) 626-6325, open 11 A.M.-11 P.M. daily.

Spill the Beans Coffee Shop, 43 East Main Street, (717) 627-7827, Mon.-Sat., 11 A.M.-6 P.M.

Donecker's Restaurant, 333 North State Street, Ephrata, (717) 738-9501, Thur.-Tues., 11 A.M.-10 P.M.

Ten Thousand Villages Tea Room, 240 North Reading Road, Ephrata, (717) 721-8400, lunch Mon.-Sat., dinner on Friday.

Lodging:

General Sutter Inn, 14 East Main Street, (717) 626-2115.

Alden House Bed & Breakfast, 62 East Main Street, (717) 627-3363.

Casual Corners Bed & Breakfast, 301 North Broad Street, (717) 626-5299.

Carter Run Inn, 511 East Main Street, (717) 626-8807.

Jacob Keler House, 990 Rettew Mill Road, Ephrata, (717) 733-4954.

Meadow Valley Farm Guest House, 221 Meadow Valley Road, Ephrata, (717) 733-8390.

501 Motel, Route 501 North, (717) 626-2597.

Swiss Woods Bed & Breakfast, 500 Blantz Road, (800) 594-8018.

Clearview Farm Bed & Breakfast, 355 Clearview Road, Ephrata, (717) 733-6333.

The Inn at Donecker's, 318 North State Street, Ephrata, (717) 738-9502.

Shopping:

Absolutely Balloony, 23 East Main Street, (717) 626-1188, Mon.-Sat., 10 A.M.-5 P.M.

Another Pretty Face Doll Shop, 153 East Main Street, (717) 626-9169, Mon.-Sat., 10 A.M.-5 P.M.

Donecker's, 409 North State Street, Ephrata, (717) 738-9500, Mon., Tues., Thur., and Fri., 11 A.M.-9 P.M., Sat., 9 A.M.-5 P.M.

Green Dragon Market, 955 North State Street, Ephrata, (717) 738-1117, open on Fridays.

Gypsy Hill Gallery, 47 East Main Street, (717) 626-8141, Mon.-Sat., 10 A.M.-5 P.M.

The Herb Shop, 20 East Main Street, (717) 626-9206, Mon.-Sat., 10 A.M.-5 P.M.

Hess Clothing, 11 South Broad Street, (717) 626-4609, Mon.-Sat., 10 A.M.-5 P.M.

Jewelry & Clock Works, 11 South Cedar Street, (717) 627-2560, call for hours.

Lititz Book Store, 27 East Main Street, (717) 626-7755, , Mon.-Sat., 10 A.M.-5 P.M.

Lititz Springs Outfitters, 49 North Broad Street, (717) 626-1009, Mon.-Thurs., and Sat., 10 A.M.-6 P.M., Fri., 10 A.M.-8 P.M.

Main Street Peddler, 22 East Main Street, (717) 626-4511, Mon.-Sat., 10 A.M.-5 P.M., Sun., 10 A.M.-3 P.M.

Re-Uzit Shop, 22 West Main Street, Ephrata, (717) 733-4982, Mon.-Sat., 9 A.M.-5 P.M.

Shaker Shoppe, 616 Owl Hill Road, (717) 626-9461, Tues. and Wed., noon-5 P.M., Thur. and Fri., noon-8 p.m., and Sat., 10 A.M.-3 P.M.

The Teddy Bear Emporium, 51 North Broad Street, (800) 598-6853, Mon.-Sat., 10 A.M.-5 P.M.

The Turquoise Shoppe, 25 East Main Street, (717) 626-1616, Mon.-Sat., 10 A.M.-5 P.M.

Tigers Eye, 69 East Main Street, (717) 627-2244, Mon.-Sat., 10 A.M.-5 P.M.

Ten Thousand Villages, 240 North Reading Road, Ephrata, (717) 721-8400, Mon.-Thur., and Sat., 9 A.M.-5 P.M., Fri., 9 A.M.-9 P.M.

Annual Events:

For a calendar, contact the Lititz Retailers Association, P.O. Box 10, Lititz, PA 17543.

Lititz Retailers Spring Sales Days, mid-March.

Cruise Night, Main Street, late April.

Plant Exchange & Sale, Lititz Historical Foundation, first Sunday in May.

Spring Antique Show & Sale, third Saturday in May, Main Street.

Craft Festival

Crafts in the Park, second Saturday in June.

Fourth of July Celebration, Lititz Springs Park.

Lititz Outdoor Art Show, last Saturday in July, Lititz Springs Park.

Lititz Rotary Craft Show, second Saturday in August, downtown.

Fall Antique Show, Saturday before Labor Day, Lititz Springs Park.

Lancaster YMCA Triathlons, Saturday after Labor Day, Speedwell Forge Lake, (717) 397-7474.

Lititz Historical Foundation Apple Festival, first Sunday in October, Linden Hall campus, Main Street.

Hometown Christmas Weekend, first weekend in December, downtown.

Moravian stars in houses and businesses, December.

The Active Life:

Lititz is a great town for walking, and the roads around Lititz are excellent for bicycling. The flattest direction to head is west, toward Manheim. A **45.9-mile bike tour** begins at the Ephrata Cloister and takes riders to the Landis Valley Farm

Erb's Bridge

Museum in Lancaster and the Railroad Museum of Pennsylvania in Strasburg. Direction sheets are available at all three museums. **Middle Creek Wildlife Management Area** has hiking trails of easy and moderate steepness.

A Great Place to Relax:

   Lititz Springs Park is an oasis of tranquility right in the center of town. Bring a picnic lunch and sit beneath the tall trees. You can watch the little stream and the ducks.

Covered Bridges:

   Several are fairly close to Lititz. The easiest to find is **Erb's Bridge.** From Lititz, go east on PA 772 to Rothsville. In Rothsville, turn left on Picnic Woods Road and go straight ahead for about a mile. The bridge is in a scenic spot, and it's in excellent condition.

Tourist Information:
- Pennsylvania Dutch Visitors Bureau, (800) PA-DUTCH, or
- Lititz Retailers Association, P.O. Box 10, Lititz, PA 17543.

Where is it? Southeast quadrant, along PA Route 501.

Getaway Rating: 2

Lititz Springs Park

20

MARIENVILLE . . .
STOPPING BY WOODS
(N, R&R)

Marienville is truly a getaway from the frantic pace of modern life. The town lies in **Forest County,** and the name accurately describes the place because forests still cover most of the land. Marienville is the largest town in the county, and with 1,300 residents it has about 25 percent of Forest County's population.

A good way to describe Forest County is to list some of the things that it doesn't have. Absent are **traffic lights, four-lane highways, television and radio stations,** and **shopping centers.** The county does have a weekly newspaper, but the main attractions are trees, water, wildlife, and cool temperatures. The **Allegheny National Forest** covers much of the county, and **Tionesta Lake** and the **Allegheny River** offer water sports. If you want to get away from it all, Pennsylvania has no better county.

Marienville itself doesn't have a lot of attractions. Visitors find food and lodging here, and it's a nice place to take a walk or ride a train, but the biggest attraction is the adjacent Allegheny National Forest. There people can bike, backpack, camp, swim, boat, canoe, water ski, cross-country ski, and ride mountain bikes, ATV's, and snowmobiles. And, there are plenty of places that are ideal for sitting and doing nothing.

Allegheny National Forest

The Allegheny National Forest covers 513,000 acres, or about 780 square miles, and it's most dazzling in autumn when the leaves turn the mountains into spectacular panoramas of red, orange, yellow, and gold.

The most prized tree in the forest is the black cherry, and the town of **Kane,** 25 miles north of Marienville, calls itself the **"Black Cherry Capital of the World."** So prized is the wood that local residents tell stories of single trees being worth as much as $5,000.

Throughout the forest, colorful wildlife abounds. White-tail deer, black bears, red foxes, and snowshoe rabbits are common, as are weasels and porcupines. In winter, snow falls abundantly and it's slow to melt. If you love snow sports, with the exception of downhill skiing, you'll enjoy Forest County.

If you like to watch birds, pay a visit to **Buzzard Swamp,** which is about a mile south of Marienville on Forest Road 157. Eleven miles of trails offer excellent opportunities to view various varieties of wildlife, and the **Songbird Sojourn Interpretative Trail** is a marked 1.5-mile trail that may provide a melodious walk.

During spring migrations, more than 20 species of waterfowl may visit the area, and bears, deer, beavers, and coyotes live in the neighborhood. Many species of fish thrive in the nearby ponds.

The primary attraction in downtown Marienville is the **Knox & Kane Railroad.** The K & K makes a 96-mile round trip through forests and meadows to the **Kinzua Bridge,** which is the second highest railroad bridge in the United States. The Kinzua Bridge is 2,053 feet wide and 301 feet high, and before the train crosses the bridge, it stops to let squeamish passengers off. After the train crosses the bridge, the other passengers have time for a picnic lunch while the crew moves the steam engine from one end of the train to the other. Then, the squeamish riders can get back on the train after it crosses the bridge on its return trip.

One interesting aspect of the bridge is that Kinzua Creek, which runs through the valley, is a stream so small that people can jump across it.

The train ride from Marienville to the bridge and back takes up an entire day, from 8:30 A.M. to 4:30 P.M., so the railroad offers a shorter option. Riders can board in Kane at 10:45 A.M. and return there at 2:15 P.M. The train operates from June through October.

One other attraction in Kane is the **Holgate Toy Company,** which makes wooden toys and has a factory store and toy museum. Kane also has a big athletic presence for a small town. It's the original home of basketball coach Chuck Daly and Olympic runner Amy Rudolph.

South of Marienville is **Clarion,** which likes to call itself the **"Autumn Leaf Capital of The World."** Clarion is home to Clarion University and **Cook Forest State Park,** which is known for its virgin stands of white pine and hemlock. The park lies beside the Clarion River, and it offers a full range of outdoor activities, including a swimming pool. The park is open all year, and it has facilities for winter activities such as a lighted skating pond, cross-country ski trails, sledding areas, and snowmobile trails. Snow is plentiful here, so winter sports enthusiasts have a long season.

The woods are lovely and deep, and they're everywhere. Marienville is an excellent place to escape from everything.

Knox & Kane Railroad

Attractions:

Allegheny National Forest, (814) 723-5150.

Knox & Kane Railroad, (814) 927-6621, opens at 8:30 A.M.,
Tues.-Sun., June through October.

Dining:

Americo's, Cooksburg/Vownickel Road in Cook Forest, (814)
927-8516.

Carol's Café, Route 66, Marienville, (814) 927-8646, open 5:30
A.M.-10 P.M. daily.

Guisippe's Country Villa, Route 66, Marienville, (814) 927-6623,
opens at 7 A.M. daily.

Kelly Hotel, 102 South Forest Street, Marienville (814) 927-6652,
open 8 A.M.-10 P.M. daily.

Clarion River Lodge, River Road, Cooksburg, (814) 744-8171,
lunch and dinner daily.

Cook Forest Country Inn, Vownickel/Cooksburg Road,
Cooksburg, (814) 927-8925, Wed.-Fri., 11 A.M.-9:30 P.M., Sat.
and Sun., 8 A.M.-11:30 P.M.

Forest Hills Restaurant, Route 36, Tionesta, (814) 755-8886, open 11 A.M.-9 P.M. daily.

Gateway Lodge, Route 36, Cooksburg, (814) 744-8017, open 11 A.M.-10 P.M. daily.

Ray's Hot Spot, Route 66, Marienville, (814) 927-8689, Fri. and Sat., 11 A.M.-2 A.M.

Sawmill Restaurant, Route 66, Leeper, (814) 744-8578, open 7 A.M.-midnight daily.

Lodging:

Bucktail Lodge, Route 66, Marienville, (814) 927-6676.

Cook Forest Country Inn, just off Route 66, Vownickel, (814) 927-8025.

Forest Ridge Campgrounds & Cabins, Loleta Road, Marienville, (814) 927-8340.

Gateway Lodge, Route 36, Cooksburg, (800) 843-6862 in Pennsylvania and Maryland, or (814) 744-8017.

Comfort Inn, Clarion, I-80 and PA 66, (814) 226-5230.

Holiday Inn of Clarion, I-80 and PA 68, (800) 596-1313.

Kane Motel, 80 Greeves Street, Kane, (814) 837-6161.

Kane View Motel, Route 6, Kane, (814) 837-8600.

Kelly Hotel, 102 South Forest Street, Marienville, (814) 927-6652.

Pigeon Loft Motel, Route 66, north of Marienville, (814) 927-8485.

Ronald McDonald Pioneer Lodge Bed & Breakfast, Box 447, Marienville, (814) 927-6654.

Skip Away Lodge, Route 66 North, Snyder Lane, Marienville, (814) 927-6903.

Snyder's Four Season Cottage, Route 66, Marienville, (814) 927-8813.

Stone's Throw Cottage, Route 66 South, Marienville, (814) 724-6331.

Whistling Pines, RD #3 Guitonville/Marienville, (814) 927-8837.

Camping in the **Allegheny National Forest,** (800) 280-CAMP.

Camping in **Cook Forest State Park,** (814) 744-8407.

Deer Meadows Campground, Cooksburg, (814) 927-8125.

Note on Lodging:

Forest County doesn't have an abundance of motel rooms and cabins, and "No Vacancy" signs are common sights, especially on weekends. Calling ahead is wise.

Shopping:

Shopping isn't a major attraction in this area. You'll be able to find items that you need, as well as souvenirs, but you won't find malls or outlets.

Baughman's Market, Route 66, Marienville, (814) 927-6624, opens at 8 A.M. daily.

Marienville Power Sports, Route 66, Marienville, (814) 927-8543, opens at 9 A.M. daily.

Mountain Mercantile, Route 36, north of Cook Forest State Park, (814) 744-8150, Tues.-Sun., 10 A.M.-5 P.M.

North Country Antiques, Route 66, Marienville, (814) 927-8995, Fri.-Sun., 11 A.M.-5 P.M.

Rizer's Wholesale Fireworks, Route 66, south of Marienville, (814) 927-6637, seasonal hours.

Shoup's ServiStar Hardware, Cherry Street, Marienville, (814) 927-6683, Mon.-Sat., 8 A.M.-5 P.M.

Annual Events:

Marienville Winterfest, late January, (814) 755-4598.

Clarion River Half Marathon, Cook Forest, early April, (814) 764-5215.

Marienville Fire Company Tour-de-Forest ATV Ride, (814) 755-4598.

Town Square

Marienville Firemen's Festival, July 4, (814) 755-4598.

Clarion County Fair, July, (814) 275-3929.

Cook Forest Sawmill All-Wood Festival, July, (814) 744-8407.

Tionesta Indian Festival, August, (814) 755-4598.

Marienville Oktoberfest, late September, (814) 755-4598.

Autumn Leaf Festival, Clarion, early October, (814) 755-4598.

The Active Life:

That's why people come here. Hiking, biking, snowmobiling, hunting, fishing, boating, and other outdoor activities are readily available here. One good place to stop when you arrive is the **Marienville Ranger Station** on Route 66, just north of town. For information, call (814) 927-6628.

Pickin' Berries:

Wild raspberries, blackberries, and blueberries grow throughout the forests, frequently by the side of a road. In this region, they mature in late July and in August. Keep your eyes open and you'll find some delicious free snacks.

A Great Place to Relax:

The whole county fits the description. Walk in the forest or ride the train. Sit outside your motel room or relax by a lake. Forest County is the ideal place to get away from stress and congestion.

Covered Bridges:

None nearby.

Tourist Information:

• Forest County Tourist Promotion Agency, (814) 755-4598.

Where is it? Northwest quadrant, on PA 66.

Getaway Rating: 5

21

MOUNT GRETNA . . .
A SUMMER PLACE
(A, N, R, R&R)

Ladies in the long dresses of the 19th century and men in suits and top hats are images that come quickly to mind in the genteel settings of Mount Gretna. On summer afternoons, the relentless pace of the modern world seems a million miles away to diners who enjoy shakes and fries beneath tall pines and mighty oaks at the **Jigger Shop.**

Built into the woods in southern Lebanon County, Mount Gretna is a both a place and an attitude. For residents and summer visitors, Mount Gretna provides a quiet escape and invites everyone to slow down for a while. The trees are tall, and they hide most of the houses. Streets are narrow, hilly, and winding. Commercial establishments are few, and just about every home has a porch or a deck where people can sit and sip. Mount Gretna is a pleasant reminder of an era when life moved at a slower pace.

Once, Mount Gretna had three large hotels and two railroads. The Cornwall and Lebanon Railroad connected to the main line of the Pennsylvania Railroad at Elizabethtown, and the Mount Gretna Narrow Gauge Railroad carried passengers from "downtown" to the top of a ridge called **Governor Dick.** Today, a tower on top of Governor Dick offers spectacular views in all directions.

Jigger Shop

A century ago, Mount Gretna was a summer getaway for religious groups and a daytime getaway for the masses. In the last 100 years, however, it has changed somewhat, but the feeling remains the same, and the trees are taller and thicker than they were in the late 1890s.

Mount Gretna is a perfect place to do nothing, and it's also an excellent place to enjoy a little sun, water, and culture. After a leisurely day at the lake, evenings offer concerts, plays, and dinner theater. Many homes in Mount Gretna are summer cottages, and some are available for rental. For day-trippers or evening visitors, Mount Gretna extends a quiet welcome.

Summer is Mount Gretna's season. From Memorial Day weekend until Labor Day, the playhouse, the dinner theater, and the community building present a full lineup of stage productions, concerts, and bridge matches. For one weekend in August, the town becomes a crowded place as the art show brings thousands of visitors. Then, after Labor Day, Mount Gretna goes back to its quiet disposition, and that's just how the permanent residents like it.

The man behind the rapid development of Mount Gretna was Robert Coleman, who was the owner of the **Cornwall Iron**

Furnace and whose wealth exceeded that of such tycoons as J. P. Morgan and Marshall Field.

Mount Gretna began life in 1882 as the **Camp Meeting,** a tent site for summer religious activities, and the following year Coleman selected it as a site for a picnic grove along his Cornwall and Lebanon Railroad. Growth came quickly, and in 1885, the Pennsylvania National Guard established a camp. In that same year, Coleman began work to dam the Conewago Creek, creating **Conewago Lake,** which opened in the autumn of that year.

By 1886, Mount Gretna was a flourishing summer place, and on June 2, 1886 the *Lebanon Daily News* offered this description:

> "Mount Gretna was never so lovely as it is this summer. Disinterested, impartial people have declared it the finest mountain park in the State. Certainly there is none covering such an immense area. It is unexcelled as to location, accessibility, conveniences, scenery, elevation, rambles, drives, soil, water, and management. New and picturesque walks have been laid out . . . so that there are miles of shaded paths so directed as to lead to the most beautiful spots, past the coolest springs, along the mossy banks of a mountain stream, down to Lake Conewago."

With such pleasing amenities, Mount Gretna began to draw visitors who wanted to stay for more than a day. Wealthy people built summer cottages, many of which were elegant Victorian homes, and in 1892 the **Pennsylvania Chautaqua** made Mount Gretna its official home. Chautaqua is a movement that began in New York state in 1874 as a summer school for Sunday school teachers. It grew and expanded, and still operates in Mount Gretna today.

Every summer, the **Chautaqua Village** springs to life as a place of education, the arts, recreation, and religion. Also operating is the Camp Meeting, home of **The Tabernacle** and a program of cultural activities. Thus, while the means of transportation have changed in the past 100 years, visitors come to Mount Gretna today for many of the same reasons as they came for in the past.

Cornwall Iron Furnace

The general feeling of Mount Gretna is calm and quiet, but the little town is also a haven for those who enjoy vigorous outdoor recreation. The adjacent woodlands are full of trails that are popular with runners, hikers, mountain bikers, and horseback riders.

In summers, Mount Gretna is a destination for many bicyclists who enjoy the challenge of the hills and the cool drinks available at the Jigger Shop. In October, a 50K trail race takes place in the hills around town, and throughout the year local residents enjoy the recreational opportunities.

For many visitors, the primary attractions are the plays and the concerts at the **Mount Gretna Playhouse.** Throughout the summer, professional stage productions and musical events attract patrons to the playhouse. Walkers in the woods and diners at the Jigger Shop can hear the sounds.

Despite its relaxed atmosphere, Mount Gretna really isn't an isolated place. **Lebanon** is less than 10 miles away, and **Lancaster** and **Hershey** aren't much farther. On the southern side of the "mountain" is the **Mount Hope Estate and Winery,** home of the **Pennsylvania Renaissance Faire,** a re-creation of medieval England held on weekends from August through October.

Mount Gretna Playhouse

Five miles east of Mount Gretna is the **Cornwall Iron Furnace,** which was once one of the major economic forces in Lebanon County. Iron ore came out of the ground in Cornwall, and, in Lebanon, Bethlehem Steel operated a huge plant.

The Cornwall Iron Banks were once the greatest known deposit of iron ore in the United States. The furnace operated until 1883, and the mine produced ore until Hurricane Agnes flooded the open pit mine and destroyed equipment in 1972.

The mine and the furnace were part of a 10,000-acre iron plantation, a self-sufficient community that existed solely to produce iron. The village still exists, and the handsome stone houses are private residences. The furnace is now a state museum with guided tours.

If you're looking for a quiet place in the woods with just enough activities to hold your interest, come to Mount Gretna.

Attractions:

Mount Gretna Playhouse, (717) 964-3322.

The Lake at Mount Gretna, (717) 964-3130, opens daily at 11:30 A.M. in summer.

Cornwall Iron Furnace, (717) 272-9711, Tues.-Sat., 9 A.M.-5 P.M., Sun., noon-4 P.M.

Mount Hope Estate & Winery/PA Renaissance Fair, (717) 665-7021, call for days and hours.

Dining:

The most popular place in town is the Jigger Shop, which has been in business since 1895. On warm summer weekends, it's a busy place, but it's only open in summer. It's along Route 117. Call (717) 964-9686 for details.

The Timbers Restaurant & Dinner Theater, 10 Timber Road, Mount Gretna, (717) 964-3601, Tues.-Sat., opens at 6 P.M., Wed. and Sat. matinees open at noon

The Hideaway in Mount Gretna, Boulevard Street, just off Route 117 (look for signs). Hideaway has a large outdoor deck and patio. Open daily, call (717) 964-3170 for information.

The Porch & Pantry Café, Route 117, Mount Gretna, (717) 964-3771, Wed.-Sat., 7 A.M.-1 P.M., Fri.-Sat., 6 P.M.-8 P.M.

Tony's Mining Company, 211 Rexmont Road, Cornwall, (717) 273-4871, Tues.-Fri., 5:30 P.M.-9 P.M., Sat., 5 P.M.-9:30 P.M.

Mount Gretna Corner Deli, Route 117, Mount Gretna, (717) 964-3182, open 7 A.M.-7 P.M. daily.

Lodging:

The Mount Gretna Inn, (800) 272-6602, a bed and breakfast, is the only lodging in Mount Gretna.

Weekly home rentals in Mount Gretna are available through Penn Realty, (717) 964-3800.

Inn at Mount Hope, 2232 East Mount Hope Road, Manheim, (717) 664-4708.

Rexmont Inn, 299 Rexmont Road, Rexmont, (800) 626-0942.

Mount Vernon Motel, 980 Lebanon Road (Route 72), Manheim, (717) 665-2938.

Rodeway Inn, 2931 Lebanon Road (Route 72) Manheim, (717) 665-2755.

Mount Gretna Inn

Quality Inn Lebanon, 625 Quentin Road (Route 72), (717) 273-6771.

Shopping:

Mount Gretna isn't a shopping destination. You could easily spend a weekend in the town and go home without any new items, but the town does have several antique and craft shops.

Memory Lane, Route 117, beside miniature golf course, (717) 964-3303, flexible hours.

Gretna Sampler, Route 117, beside the Jigger Shop, (717) 964-2210, open daily in summer, from noon-10 P.M.

Annual Events:

Music at Gretna, summer, (717) 361-1508.

Mount Gretna Outdoor Art Show, third weekend in August, (717) 964-2340.

Pennsylvania Renaissance Faire, weekends, August through October, Mount Hope Estate & Winery, (717) 665-7021.

Stan & Dan's 25K & 50K trail runs, Mount Gretna, first Sunday in October.

Edgar Allen Poe Evermore, Mount Hope Estate & Winery, weekends in November, (717) 665-7021.

Charles Dickens Victorian Christmas, Mount Hope Estate & Winery, weekends from Thanksgiving to Christmas, (717) 665-7021.

The Active Life:

Mount Gretna is popular with mountain bikers and trail runners. They enjoy the trails through the woods and the abandoned railroad bed that runs just north of Route 117. Swimming and boating are available at the lake, and the town has tennis courts and a playground.

A Great Place to Relax:

At the Jigger Shop or at the lake.

Covered Bridges:

None in Lebanon County.

Tourist Information:

• (717) 272-8555.

Where is it? Southeast, on PA 117 and U.S. 322.

Getaway Rating: 4

22

NEW HOPE/DOYLESTOWN . . . CURTAIN CALLS AND STATELY WALLS

(A, R, R&R)

New Hope and Doylestown cater to crowds that enjoy art and good food, and your stop here will be a time of pleasant shopping and relaxing.

Antique shops and art galleries line the streets of New Hope. Some visitors come to stroll and to buy. Others come to ride on the **New Hope & Ivyland Railroad.** In warm weather, just about every restaurant offers outdoor dining, and visitors can see the sights on foot, by boat, by train, and on a mule-drawn barge.

Doylestown is another small town with an artsy atmosphere. **James Michener** called Doylestown home, and the **Michener Museum** houses a fine collection of 19th- and 20th-century American art. The museum also houses exhibits with displays on famous figures such as **Pearl Buck** and **Dorothy Parker.**

Doylestown and New Hope are both charming little towns where the walking is pleasant. They're about 20 miles north of Philadelphia and 10 miles apart, and the region between them is distinctly different from the towns themselves. Suburban sprawl has come to Bucks County, but it can't affect the downtowns, so the atmosphere in New Hope and Doylestown is different from the places where new houses and stores seem to sprout up every hour.

Traffic can be an annoyance in both New Hope and Doylestown, so it's a good idea to stay somewhere in the downtown area and forget the car for a day or two. Both downtowns are compact enough to allow you to park the car and easily walk to all the attractions.

New Hope is a quaint place today, but it wasn't that way during the American Revolution. George Washington and his Continental Army launched their attack on Trenton on Christmas night, 1776, from a site a few miles south of New Hope. **Washington Crossing Historic Park** covers 500 acres and includes **McConkey's Ferry Inn, Bowman's Tower,** and **Bowman's Hill Wildlife Preserve.**

New Hope itself is a busy place, but the business ends abruptly on the edge of town, and the land immediately becomes pastoral and quiet. Bucks County has 12 covered bridges, and one is just west of Washington Crossing Historic Park.

Back in New Hope, visitors stroll the streets and browse at more than 200 art galleries, antique shops, boutiques, and specialty shops, such as **Gothic Creations,** which features gargoyles and angels, and **New Hope Miniatures,** which sells hand-crafted collectibles, miniatures, and dollhouse kits. **Meow, Meow** has everything for cats and cat lovers. Downtown New Hope is a shopper's delight if you're looking for unusual items.

If you'd rather travel by something other than shoe leather, New Hope offers good choices. You can head out on the river at the **Boat Rides at Wells Ferry** for a comfortable tour on the *Star of New Hope* or **Coryell's Ferry Boat Rides** will take you out on the river aboard a sternwheeler reminiscent of the boats that plied the Mississippi in the 19th century. For a wetter view of the river, **Bucks County River Country** in Upper Black Eddy will take you rafting, tubing, or canoeing on the river.

The **New Hope & Ivyland Railroad** offers excursions through the scenic countryside, and shoppers can take the train to Lahaska, get off there, and take a bus to **Peddler's Village** to shop and dine, and then catch a later train back to New Hope. The train runs specials on weekends, with dinner trains on Saturdays and brunches on Sunday mornings.

Michener Museum, Doylestown

The most unusual mode of transportation is the canal boat. Pulled by mules, the boats will take you on a slow ride down the canal, and you'll get a glimpse at New Hope life as it was in the 1800s.

Culture and the arts have a large presence in New Hope, and the **Bucks County Playhouse** is a focal point for the performing arts. Housed in a mill that dates to the 1780s, the playhouse gives productions from May through December.

Doylestown is a college town **(Delaware Valley College)**, and a town of museums. The **Fonthill Museum** is the creation of Dr. Henry Mercer who, in 1908 to 1910, built this home that looks like a fortress. Constructed of concrete, it has 44 rooms, 32 stairways, and more than 200 windows.

The **James A. Michener Art Museum** is in the renovated Bucks County Prison. The museum houses a large collection of 20th-century American art, sculpture, and cultural programs. An exhibit focused on Michener himself shows the Bucks County office where he wrote *Tales of the South Pacific*.

The **Mercer Museum** documents the early history of the United States, from the days of the colonies to the Civil War. Artifacts from the 1700s and the 1800s show how more than 60 types of craftspeople performed their jobs.

The building formerly used by Dr. Henry Chapman to produce decorative tile and mosaics now houses the **Moravian Pottery and Tile Works.** A video presentation shows Mercer and his production methods, and a walking tour shows the tile-making process.

The **National Shrine of Our Lady of Czestochowa** is a shrine to Polish Christianity. On exhibit is a painting of the Virgin Mary, and the upper church's stained glass windows depict a millennium of Polish Christianity.

Like New Hope, Doylestown's streets are full of antique and craft shops, as well as cafés and restaurants that offer outdoor dining. **Crossroad Crafts** sells international handcrafts such as jewelry and decorations from Ten Thousand Villages and other trade organizations. **Dragon's Den of Antiques** is a co-op that sells art and textiles, as well as Victorian, Primitive, and Deco items. **Frog Pond Antiques** features carved Santas and painted birdhouses. The **Leleu Gallery** has artworks and crafts by local and national artists.

For a weekend of sophistication and shopping, pay a visit to New Hope or Doylestown. Both little towns offer a healthy dose of fun and relaxation.

Attractions:

Downtown New Hope.

Downtown Doylestown.

Michener Art Museum, 138 South Pine Street, Doylestown, (215) 340-9800, Tues.-Fri., 10 A.M.-4:30 P.M., Sat. and Sun., 10 A.M.-5 P.M.

New Hope & Ivyland Railroad, (215) 862-2332, varying schedule, open all year.

New Hope Canal Boat Company, (215) 862-0758, opens at 11 A.M., May through October.

James A. Michener Art Museum, (215) 340-9800, Tues.-Fri., 10 A.M.-4:30 P.M., Sat. and Sun., 10 A.M.-5 P.M.

Moravian Pottery & Tile Works, 130 Swamp Road, Doylestown, (215) 345-6722, open 10 A.M.-4:45 P.M. daily.

Philadelphia Park Racetrack, 3001 Street Road, Bensalem, (215) 639-0000, racing begins at 12:30 P.M. and dates vary throughout the year.

Sesame Place amusement park, (215) 752-7070, open mid-May through October.

Washington Crossing Historic Park, (215) 869-2924, open 9 A.M.-5 P.M. daily.

Dining:

B. Maxwell's Restaurant, 37 North Main Street, Doylestown, (215) 348-1027, Mon.-Thur., 11 A.M.-11 P.M., Fri. and Sat., 11 A.M.-midnight.

Chong's Garden, 22 North Main Street, Doylestown, (215) 345-9444, Tues.-Thur., 11:30 A.M.-9:30 P.M., Fri., 11:30 A.M.-10:30 P.M., Sat., noon-10:30 P.M., and Sun., noon-9:30 P.M.

Doylestown Inn, 18 West State Street, (215) 345-6610, lunch and dinner daily.

Forager Restaurant & Bar, 1600 River Road, New Hope, (215) 862-9477, open daily for dinner.

Gerenser's Exotic Ice Cream, 22 South Main Street, New Hope, (215) 862-2050, open 10:30 A.M.-7 P.M. daily.

Havana, Inc., 105 South Main Street, New Hope, (215) 862-9897, Mon.-Fri., noon-midnight, Sat. and Sun., opens at 11 A.M.

Inn on Blueberry Hill, Route 611, Doylestown, (215) 453-0379, opens Mon.-Sat. at 5 P.M.

Karla's, 5 West Mechanic Street, New Hope, (215) 862-2612, open 11 A.M.-10 P.M. daily.

Kelly's Bar & Grill, 29 South Main Street, Doylestown, (215) 345-8108, lunch and dinner, Mon.-Sat.

La Bonne Auberge, Mechanic Street, New Hope, (215) 862-2462, open daily for dinner.

The Landing, 22 North Main Street, New Hope, (215) 862-5711, lunch and dinner daily.

Logan Inn Restaurant, 10 West Ferry Street, New Hope, (215) 862-2300, lunch and dinner daily.

Luigi's at the Canal House, 28 West Mechanic Street, New Hope, lunch and dinner daily.

Mothers Restaurant, 34 North Main Street, New Hope, (215) 862-9354, breakfast, lunch, and dinner daily.

New Hope Country Diner, 6522 Route 202, New Hope, (215) 862-5575, open 1 A.M.-10 P.M. daily.

Odette's Restaurant, South River Road, New Hope, (215) 862-2432, open daily for lunch and dinner, Sunday brunch.

Paganini Ristorante, 81 West State Street, Doylestown, (215) 348-9522, open 11:30 A.M.-10:30 P.M. daily.

River's Edge Inn, 50 South Main Street, New Hope, (215) 862-5085, lunch and dinner daily.

River City Pizza, 82 South Main Street, New Hope, (215) 862-9956, Sun.-Thur., 11 A.M.-11 P.M., Fri. and Sat., 11 A.M.-midnight.

Roosevelt's Blue Star, 52 East State Street, Doylestown, (215) 348-9000, opens at 11 A.M. daily.

Russell's 96 West, 96 West State Street, Doylestown, (215) 345-8746, lunch and dinner, Mon.-Sat.

Tilley's, 120 Veterans Lane, Doylestown, (215) 345-7778, Mon.-Sat., 6 A.M.-8 P.M., Sun., 6 A.M.-1 P.M.

Lodging:

Doylestown Inn, 18 West State Street, (215) 345-6610.

New Hope Inn, 36 West Mechanic Street, (215) 862-2078.

Logan Inn, 10 West Ferry Street, New Hope, (215) 862-2300.

Aaron Burr House Inn, 80 West Bridge Street, New Hope, (215) 862-2343.

Fox & Hound Bed & Breakfast, 246 West Bridge Street, New Hope, (215) 862-5082.

The Mansion Inn, 9 South Main Street, New Hope, (215) 862-1231.

Pineapple Hill Bed & Breakfast, 1324 River Road, New Hope, (215) 862-1790.

Porches on the Towpath Bed & Breakfast, 20 Fisher Alley, New Hope, (215) 862-3277.

Peace Valley Bed & Breakfast, 75 Chapman Road, Doylestown, (215) 230-7711.

Wedgewood Inn of New Hope, 111 West Bridge Street, (215) 862-2520.

Best Western New Hope Inn, Route 202, (215) 862-5221.

New Hope Motel in the Woods, 400 West Bridge Street, (215) 862-2800.

Shopping:

Appalachian Trail Outfitters at Rudolph's, Main Street and Oakland Avenue, Doylestown, (215) 348-5230, Mon.-Sat., 10 A.M.-6 P.M., Sun., 11 A.M.-5 P.M.

Bucks County Antiques Mall, Route 202, Chalfont, (215) 997-3227, Wed.-Sun., 10 A.M.-6 P.M.

Consignment Galleries, Clemens Town Center, New Britain, (215) 348-5244, Mon.-Fri., 10 A.M.-8 P.M., Sat., 10 A.M.-5 P.M., and Sun., noon-5 P.M.

Crown & Eagle Antiques, Route 202, New Hope, (215) 794-8277, open noon-4 P.M. daily.

Darby-Barrett Antiques, Route 202, Lahaska, (215) 794-8277, open noon-5 P.M. daily.

Dragon's Den of Antiques, 135 South Main Street, Doylestown, (215) 345-8666, open daily.

Frog Pond Antiques, 70 West State Street, Doylestown, (215) 348-3425, Wed.-Sun., noon-5 P.M.

Gould's Country Accents, Route 202, Lahaska, (215) 766-7428, Fri.-Sun., 10 A.M.-5 P.M.

Olde Mill Flea Market, Hulmeville, near PA Turnpike 7, I-95, (215) 757-1777, Thur. and Fri., 6 P.M.-9 P.M., Sat., noon-9 P.M., and Sun., noon-5 P.M.

Alfred B. Patton, 64 Swamp Road, Doylestown, (215) 345-0700, Mon.-Wed. and Fri., 8 A.M.-5 P.M., Thur., 8 A.M.-8 P.M., and Sat., 9 A.M.-4 P.M.

Penn's Purchase Factory Outlet Stores, Route 202, Lahaska, (215) 794-0300, Mon.-Sat., 10 A.M.-8 P.M., Sun., 10 A.M.-6 P.M.

Rice's Sale & Country Market, 6326 Greenhill Road, New Hope, (215) 297-5993, open Tuesdays.

Salad Garden Farm Market, 527 Center Hill Road, Upper Black Eddy, (610) 847-2853, Fri.-Sun., 10 A.M.-6 P.M.

Scarlett, 129 South Main Street, New Hope, (215) 862-9408, Mon.-Fri. and Sun., 11 A.M.-6 P.M., Sat., 11 A.M.-10 P.M.

Annual Events:

Food, Fun, & Fitness Day, Saturday before Memorial Day, Doylestown, (215) 340-9988.

Legacy Lawn Party, Mercer Museum, Doylestown, June, (215) 345-0210.

Bucks County Covered Bridges & Garden Tour, first Saturday in June, (215) 766-2211.

Outdoor Film Festival, Mercer Museum, Doylestown, July and August, (215) 345-0210.

Fourth of July Colonial Day Celebration, Washington Crossing Park, (215) 493-4076.

Bucks County Wine & Food Festival, Doylestown, (215) 230-7533.

Juried Art Exhibition, late September through October, New Hope, (215) 862-0582.

New Hope Outdoor Arts & Crafts Festival, first weekend in October, (215) 598-3301.

Canal, New Hope

Harvest Festival, New Hope Winery, second weekend in October, (800) 592-9463.

Halloween Party, Parry Mansion, New Hope, (215) 862-5652.

Twelve Trees Holiday Display, Mercer Museum, Doylestown, November, (215) 345-0210.

Washington Crossing Re-enactment, Christmas Day, Washington Crossing Park, (215) 493-4076.

The Active Life:

You'll probably do a fair amount of walking during a day or a weekend in New Hope or Doylestown. The Delaware River is ideal for floating on a hot summer day. **Bucks County River Country** on Route 32 in Upper Black Eddy rents tubes, rafts, canoes, and kayaks. Call (215) 297-5000 for details. Country roads around New Hope are less crowded than the highways and are good for bicycling.

In Langhorne is **Sesame Place,** a theme park for children that features Sesame Street characters.

A Great Place to Relax:

The outdoor restaurants in New Hope have a pleasant atmosphere, and sitting down by the river is always relaxing.

Covered Bridges:

Bucks County has 12. The **Van Sant Bridge** is close to New Hope, about a mile west of Washington Crossing Park on Township Route 392.

Tourist Information:

• (215) 345-4552.

Where is it? Southeast, on U.S. 202.

Getaway Rating: 3

Boat rides, New Hope

23

OHIOPYLE . . .
THE WRIGHT BLUFF
(N, R, R&R)

Ohiopyle is a part of an area known as the **Laurel Highlands.** It's a place of great natural beauty, important American history, and vigorous outdoor activities. For weekend visitors, Ohiopyle offers a long list of activities, and excellent opportunities for uninterrupted relaxation.

George Washington fought near here in 1754. At **Fort Necessity,** Washington, then only 22 years old, engaged in a battle that marked the beginning of the French and Indian War. Washington was heading for the forks of the Ohio River, now Pittsburgh, an important area claimed by both the British and the French. On July 3 a force of French soldiers and Indians surrounded Washington and his troops in their "fort of necessity" at **Great Meadows,** a small open area in the vast forest. Washington called the spot "A charming field for an encounter." Washington and his men were no match for the French and Indians from Fort Duquesne. Badly defeated, the Americans were forced to withdraw east of the mountains.

In the 1750s, this area of southwestern Pennsylvania was a completely uncharted wilderness with few inhabitants. The land is rugged, and Washington was hoping to establish a water route to the forks of the Ohio, but he had to abandon that idea

The falls at Ohiopyle

when he encountered the falls on the **Youghiogheny (Yuck' a gay nee) River.** In the 1750s, those falls proved an almost insurmountable obstacle to westward expansion, but today they're a major attraction and the main economic force in Ohiopyle, a town devoted almost entirely to recreation.

Ohiopyle is a major starting point for river adventurers and bicyclists. They come by the hundreds to get on the river and the hiking and biking trails in the region. Visitors looking for a more relaxing getaway can sit and watch the river and visit two of Frank Lloyd Wright's masterpieces, **Kentuck Knob** and **Fallingwater,** which is a spectacular example of architectural innovation.

On a summer Saturday morning, the tiny town of Ohiopyle is a bustling place. The water in the Yuck is pretty low, but that's good for novices, and the crowds are pretty big. Nearby, bicyclists are putting their wheels on the **Yough River Trail,** and a few runners are enjoying the beauty and the challenge of the **Laurel Highlands Trail.** In **Ohiopyle State Park,** many people are just watching the river. The shrill whistle of a CSX freight train briefly interrupts the quiet as the cars thunder down the rails. Up the mountain, hundreds of visitors are marveling at the beauty of **Fallingwater** and its grounds. Meanwhile, over in Farmington, guests are enjoying just about every possible pampering at the **Nemacolin Woodlands Resort & Spa** and at the **Summit Inn Resort.** A weekend hardly seems enough time to do everything around here.

The most famous of the attractions is Fallingwater, the best-preserved house designed by Frank Lloyd Wright. From 1937 until 1963, Fallingwater was the weekend home of the Kaufmann family of Pittsburgh, the founders of Kaufmann's department stores. In 1963, Edgar Kaufmann, Jr., presented the home to the Western Pennsylvania Conservancy, which has maintained it since then in the same condition, with its contents intact.

The home is a beautiful example of Wright's "organic architecture," a concept that blends buildings in with their natural settings. In this setting, that meant building the house right over boulders instead of removing them. It also meant building right up to the stream bed, which gives the house its name.

Fallingwater was an early use of cantilevering in construction. Concrete decks appear to be unsupported, and they look as though they should collapse, but the cantilevering and reinforced concrete allow the house to defy gravity. The result is a stunning home in a pristine natural setting. Tour guides lead visitors through all rooms in the home, and visitors may then roam the grounds on trails through the 1,500-acre property.

A few miles south, **Kentuck Knob** represents a refinement of Wright's organic architecture concept. The home appears to be part of the hill itself. Constructed of red cypress and native fieldstone, the home is just a few yards from a hilltop that provides a stunning view of the **Youghiogheny River Gorge** and the mountains that surround it.

History lovers will enjoy a ride down **Route 40,** known in this area as the **National Road.** Along the road, stone markers tell the distances to Wheeling, West Virginia, and Cumberland, Maryland. Route 40 was the first federally funded road in the United States. Built in the first half of the 19th century, it helped to open up the territories west of the Allegheny

Fallingwater

Mountains and gave a young nation room to grow. Even with the opening of the National Road, travel in the region wasn't easy.

The mountains are steep, and they're still a challenge for motor vehicles. Trucks crawl up and down the mountains, and in several places you'll see "Runaway Truck" ramps, places for trucks to bail out when their brakes fail on a downhill.

A 90-mile section of Route 40 has become the **National Road State Heritage Park,** a corridor that commemorates the role the road played in the country's development. Along the route, many structures offer a brief glimpse back to an era when travel was much harder than it is now. Forty-eight buildings that were either taverns or inns during the National Road era from 1818 to 1853 are still standing, and many are still in use.

Route 40 passes through many small towns, and the city of **Uniontown,** where visitors can find shopping malls and many restaurants. East of Uniontown is **Laurel Caverns,** Pennsylvania's largest cave. Visitors can go deep into the earth to see limestone formations in a place that maintains a constant temperature of 52°.

Because of the steepness of the mountains, most of the land never allowed farming, and it's almost impossible to find a spot that doesn't provide a view of a wooded hillside. Such a setting invites outdoor activities, and Ohiopyle is an excellent place to enjoy them. Many of the businesses have bike racks outside, and kayaks and rafts are common sights. Ohiopyle State Park covers almost 30 square miles, and it's spectacular in every season. Trails run throughout the park, and the easiest is definitely the **Youghiogheny River Trail,** which extends about 28 miles. This trail is an abandoned railroad right-of-way, and its grade is gentle. It's ideal for leisurely biking or walking, and it provides excellent views of the river and the rafters floating by.

Considerably more challenging is the **Laurel Highlands Trail,** which begins at Ohiopyle and extends 70 miles to Johnstown. The Laurel Highlands Trail has serious hills, and every June a select group of runners undertakes the challenge of running all 70 miles.

But it's the river that has given the region its identity among adventurers, and Ohiopyle is home to four different whitewater rafting guide services. The river isn't wide, but it runs very fast, and it has rapids ranging from Class I, the easiest, to Class V, the most difficult. Traditional whitewater season begins in March and runs until October, although experienced rafters, canoeists, and kayakers will head out on the river whenever conditions allow. If you do choose to take a ride with one of the tour services, you can save a lot of money by riding on a weekday. Prices are much lower during the week, with the lowest prices available on Tuesdays, Wednesdays, and Thursdays.

If you'd like a getaway that's more gentle than bouncing around on the river, book a weekend at **Nemacolin Woods** or the **Summit Inn.** Nemacolin is a modern resort with a championship golf course, an equestrian center, tennis, swimming, a culinary staff, and plenty of pampering. The Summit Inn is an older mountain resort with indoor and outdoor pools, golf, tennis, entertainment, and pampering. These resorts will cost

Yough River Trail

you a few dollars more than the hostel at Ohiopyle, and they're destinations in themselves. You can stay for a weekend or a week without leaving the grounds.

For relaxation or grueling activities, Ohiopyle and the mountains surrounding it are an excellent destination.

Attractions:

Fallingwater, PA Route 381, (724) 329-8501, Tues.-Sun., 10 A.M.-4 P.M., April through November.

Fort Necessity Battlefield, U.S. Route 40, (724) 329-5512, open 8:30 A.M.-5:30 P.M. daily.

Outdoor activities along Youghiogheny River.

National Road Heritage Park, Route 40.

Laurel Caverns, Route 40 East, Uniontown, (724) 438-3003, open 9 A.M.-5 P.M., seven days a week, May through October, and Sat. and Sun. in March, April, and November.

Dining:

Chez Garard, Route 40 East, Hopwood, (724) 437-9001, opens at 5 P.M. daily.

Ruse's, Route 40 East, Hopwood, (724) 437-2796, opens at 7 A.M. daily.

Sun Porch, Route 40 East, Hopwood, (724) 437-5734, opens at 7 A.M. daily.

Smokehouse, Route 381, Ohiopyle, (724) 329-1810, Tues.-Sun., 11 A.M.-9 P.M.

Falls Market Inn, Ohiopyle, (724) 329-4973, open 7 A.M.-9 P.M., seven days a week.

Big Dipper, Sherman and Sheridan Streets, Ohiopyle, open 9 A.M. to dusk, seven days a week.

Fox's Den Pizza, Sherman Street, Ohiopyle, (724) 329-1111, open 11 A.M.-10 P.M., seven days a week.

River's Edge Restaurant, 203 Yough Street, Confluence, (814) 359-5059, open 11 A.M.-9 P.M. daily.

Stone House Restaurant, Route 40, Chalk Hill, (724) 329-8876, open 11:30 A.M.-11 P.M., seven days a week.

Titlow Grille, 92 West Main Street, Uniontown, (724) 437-6749, Tues.-Thur., 4 P.M.-9 P.M., Fri. and Sat., 4 P.M.-10 P.M.

Canton Chinese Restaurant, 145 East Fayette Street, Uniontown, (724) 439-1770, open 11 A.M.-9 P.M., seven days a week.

Lodging:

Hopwood Motel, Route 40, Hopwood, (724) 437-7591.

Stone House Hotel, Route 40 East, Chalk Hill, (724) 329-8876.

River's Edge Bed & Breakfast, 203 Yough Street, Confluence, (814) 395-5059.

The Point, 221 Jacobs Street, Confluence, (814) 395-3082.

Ferncliff Guest House, Grant Street, Ohiopyle, (724) 329-8531.

Ohiopyle Guest House, Sheridan Street, (724) 329-8531.

Ohiopyle Hostel, Ferncliff Road, (724) 329-4476.

Rafferty Manor, Garrett Street, Ohiopyle, (724) 329-1732.

Yough Plaza Motel, Sherman Street, Ohiopyle, (800) 992-7238.

Hampton Inn, 698 West Main Street, Uniontown, (724) 430-1000.

Nemacolin Woods Resort, Route 40, Farmington, (800) 422-2736.

Summit Inn Resort, 2 Skyline Drive, Farmington, (724) 438-8594.

Benner's Meadow Run Camping and Cabins, Nelson Road, Farmington, (724) 329-4097.

Scarlett Knob Campground, Route 381, Farmington, (724) 329-5200.

Shopping:

Youghiogheny Trading Post, 203 Yough Street, Confluence, Wed., Sat., and Sun., 11 A.M.-7 P.M.

Bittersweet Antiques, Route 381, Farmington, (724) 329-4847, call for hours.

The Christmas Shop, Route 40, Chalk Hill, (724) 439-6500, Mon.-Fri., 10 A.M.-5 P.M., Sat. and Sun., 10 A.M.-6 P.M.

Wayne's Collectibles, Route 40, Markleysburg, (724) 329-0411, call for hours.

Youghiogheny Station, 900 Crawford Avenue, Connellsville, (724) 628-0332, Mon.-Sat., 10 A.M.-5 P.M., Sun., noon-5 P.M.

Big Summit Outlet, Route 40 East, Uniontown, (724) 439-8087, Mon.-Sat., 9 A.M.-9 P.M., Sun., noon-5 P.M.

Uniontown Mall, 1368 West Main Street, Uniontown, (724) 437-9411, Mon.-Sat., 9:30 A.M.-9 P.M., Sun., noon-5 P.M.

Annual Events:

National Road Festival, spring, Route 40, (800) 840-0274.

Lafayette Week, July, Fayette County, (724) 437-9001.

Fayette County Fair, July, Uniontown, (724) 438-0502.

The Active Life:

Whitewater rafting, mountain biking, and hiking top the list. Ohiopyle is home to many rafting and biking companies:
Laurel Highlands River Tours, (800) 472-3846.

Mountain Streams, (800) 723-8669.

Wilderness Voyageurs, (800) 272-4141.

Yough River Raft Rental, (800) 967-2387.

Youghiogheny Outfitters, (724) 329-4549.

Yough Trail Bike Rentals, (724) 329-8833.

For an easy bike ride or a flat, scenic hike, pick up the Yough River Trail in Ohiopyle. Golfers can play their rounds at Nemacolin Woods, (800) 422-2736, and Summit Inn, (800) 433-8594.

A Great Place to Relax:

Ohiopyle State Park, in the center of Ohiopyle, has nice benches and beautiful waterfalls. Occasionally, a long freight train rolls by. It's a nice place to while away an hour or a day.

Covered Bridges:

None Nearby

Tourist Information:

• (724) 329-1127 or (724) 238-5661.

Where is it? Southwest quadrant, on PA 381.

Getaway Rating: 5

Fort Necessity

24

POCONO MOUNTAINS . . . HONEYMOON HAVEN
(N, PT, R, R&R)

The business of the Poconos is recreation. The region has poor soils and a short growing season, so it's not good for agriculture. The mineral resources are small, so there's little mining, and the steep terrain traditionally made the building of highways and railroads difficult, although the Northeast Extension of the Pennsylvania Turnpike and two interstate highways—I-80 and I-84—now run through the Poconos and make the area easily accessible from all directions.

In fact, Pike County has become Pennsylvania's fastest-growing county, and some of the newcomers are reportedly New Yorkers who work in the city and make the 90+ mile commute twice a day. That doesn't mean that Pike County is becoming crowded. The population is still small enough that an influx of 3,000 newcomers will give the county a high rate of growth without bringing huge throngs into the lightly populated region.

Because of the tough terrain and the limited resources, no large cities have ever grown up in the Poconos, and the mountains are an excellent place to come for a getaway. Vacations are the main industry here, in all seasons of the year. People come for weekends and weeks, and many own vacation homes

Delaware River, Matamoras

and time-share packages. Whether you like waterfalls, skiing, auto racing, or just sitting on a mountain and pondering the universe, you can do it in the Poconos. Name your pleasure and you'll find it here.

The Poconos cover roughly 2,400 square miles, although nobody can define exactly where the Poconos begin and end, and most of the region is heavily wooded. Drive across Route 80 from **Stroudsburg** to **White Haven** and you'll pass through almost unbroken forest for 30 miles, but lots of activities take place in the clearings and around the lakes.

Lakes are numerous in the Poconos, and resorts and vacation homes surround many of them, such as **Big Bass Lake.** Big Bass Lake is a planned community that has a heated indoor swimming pool, sauna, and private ski area. The Poconos are home to many similar communities, and many of them are built around the lakes. Away from the **Delaware River,** the land rises steeply, and many Pocono names reflect the region's terrain. Mountainhome, Mount Pocono, Pocono Summit, and Skytop are a few examples.

The biggest urban area in the Poconos is the **Stroudsburg/ East Stroudsburg** area, and they're both small cities surrounded by green mountains. Between them they have fewer than 20,000 residents. So you'll never have the feeling of being in a big city in the Poconos, but you will find lots of golf courses, waterfalls, hiking trails, ski slopes, outlet shopping malls, campgrounds, and posh resorts.

East Stroudsburg is a good place to start a Poconos getaway. It's accessible by I-80, and it's close to many of the big attractions. East Stroudsburg is a college town (East Stroudsburg University, a state-supported institution) whose downtown suffered a major fire in 1996. The region is rebuilding and rebounding with shops and restaurants.

One popular restaurant is **Dansbury Depot** in the renovated railroad station. (East Stroudsburg currently has no rail passenger service, but plans to resurrect it surface periodically, with hopes of running trains from New York to the Poconos.) Also in the old depot is **The Green Caboose,** a toy and gift shop that specializes in Thomas the Tank Engine items.

Stroudsburg's Main Street combines traditional shopping for clothes and hamburgers with antiques, art galleries, and historic buildings. The **Chamber of Commerce,** the **Monroe County Historical Association,** and the **Monroe County Arts Council** are on Main Street. At South 9th and Ann Streets is the **Pocono Outlet Complex,** housed in historic **Ribbon Mill** and several other factory buildings. The **Pocono Outlet Complex** allows you to participate in outlet shopping and then to enjoy the restaurants and other shops in the downtown district.

Outside Stroudsburg on Turkey Hill Road is **Quiet Valley Living Historical Farm,** an attraction that remembers the hard work required of an early farm family in the area. The farm offers daily demonstrations of spinning, gardening, cooking, and many other activities required to run a farm.

The Stroudsburgs are near the southern end of the **Delaware Water Gap National Recreational Area.** The Delaware River has cut a gap that's 1,200 feet deep and only a mile wide. The Delaware Water Gap National Recreational Area is a 73-mile stretch of the Delaware River that's popular with canoeists who enjoy the swift and usually shallow waters.

Delaware Water Gap

Delaware Water Gap is also the name of a small town that was one of the early destinations in the Poconos, primarily because trains served it directly from New York and Philadelphia. Today Delaware Water Gap is an artsy town whose business district features many galleries and boutiques. The **Water Gap Trolley** leaves from a station on Route 611, and buses designed to look like trolleys take visitors to scenic sites while guides explain the area's geology and history. On summer Sunday evenings, the **Church of the Mountain,** on Route 611 in Delaware Water Gap, presents free jazz concerts in the gazebo, with snacks and lemonade available.

Perhaps the prettiest little town in all of the Poconos is **Milford,** which lies on the Delaware River at the junction of Route 6 and Route 209, very close to Route 84. Milford is the kind of place where people stroll tree-lined streets, shop for antiques, and dine at outdoor cafés. The town has a touch of sophistication, in part because of the bluestone used in the construction of many buildings.

The largest collection of shops is right in the center of town, and an easy walk will take you to shops, restaurants, and historic attractions. **Hare Hollow** on Broad Street sells country gifts, furniture, and collectibles. The **Dimmick Inn,** located right on the town square, offers fine lunches and dinners and comfortable outdoor dining.

The **Columns on Broad Street** houses the museum of the **Pike County Historical Society,** whose collection includes the blood-stained flag used to cradle President Lincoln's head as he was dying.

Grey Towers is the French-style chateau that was home to Gifford Pinchot, a former Pennsylvania governor who founded the United States Department of Agriculture Forest Service. The mansion offers beautiful views of Milford and the Delaware River. The USDA maintains the property, and it's open daily from Memorial Day to Labor Day.

Five miles upriver from Milford is **Matamoras,** another small town that's a favorite spot for river users. **Tri-State Canoe & Boat Rentals** on Shay Lane rents canoes, rafts, and rowboats. On good summer days, the river at Matamoras seems to carry as many vehicles as the bridge that connects Pennsylvania and New York. On this stretch, the river is shallow and gentle, and you don't need any special athletic abilities to enjoy a day on the water.

One of the biggest concentrations of attractions and resorts is the region around **Mount Pocono,** which lies at the junction of Routes 940 and 611. Route 611 is actually Broad Street in Philadelphia, so a drive from Philadelphia to the Poconos on 611 would be interesting, but very slow.

Within 10 miles of Mount Pocono are such towns as Cresco, Paradise Valley, Mountainhome, Swiftwater, Tannersville, Scotrun, and Pocono Summit. They're home to a high concentration of resorts, restaurants, and shopping opportunities. Tannersville has a heavy outlet shopping presence with many individual stores and **The Crossings,** an outlet mall housed in eight different buildings. Just down the road from The Crossings is **The Persnickety Cat,** a shop devoted to cats and their human servants.

In Cresco, on Route 390, taste buds get a treat at **Callie's Candy Kitchen** and **Callie's Pretzel Factory**. Visitors can watch as workers create candies and pretzels, and ample samples are available for tasting.

If you're looking for a distinctly different weekend activity, stop by **Jack Frost Mountain** in Blakeslee for a game of **Paintball** at Splatter. Paintball is a war game played with paint instead of bullets. Different versions of the game, at different levels of intensity, are available, and the game is quickly developing a loyal following. All necessary equipment, including protective gear, is available for rental.

When you really want to get away from it all, the Poconos' 175 square miles of parks make the region ideal. **Big Pocono State Park** is a rugged area that covers only two of those square miles, but it offers spectacular views from the top of **Camelback Mountain** and ten miles of hiking trails.

Promised Land State Park offers a full range of activities, more than 30 miles of hiking trails, and rustic cabins. In addition, most of the resorts own large wooded tracts where it's easy to get away from it all before heading back for some more pampering.

With no big cities, the Poconos don't have much to offer sports teams, but the region does have one big spectator sports attraction—**Pocono Raceway**. Several times a summer, stock cars come to the Poconos to race around the 2.5-mile course that's built more like a triangle than the traditional oval. The Pocono Raceway track has three turns, and that factor adds an extra element to racing here.

The big races are the **Pocono 500** in June and the **Pennsylvania 500** in July, and if you're planning a trip to the Poconos, be aware of these races. They bring tens of thousands of fans to the region and fill up hotels, motels, campgrounds, and restaurants. They're good for the local economy, but if you're looking for a quiet getaway, come some other weekend.

If you've ever though that you'd like to know what it feels like to zoom around a track at 170 m.p.h., the Pocono Raceway has a program for you. Called the **Stock Car Racing Experience,** it allows regular people to ride in stock cars. The different programs range from simply taking a ride with an instructor to taking driving lessons. You'll never go this fast on an American road, so if traveling at scary speeds appeals to you, come to Pocono Raceway and buy a ride in a stock car.

If 18 is the most important number in your life, you'll like the Poconos. Many resorts have "Golf" in their names and 18 or more holes on their grounds. And if you don't have time for 18, you can play one of the numerous 9-hole courses in the region. One of the newest courses is the **Great Bear Golf & Country Club** on Route 209 in Marshalls Creek, designed by Jack Nicklaus.

Many of the courses and resorts are much older. **Buck Hill** dates back to 1906 and **Shawnee Inn** goes back to 1907. Wherever you play, you can expect to find the course lined with trees, a creek or two, and some nice views. Many of the resorts also offer special packages, such as reduced rates for 3-day midweek stays.

When golf season ends, the pace in the Poconos changes, but it doesn't slow down. In fact, it picks up speed as skiers race down hundreds of slopes. Snowboarders, snow tubers, skaters, and sledders also find plenty of places for fun, but skiing is the glamour sport of winter.

The Poconos have many ski areas and ski resorts, and most of the facilities can make snow when nature is either warm or dry. For less crowded conditions and lower prices, come during the week or ski early in the morning or at night on one of the lighted slopes.

Many of the ski resorts also have cross-country trails and equipment rentals. If you're not staying at such a resort, you can find plenty of trails in state and local parks.

So, with so many attractions, how can you choose a place for a weekend getaway? One good step is to call the visitors' bureau and get as much information as possible. Or, you can just identify your favorite activity and plan accordingly. For instance, if you enjoy a relaxed weekend of strolling and antique shopping, head to Milford. If you like noise, fumes, and big crowds, visit Pocono Raceway, and if it's your honeymoon, book a week at one of the honeymoon resorts.

The Poconos have plenty of attractions and shops to keep you busy, and plenty of secluded places for you to relax. Pay a visit, do a little exploring, and you're sure to find a place that you'll want to visit more than once.

Attractions:

Mountain resorts.

Honeymoon resorts.

Lakes.

Golf courses.

Pocono Raceway, (800) RACE-WAY, NASCAR races in June and July.

Ski lodges.

Delaware Water Gap.

Quiet Valley Living Historical Farm, Turkey Hill Road, Stroudsburg, (570) 992-6161, Tues.-Sat., 10 A.M.-5:30 P.M., Sun., 1 P.M.-5:30 P.M.

Dining:

Bamboo House, Route 209 North, East Stroudsburg, (570) 424-2460, Mon., 3 P.M.-9:30 P.M., Wed. and Thur., noon-9:30 P.M., Fri. and Sat., noon-10:30 P.M., and Sun., 1 P.M.-9:30 P.M.

Beaver House, 1001 North 9th Street, Stroudsburg, (570) 424-1020, opens at 4:30 P.M. Mon.-Fri., at 4 P.M. on Sat., and at noon on Sun.

Besecker's Diner, 1427 North Fifth Street, Stroudsburg, (570) 421-6193, open 6 A.M.-10 P.M. daily.

Brownlee's in the Burg, Seventh and Main, Stroudsburg, (570) 421-2200, open 11:30 A.M.-10 P.M. daily.

Dana's, Route 196, Tobyhanna, (570) 894-9808, Tues.-Sat., 4 P.M.-10:30 P.M., Sun., 11 A.M.-9 P.M.

Dansbury Depot, 50 Crystal Street, East Stroudsburg, (570) 476-0500, Mon.-Sat., 11 A.M.-10 P.M., Sun., 11 A.M.-9 P.M.

Dimmick Inn, Broad and Harford Streets, Milford, (570) 296-4021, opens at 11 A.M. daily.

Francesco's, Saylor's Lake, Saylorsburg, (570) 992-7018, Mon.-Sat., 4 P.M.-10 P.M., Sun., noon-9 P.M.

Frog Town Restaurant, Route 390 Canadensis, (570) 595-6282, open Thur.-Sun., 5 P.M.-9:30 P.M.

Jaegermeister, Route 390, Mountainhome, (215) 595-7525, opens at 11 A.M. daily.

Jubilee Restaurant, Route 940, Pocono Pines, (570) 646-2377, open Sun.-Thur.,7 A.M.-9 P.M., Fri.-Sat., 7 P.M.-10 P.M.

Laurel Villa Country Inn, Second and Ann Streets, Milford, (570) 296-9940, opens at 5 P.M. Fri.-Sun.

Memorytown, Grange Road, Mount Pocono, (570) 839-1680, lunch and dinner daily.

Naturally Rite Restaurant & Café, Route 209, Marshals Creek, (570) 223-1133, lunch and dinner, Wed.-Mon.

Pepper's Ristorante, Engle Valley Mall, East Stroudsburg, (570) 421-4460, Mon.-Fri., 11:30 A.M.-2:30 P.M. and 5 P.M.-10 P.M., Sat., 4 P.M.-11 P.M, and Sun., 3 p.m.-9 P.M.

Scotrun Diner, Route 611, Scotrun, (570) 629-2430, open 6 A.M.-10 P.M. daily.

Swiftwater Inn, Route 611, Swiftwater, (570) 839-7206, open for dinner, Tues.-Sun., May through October, and Fri.-Sun., November through April.

Tokyo Tea House, Route 940, Pocono Summit, (570) 839-8880, open noon-3 P.M. and 5 P.M.-10 P.M. daily.

Tom Quick Inn, 411 Broad Street, Milford, (570) 296-6514, opens at 11:30 A.M. daily.

Uinnyds Upscale New York Style Deli, Strawberry Fields Plaza, East Stroudsburg, (570) 421-6868, breakfast, lunch, and dinner daily.

Dansbury Depot, East Stroudsburg

Lodging:

Black Walnut Country Inn, Firetower Road, Milford, (570) 296-6322.

Blueberry Mountain Inn, Thomas Road, Blakeslee, (570) 646-7144.

Brtittania Country Inn, Swiftwater, (570) 839-7243.

Brookview Manor Bed & Breakfast, Canadensis, (570) 595-2451.

Crescent Lodge, Route 191 and Route 940, Cresco, (570) 595-7486.

Dreamy Acres, Route 447, Canadensis, (570) 595-7115.

Farmhouse Bed & Breakfast (for non-smokers only), Grange Road, Mount Pocono, (570) 839-0796.

Mountaintop Lodge, Route 940, Pocono Pines, (570) -646-6636.

Pine Hill Lodge, 42 Pine Hill Road, Mount Pocono, (570) 839-8060.

The Shepard House, 108 Shepard Avenue, Delaware Water Gap, (570) 424-9779.

Stroudsmoor Country Inn, Stroudsmoor Road, Stroudsburg, (570) 421-6431.

Caesar's Cove Haven, Route 590, Lakeville, (800) 233-4141.

Caesar's Pocono Palace, Route 209, Marshall's Creek, (800) 233-4141.

Mount Airy Lodge, Mount Pocono, (888) 415-9053.

Pocono Gardens Lodge, Mount Pocono, (888) 415-9053.

Summit Resort, I-80, Exit 45, Tannersville, (800) 233-8250.

Budget Motel, I-80, Exit 51, East Stroudsburg, (800) 233-8144.

Colony Motor Lodge, 1863 West Main Street, Stroudsburg, (570) 421-3790.

Days Inn, 100 Park Avenue, Stroudsburg, (570) 424-1771.

Garden Motel, 546 Pocono Boulevard, Mount Pocono, (570) 839-9466.

Harmony Lakeshore Inn, Lake Harmony, (570) 722-0522.

Mount Pocono Motel, 25 Knob Road, Mount Pocono, (570) 839-0700.

Pocono Mountain Lodge, Route 940, White Haven, (570) 443-8461.

Daniels Top-O-The Poconos Resort, Route 447, Canadensis, (570) 595-7531.

Delaware Water Gap KOA, 6196 Hollow Road, East Stroudsburg, (570) 223-8000.

Mount Pocono Campground, Route 196, Mount Pocono, (570) 839-7573.

Shopping:

American Candle, Route 611, Bartonsville, (570) 629-3388, Mon.-Thur., 9 A.M.-8 P.M., Fri. and Sat., 9 A.M.-9 P.M., and Sun., 9:30 A.M.-5:30 P.M.

Bendixen's Giftware, Route 940, Pocono Summit, (570) 839-8795, open 10 A.M.-5 P.M. daily.

Buttermilk Falls Antiques, Route 209, East Stroudsburg, (570) 421-3326, Thur.-Mon, 10 A.M.-5 P.M.

Dimmick Inn, Milford

Clockworks, 319 Broad Street, Milford, (570) 296-5236, Sat., 10 A.M.-5 P.M.

Crossings Factory Store, Tannersville, (570) 629-4650, Mon.-Sat., 10 A.M.-9 P.M., Sun., 10 A.M.-6 P.M.

Enchanted Cottage, Route 115, Blakeslee Corners, (570) 646-7464, Sat. and Sun., 10 A.M.-5 P.M.

Ehrardt General Store, Route 191 and Route 507, Newfoundland, Fri.-Mon., 10 A.M.-5 P.M.

House of Candles, Route 715, Tannersville, (570) 629-1953, Mon.-Sat., 10 A.M.-5 P.M.

Odd Lot Outlet, Route 209, Marshalls Creek, (570) 223-1844, Mon.-Thur., 10 A.M.-8 P.M., Fri., 10 A.M.-8:30 P.M., Sat., 9:30 A.M.-8:30 P.M., and Sun., 10 A.M.-6 P.M.

Olde Engine Works, 62 North Third Street, Stroudsburg, (570) 421-4340, open 10 A.M.-5 P.M. daily.

Pocono Outlet Complex, South 9th and Ann Streets, Stroudsburg, (570) 421-7470, Mon.-Sat., 10 A.M.-5 P.M., Sun., noon-5 P.M.

Pocono Peddler's Village, Route 611, Tannersville, (570) 629-6366, Fri.-Mon., 9 A.M.-5 P.M.

Schouppe's Antiques, 100 Benett Avenue, Milford, Mon.-Sat., 10 A.M.-5 P.M., Sun., noon-5 P.M.

Selma's Art Needlework, Route 940, Pocono Summit, (570) 839-8729, Mon.-Sat., 11 A.M.-4 P.M., Sun., noon-5 P.M.

Annual Events:

Winter—skiing and sitting by the fire.

Spring—mountains in bloom.

Summer—lazy days by the lake.

Fall—Autumn's golden gown.

Learn To Ski Free Day, January, many resorts, (800) 762-6667.

Festival of Ice, January, Mountain Laurel Resort Hotel, White Haven, (800) 458-5921.

Snowy Mountain Craft Fair, February, Stroudsmoor Country Inn, Stroudsburg, (570) 424-1199.

Maple Sugaring Program, March, Monroe County Environmental Education Center, Bartonsville, (570) 629-3061.

Horse-drawn hay rides, April, Split Rock Resort, Lake Harmony, (570) 722-9111.

Country Sampler Fair, May, Stroudsmoor Country Inn, Stroudsburg, (570) 424-1199.

Cranberry Bog Nature Walks, June, Monroe County Environmental Education Center, Bartonsville, (570) 629-3061.

Great Tastes of Pennsylvania Wine and Food Festival, Split Rock Resort, Lake Harmony, (570) 722-9111.

Miller 500, July, Pocono Raceway, Long Pond, (570) 646-2300.

Cajun Fest, August, Tannersville Inn, (570) 629-3131.

Celebration of the Arts, September, Delaware Water Gap, (570) 424-2210.

Pike County Agricultural Fair, September, Matamoras, (570) 296-8790.

Lumberjack Festival, October, Shawnee-on-Delaware, (570) 421-7231.

Great Brews of America Classic Beer Festival, Split Rock Resort, Lake Harmony, (570) 722-9111.

Old Time Christmas, December, Quiet Valley Living Historical Farm, Stroudsburg, (570) 992-6161.

The Active Life:

In all seasons, the Poconos are a place of outdoor fun. The region boasts:

- 35 golf courses (for a brochure, call (800) 762-6667),
- 175 square miles of park land,
- 12 ski resorts,
- 170 river miles, and
- 150 lakes.

Uncounted swimming pools, tennis courts, and miles of trails for riding horses and snowmobiles

The Poconos are a good place to be active all day and relax by the fire or the air conditioner at night. Many of the resorts also have dancing, entertainment, and active nightlife. Wherever you stay in the Poconos, you'll find plenty of opportunities to have fun or work up a good sweat.

A Great Place to Relax:

In an area that's mostly woods and lakes, fine places to sit and do nothing are easy to find. Climb to the top of a mountain or sit by the water, and you'll be far from noise. A good spot in a town is the public library in Milford, at Broad and Harford. Under spreading trees is a bench where it's nice to sit and watch the other visitors walk by.

Covered Bridges:

None nearby.

Tourist Information:

- Contact the Pocono Mountains Vacation Bureau at 1004 Main Street, Stroudsburg, PA 18360, (800) POCONOS. Your mailbox will soon fill with information on Poconos attractions.

Where is it? Northeast, along the Delaware River and west toward Scranton.

Getaway Rating: 3

Lake Conneaut

25

PYMATUNING/
MEADVILLE . . .
A WATER WONDERLAND
(N, R, R&R)

Pymatuning Lake is a man-made body of water whose stated purpose is to conserve the waters entering Pymatuning Swamp. The lake is in both Pennsylvania and Ohio, with about three-quarters of the water on the Pennsylvania side.

Pymatuning Lake State Park covers almost 33 square miles, and it's a playground with just about every sort of outdoor activity. **Meadville,** about 10 miles to the east, is a historic city with plenty of lodging, dining, and shopping. **Grove City** and **Sharon** offer lots of interesting shopping possibilities.

A quick assessment of Pymatuning is that it's a getaway kind of place. Whether you want to frolic in the water or just sit by the camper or the tent, Pymatuning has such a peaceful atmosphere that it seems as though signs at the park's entrances must say, "No Tension Allowed." Water covers more than 20 square miles, and the park is ideal for both activities and inactivities.

The word Pymatuning comes from the Iroquois Indians, and it means "The Crooked-Mouthed Man's Dwelling Place." In this instance, crooked refers to deceit rather than to a disfigurement. Before the Iroquois occupation, the Erie tribe, ruled at the time by a queen noted for her cunning and crooked dealings, lived on the land.

The beach in Pymatuning Lake State Park

The Pymatuning Swamp covered more than 10,000 acres, and scientists spent much time studying plant and animal life there, but the swamp had a problem with the Shenango, the river that drained it.

The river had a habit of flooding in spring and drying up in summer, so the authorities built a dam at the southern end of the swamp in 1934, and the reservoir slowly filled in. As the reservoir filled, a vacation industry developed around it.

Visitors to the park can stay in either modern cabins with showers, kitchens, and furnishings, or in campgrounds. Two different campsites in the park have hookups for recreational vehicles. Several parts of the lake have recreational facilities, but many miles of shoreline are undeveloped and rarely visited. Quiet places are numerous.

You can swim at four different guarded beaches from Memorial Day through Labor Day, and boats with a 10-horse-power limit are permitted. The roads in and around the park are relatively flat and good for bicycling. The major roads carry heavy traffic, but the surrounding roads are rural and pleasant.

Birdwatching is a popular pastime around the lake. Many species of birds, especially waterfowl, either live here or stop by on their migratory flights. At the wildlife museum in **Linesville,** visitors can sometimes view Pennsylvania's largest colony of nesting eagles. In addition, many types of wildlife, such as the white-tail deer, inhabit the region. The museum has over 300 mounted specimens of birds and animals in its collection.

The single biggest attraction in the park is the **spillway** on Route 18, south of Linesville. There, visitors feed the fish and ducks, and the schools of fish are so large that the ducks walk on the backs of the fish.

Pymatuning Reservoir isn't the only popular body of water in this area. Five miles to the east is **Conneaut Lake,** a natural body of water that's also the name of a small town on Routes 6 and 322.

The lake itself is a busy place, with attractions all around it. They include **Conneaut Lake Amusement Park,** golf courses, motels, restaurants, and stores. Grapes grow well in this area, and **Conneaut Cellars Winery** offers tours and tastings.

At the amusement park, the most famous ride is the **Blue Streak,** an old-fashioned wooden roller coaster. Prowling the waters of the lake is the *Barbara J,* a sternwheeler that gives 45-minute cruises around the lake. You can sit in the sun or the shade, and the boat has a snack bar.

The biggest city in the region is **Meadville,** which is easy to reach via Interstate 79. Meadville is an attractive city where mass production of the zipper began in the 1920s. Meadville is the home of **Allegheny College** and many historic sites. The **Market House** on Market Street has provided a location for farmers to sell their goods since 1870. The Market House is open six days a week throughout the year, and it sells baked goods, candies, crafts, gifts, and many other items. The second floor of the Market House is home to **The Meadville Council on the Arts.** The space holds an art gallery, a small theater, and a dance studio. Throughout the year, the gallery and the theater host exhibits and performances.

A placid spot on Lake Pymatuning

The **David Mead Log Cabin** is a replica of the home of Meadville's founder. In 1787, Mead and his brother John came to the wilderness of northwestern Pennsylvania looking for a place to settle. They chose a spot beside French Creek where they built a cabin and spent the next winter with their families. If winters then were as cold as they are now, the Meads spent the time looking at a lot of snow.

The **Baldwin-Reynolds House** is considerably more comfortable than a log cabin. Henry Baldwin, a Supreme Court Justice, built the house in the early 1840s. It's a four-story mansion still furnished with the possessions of former owners. The home sits on a three-acre plot, and an herb garden, flowering trees, and shrubs produce the atmosphere of a park.

East of Meadville on Route 198 is a great wild area, the **Erie National Wildlife Refuge,** an 8,750-acre natural plot that's home to more than 200 species of birds, as well as mammals such as beavers, foxes, and muskrats. Nature and skiing trails run through the area, and it offers scenic overlooks and excellent opportunities for wildlife photography.

Northeast of Meadville is **Cambridge Springs,** where hundreds or thousands once came to seek healing in the town's spring waters. Many hotels served that clientele. Most are gone, but the **Riverside Inn** remains, and it offers a chance to experience a hotel stay similar to hotel stays of 100 years ago. The large wooden hotel has an expansive porch and a welcoming lounge, and it offers dinner theater and golf packages.

When your getaway demands some serious shopping, Meadville offers the best fixes. The **Downtown Mall** at Water and Chestnut Streets has a variety of stores, and many more are nearby on the downtown streets. The **Meadville Mall** on Route 6 provides a mall experience.

If you to do some even more serious shopping, head down Route 79 to Exit 31 and go to Grove City. There you'll find the **Grove City Factory Shops,** an outlet center with more than 130 stores.

This is the kind of place that a serious shopper will enjoy. It's so big that shuttle buses take shoppers around the grounds, a food park, and even a children's playground. Also in Grove City is a showroom for **Wendell August,** a retailer of gifts such as limited edition plates and ornaments.

You can find many enjoyable things to do in the area surrounding Pymatuning State Park, and you can also find excellent opportunities to sit back and forget about the hectic pace of modern life. Come out and take a look at the water, the birds, and the fish.

Attractions:

Academy Theatre, 275 Chestnut Street, Meadville, (814) 337-8000.

Baldwin-Reynolds House, 639 Terrace Street, Meadville, (814) 724-6080, Wed.-Sun., 1 P.M.-5 P.M., Memorial Day through Labor Day.

Conneaut Lake.

Meadville Market House, 910 Market Street, (814) 336-2056, opens 6 A.M., Mon.-Sat.

Pymatuning State Park, (724) 932-3141.

Spillway, Route 18, south of Linesville.

Wild Waterfowl Museum, Pymatuning Lake, Linesville, open 10 A.M.-5 P.M., May 1 through November 30.

Dining:

Carini Restaurant, 110 Liberty Street, Jamestown, (724) 932-5047, open 7 A.M.-11 P.M. daily.

Half-Way Country Store, 14770 Harmonsburg Road, Meadville, (814) 333-2815, Mon.-Sat., 11 A.M.-8 P.M.

Hoss's, 18817 Smock Highway, Meadville, (814) 333-4333, Sun.-Thur., 11:30 A.M.-9:30 P.M., Fri. and Sat., 11:30 A.M.-10:30 P.M.

Jamestown Boat Livery Restaurant, Pymatuning State Park, (724) 932-3267, breakfast and lunch.

Main Street Dinette, 1004 Main Street, Conneautville, (814) 587-3447, opens at 11:30 A.M. daily.

Mama Bear's Restaurant, Route 322, Conneaut Lake, (814) 382-4357, Sun.-Thur., 6 P.M.-midnight, Fri. and Sat., 24 hours a day.

No. 1 China Buffet, 961 Park Avenue, Meadville, (814) 337-7509, lunch and dinner daily.

Pub on the Square, 215 Market Square, Meadville, (814) 333-3630, lunch and dinner daily.

Rose Marie's Restaurant, 144 Erie Street, Linesville, (814) 683-4264, Mon.-Sat., 11 A.M.-9 P.M.

Spillway Inn, 493 Mercer Street, Linesville, (814) 683-2304, Sun.-Thur., 11 A.M.-10 P.M., Fri. and Sat., 11 A.M.-11 P.M.

Lodging:

Motel 6, Route 322 and I-79, Meadville, (814) 724-6366.

Days Inn, Exit 36A, I-79, Meadville, (814) 337-4254.

Just Sleep Motel, 12749 Conneaut Lake Road, Conneaut Lake, (814) 382-8246.

Adams McKinley Motel, Route 618, Conneaut Lake, (814) 382-1082.

Ski Tow Motel, Route 618, Conneaut Lake, (814) 382-3045.

Fairway 12 Motel, Route 618, Conneaut Lake, (814) 382-5775.

Hotel Conneaut, Conneaut Lake, (814) 382-5114.

Kobel's Twin Maples, 435 West Erie Street, Linesville, (814) 683-4943.

Pymatuning Camp Motel, Route 6, Linesville, (814) 683-5600.

Parkside at Pymatuning, 223 Williamsfield Road, Jamestown, (724) 932-3522.

Russel's Cottages, Route 6, Linesville, (814) 683-5176.

Willowood Inn, 215 West Lake Road, Jamestown, (724) 932-3866.

Azalea House Bed & Breakfast, 874 North Main Street, Meadville, (814) 337-8883.

Fountainside Bed & Breakfast, 628 Highland Avenue, (814) 336-5449.

Cabins and camping at Pymatuning State Park, (724) 932-3141.

Shopping:

Agney's Antiques, U.S. 322 West, Jamestown, (724) 932-5373, open 10 A.M.-6 P.M. daily, May through October.

Burkett's Country Store, Route 618, Conneaut Lake, open 10 A.M.-7 P.M. Memorial Day through Labor Day.

Downtown Mall, Water and Chestnut Streets, Meadville, (814) 724-6265, Mon.-Sat., 10 A.M.-5 P.M.

Jane's Antiques, North 2nd Street, Conneaut Lake, (814) 382-8475, Tues.-Sun., 1 P.M.-4 P.M.

J&L Bernier Gallery, Route 27, east of Meadville, (814) 789-4243, Mon.-Sat., 10 A.M.-5 P.M.

Meadville Mall, Route 322 and Route 19, (814) 333-6048, Mon.-Sat., 10 A.M.-9 P.M., Sun., noon-5 P.M.

Silver Swan Gallery, 215 Chestnut Street, Meadville, (814) 337-7997, Mon.-Sat., 10 A.M.-5 P.M., Sun., noon-5 P.M.

The Whistle Stop, Route 285, Espyville, (724) 927-6418, Sat., 11 A.M.-5 P.M., Sun., 1 P.M.-5 P.M.

Annual Events:

Bluegrass Festival, mid-January, Meadville, (814) 763-3718.

A meadow by the lake

Winter Fun Days, February, Pymatuning State Park, (724) 932-3141.

Saint Patty Gorgeous Green Day, March, Market House, Meadville, (814) 336-2056.

Conneaut Cellars Open House, April, (814) 382-3999.

Do-Wopp Fest, Conneaut Lake, late May, (814) 382-8631.

Linesville Garage Sale, late May, (814) 683-5656.

Pedal the Lakes Bike Tour, early June, Pymatuning State Park, (724) 588-1472.

Ice Cream Celebration, July, Market House, Meadville, (814) 336-2056.

Crawford County Fair, August, Meadville, (814) 337-7400.

Do-Wopp Fest, Conneaut Lake, September, (814) 382-8631.

Haunted Hotel, October, Conneaut Lake Park, (814) 832-5115.

Trees of Christmas, November, Baldwin-Reynolds House, Meadville, (814) 336-5598.

Christmas Creation, Market House, Meadville, (814) 336-2056.

The Active Life:

Pymatuning Lake is a center of activities on the water and in the woods. So is **Conneaut Lake.** Three golf courses are near Conneaut Lake: Ironwood, (814) 382-8438; Park, (814) 382-4971; and Oakland Beach, (814) 382-5665. The region around the lakes is fairly flat and good for bicycling.

A Great Place to Relax:

Many places in **Pymatuning Lake State Park** are quiet and tranquil. At the visitors center is a short nature trail and a favorite spot for bird watchers.

Covered Bridges:

None nearby.

Tourist Information:

• (724) 932-3141.

Where is it? Northwest, on Ohio Border, on U.S. 6 and U.S. 322.

Getaway Rating: 4

Visitors Center at Pymatuning Lake State Park

26

READING . . .
OUTLETS WITH A TWIST
(H, S)

Reading is city with many identities. Founded in 1748 by Thomas and Richard Penn, sons of William, Reading became an industrial city and gave its name to a railroad that has a place on the Monopoly board. The Reading Railroad is gone (although you can still see the name on some bridges), but Reading is still an industrial city. Visitors don't come to watch manufacturers, but they do come to shop. Reading is the city that popularized outlet shopping, and the outlets draw eager shoppers by the carload and the busload.

The Berks County countryside surrounding Reading is a rich agricultural area and part of Pennsylvania Dutch Country. Mennonite girls on bikes, markets full of local produce, and hex signs on barns are common sights along Berks County roads. In fact, Old Route 22 has the nickname Hex Highway.

Visually, the most striking part of Reading is Mount Penn, which is just uphill from the downtown region. Mount Penn is home to the **Pagoda,** a 7-story, 1908, Japanese-style building that is now home to the Berks Arts Council. Mount Penn affords excellent views of the surrounding Schuylkill Valley, and it's a favorite place with runners and bikers, offering a wild area right in the city.

Reading Outlet Center

The **Reading Outlet Center,** on North 9th Street in the city, popularized the idea of outlet shopping when it opened in the early 1970s. Housed in old brick warehouses, these outlets have a different atmosphere than do the more modern outlet shopping malls. Cobblestones, sidewalks, and smokestacks give the feeling of being in the city, but the stores themselves are clean and modern.

The concept of outlet shopping has changed over the decades. Originally, outlets were stores connected to factories where manufacturers could sell items directly without having to ship the goods to other stores. That's not the way it is now. Famous names such as **Ralph Lauren** and **Calvin Klein** maintain outlet stores in Reading, and shoppers love the experience. A dedicated shopper can easily make a day or a weekend of it at the outlets. The **VF Outlet Village** in West Reading even has overnight facilities for RV's.

Of course, as part of Pennsylvania Dutch Country, Reading has a strong food heritage. The city calls itself "Pretzel City," and pretzels are a favorite part of many meals. You can load up on pretzels at the Unique Pretzel Bakery Outlet in the VF Outlet Village and at the **Tom Sturgis Retail Pretzel Store** on Lancaster Pike.

Reading is about 50 miles upstream from Philadelphia along the Schuylkill River, and the river was crucial in the industrialization of America. Along its banks are mills, factories, iron furnaces, canals, and railroad tracks. The Schuylkill flows through the center of Berks County, and it was Pennsylvania's first designated **"Scenic River."**

Near the river on the north side of town is **Reading Municipal Stadium,** home of the **Reading Phillies,** an affiliate of the Philadelphia Phillies. The Reading Phillies play in the AA Eastern League, and many famous major league Phillies have spent summers in Reading.

North of Reading is the small town of **Kutztown,** which is home to a university, a tourist railroad, a cave, and a very popular antiques market.

Renninger's Antique Market on Noble Street is one of the biggest in the country. It operates only on Saturdays, and it has over 250 dealers who operate both indoors and out. On Fridays and Saturdays, Renninger's Farmer's Market offers fresh farm goods and a **Folk Art Shoppe.**

Crystal Cave, on Crystal Cave Road, takes its name from the crystalline formations found in the cave. A guided tour takes about an hour, and the grounds also have picnic facilities, an ice cream parlor, and a miniature golf course. The **Kutztown Scenic Train Ride,** at Main and Railroad Streets, takes riders on a short trip through Pennsylvania Dutch farmlands. The train operates out of a beautifully restored station in the borough on Saturdays and Sundays.

The **Kutztown Pennsylvania-German Festival** takes place at the **Kutztown Fairgrounds** in late June. The festival celebrates the area's German heritage with music, food, quilts, and folk art. The name Pennsylvania Dutch actually means German. Dutch in this instance is a variation of Deutsch, or German. So, whenever you see the term Pennsylvania Dutch, remember that it has nothing to do with Holland.

Trains played a major part in the life of Reading, and the train in Kutztown is just one of three railroad attractions in northern Berks County. In Kempton, along Routes 737 and 143, is the **Wanamaker, Kempton,** and **Southern Railroad.** The W, K & S runs steam trains beside the Ontelaunee Creek beneath **Hawk Mountain.** The ride isn't the smoothest in the world, and that's part of the charm. The engine belches steam and cinders into the air, and riders in the open car finish the trip with cinders in their hair and on their clothes. It's much cleaner inside for those who prefer not to have cinders falling on them.

The **Reading Company Technical & Historical Society** remembers the Reading Railroad with a large display of rolling stock in Leesport.

With its lengthy history, Berks County has much to remember, and the **Berks County Museum Council** consists of 11 sites. The most famous name among them is Daniel Boone, who lived at what is now known as the **Daniel Boone Homestead.** The famous frontiersman who gained fame for his adventures in Kentucky was born in a log cabin beside the Schuylkill River in 1734. He grew up in a Quaker family and lived nearby until he was in his teens. Then his father began to feel crowded by new settlers, and he moved the family to North Carolina. Today, the Daniel Boone Homestead in Birdsboro remembers his life in Pennsylvania and also gives insights into the lives of early settlers in the area.

The **Berks County Heritage Center,** reached by traveling north on Route 183 to Red Bridge Road, is a restored 19th-century wagon works displaying original tools and equipment. On the grounds is the 5-mile **Union Canal Bicycling and Walking Trail,** and nearby is **Wertz's Bridge.** At 204 feet, it's the longest single span covered bridge in Pennsylvania. The bridge is in the **Red Bridge Recreation Area,** and it's open only to foot traffic, so it's an ideal place to take a good look at a covered bridge.

The **Mary Merritt Doll Museum,** 10 miles east of Reading on U.S. 422, displays dolls dating back as far as 1725. The adjacent

Merritt Museum of Childhood contains antique toys, children's carriages, and Pennsylvania Dutch pottery and quilts. Rooms furnished with furniture from the 1780s show that furniture wasn't quite as comfortable then as it is now.

The **Mid-Atlantic Air Museum** at the Reading Airport on Route 183 contains civilian and military aircraft.

If running through the mud is one of your favorite activities, Reading has two races that will thrill you. The **Mount Penn Mudfest,** a 15K run, and the **Half-Wit Half Marathon** take runners over a mountain and through the creeks in a couple of the toughest races of their respective distances. The Mudfest is in April, and the Half-Wit is in August or September. Call Pretzel City Sports at (610) 779-2668 for details on running events in the Reading area.

Reading is an industrial city that has built a new identity with its shopping outlets. For serious shoppers, a weekend in Reading is a weekend of bliss.

Attractions:

W, K & S Railroad, Route 737, Kempton, (610) 756-6469, weekends and holidays, May through October.

Kutztown Scenic Railroad, 110 Railroad Street, Kutztown, (610) 683-9202, weekends, June through October.

Crystal Cave, Crystal Cave Road, Kutztown, (610) 683-6765, open 9 A.M.-5 P.M. daily, March through November.

Renninger's Antiques, Noble Street, Kutztown, (610) 683-6848, Sat., 8 A.M.-4 P.M.

Daniel Boone Homestead, Route 422, Birdsboro, (610) 582-4900, Tues.-Sat., 9 A.M.-5 P.M., Sun., noon-5 P.M.

Dining:

Bistro on the Green, Route 10, (610) 775-6575, Mon.-Fri., 11:30 A.M.-2 P.M. and 5 P.M.-9 P.M., Sat., 5 P.M.-9 P.M.

Café Unicorn, 116 Lafayette Street, (610) 929-9992, Tues.-Sun., 5 P.M.-9 P.M.

Train Station, Kutztown

Camelot, 220 North Park Road, Wyomissing, (610) 371-7700, lunch and dinner daily.

Canal Street Pub, 535 Canal Street, Reading, (610) 376-4009, open 11 A.M.-12:30 A.M. daily.

Carboni's Sports Pub, 1350 North 12th Street, Reading, (610) 372-9311, lunch and dinner daily.

Carini's, 1600 Elizabeth Avenue, Laureldale, (610) 929-9255, Mon.-Wed., 10:30 A.M.-10 P.M.

Corner House, 1501 Lancaster Avenue, (610) 777-7444, Mon.-Thur. and Sun., 4:30 P.M.-10 P.M., Sat., 4:30 P.M.-11 P.M.

Crab Barn, 2613 Hampden Boulevard, Reading, (610) 921-8922, serves lunch, Mon.-Fri., dinner daily.

Dempsey's American Kitchen, Route 222 and Route 724 Shillington, (610) 775-0763, open 24 hours daily.

Gangon, 8 South Fifth Street, (610) 320-9920, lunch and dinner daily.

Giulio's Italian Eatery, 3227 Perkiomen Highway, (610) 370-9660, Tues.-Thur., 11 A.M.-10 P.M., Fri. and Sat., 11 A.M.-11 P.M., and Sun., 11 A.M.-9 P.M.

Hang Thanh, 10th and Chestnut Streets, Reading, (610) 374-0434, Tues.-Thur., 11 A.M.-2:30 P.M. and 5 P.M.-9 P.M., Fri. and Sat., 11 A.M.-10 P.M., and Sun., 5 P.M.-9 P.M.

The Ironmaster, 1319 Lancaster Avenue, Mon.-Fri., 11:30 A.M.-10 P.M., Sat., 4 P.M.-10 P.M., and Sun., 4 P.M.-9 P.M.

Mohnton Navy Yard Galley, 322 East Wyomissing Avenue, Mohnton, (610) 777-6626, open 11 A.M.-9 P.M. daily.

Money's Coach House, 501 Washington Street, (610) 373-5285, breakfast and lunch daily.

Moselem Springs Inn, Route 222 and Route 662, Fleetwood, (610) 944-8213, opens at 11:30 A.M. daily.

Olive Garden, 1700 Crossing Drive, Wyomissing, (610) 373-1311, opens at 11 A.M. daily.

Peanut Bar & Restaurant, 332 Penn Street, Reading, (610) 376-8500, lunch and dinner daily.

V&S Sandwiches, 1621 Lancaster Pike, Reading, (610) 777-9182, opens at 10 A.M. daily.

Lodging:

Campus Inn, Route 222, Kutztown, (610) 683-8721.

Comfort Inn, Route 222, Reading, (610) 371-0500.

Days Inn Reading, 2299 Lancaster Pike, Shillington, (610) 777-7888.

Econo Lodge of Reading, 2310 Fraver Drive, (610) 378-1145.

Hampton Inn, 1800 Papermill Road, Wyomissing, (610) 374-8100.

The Inn at Reading, 1040 Park Road, (610) 372-7811.

Lincoln Motel, Route 222, Kutztown, (610) 683-3456.

Lincoln Plaza Hotel, 5th and Washington Streets, Reading, (610) 372-3700.

Ramada Inn Reading, 2545 North 5th Street, (610) 929-4741.

Sheraton Berkshire Hotel, 1741 Paper Mill Road, Wyomissing, (610) 376-3811.

Around the World Bed & Breakfast, 30 South White Oak Street, Kutztown, (610) 683-8885.

Brooke Mansion Victorian Inn, Washington Street, Birdsboro, (610) 582-9775.

House on the Canal Bed & Breakfast, 4020 River Road, Reading, (610) 921-3015.

Hunter House Bed & Breakfast, 118 South 5th Street, Reading, (610) 374-6608.

Reiff Farm Bed & Breakfast, 495 Old State Road, Oley, (610) 987-6216.

Sacony Park Campsites & Cabins, U.S. 222, Kutztown, (610) 683-3939.

Shopping:

Christmas Village, Route 183, Bernville, (610) 488-1110, open October to Christmas, call for hours.

Leesport Farmers Market, Route 61 North, Leesport, (610) 926-1307, open Wednesdays.

The Outlets on Heisters Lane, 755 Hiesters Lane, Reading, (610) 921-8130, Mon.-Sat., 9:30 A.M.-9 P.M., Sun., 10 A.M.-5 P.M.

Reading Outlet Center, 801 North 9th Street, (800) 5-OUT-LET, Mon.-Sat., 9:30 A.M.-8 P.M., Sun., 10 A.M.-6 P.M.

Reading Station Outlets, 951 North 6th Street, (610) 478-7000, Mon.-Thur., 9:30 A.M.-7 P.M., Fri. and Sat., 9:30 A.M.-8 P.M., and Sun., 11 A.M.-5 P.M.

Renninger's Antique & Farmers Market, 740 Noble Street, Kutztown, (610) 683-6848, Sat., 8 A.M.-4 P.M.

Unique Pretzel Bakery Outlet, 215 Bellevue Avenue, Reading, (610) 929-3172, Mon.-Sat., 8:30 A.M.-5 P.M.

VF Outlet Village, 801 Hill Avenue, (800) 772-8336, Mon.-Fri., 9 A.M.-9 P.M., Sat., 9 A.M.-7 P.M., Sun., 10 A.M.-5 P.M.

Annual Events:

Shiver by the River 5K Runs, January, February, and March, (610) 779-2668.

Shopping Outlets

Train Meet, early January, Leesport Farmers Market, (610) 926-1307.

Antique Lovers Getaway Weekend, mid-February, Antique Complex of Fleetwood, (610) 944-0707.

Berks Jazz Festival, March, (610) 371-8820.

Mount Penn Mudfest 15K Run, Reading, (610) 779-2668.

Reading Phillies, April through September, (610) 375-8469.

Kutztown Antique Show, April, (610) 987-6129.

NHRA Drag Racing, May, Maple Grove Raceway, (610) 856-7200.

Evening on the Green, June, Daniel Boone Homestead, (610) 582-4900.

Kutztown Pennsylvania German Festival, June, (888) 674-6136.

Independence Day Antiques Celebration, July, Antique Complex of Fleetwood, (610) 944-0707.

Old Time Railroad Days, August, Kutztown Scenic Railroad, (610) 683-9202.

Half-Wit Half Marathon, August, Reading, (610) 779-2668.

Labor Day Antique Celebration, September, Antique Complex of Fleetwood, (610) 944-0707.

Pumpkinland Fall Festival, October, Shoppes of Green Village, (610) 678-6711.

Christmas Craft Fair, November, Leesport Farmers Market, (610) 926-1307.

Holiday Lights, Gring's Mill Recreation Area, December, (610) 374-8839.

The Active Life:

Reading has a good assortment of public golf courses. For a brochure listing 14 of them, call (610) 370-1086. Two courses are: **Golden Oaks,** 10 Stonehedge Drive, Fleetwood, (610) 944-6000, and **Willow Hollow,** 619 Prison Road, Leesport, (610) 373-1505.

Trail running is a popular activity in Berks County. Races such as the Mudfest and the Half-Wit Half are considerably tougher than a typical 5K. Call (610) 779-2668 for racing information. **Blue Marsh Lake** in Leesport is a popular spot for water activities. Call (610) 376-6337 for information.

A good spot for easy biking and walking is the **Union Canal Towpath** in Wyomissing. Call (610) 372-8939 for information.

A Great Place to Relax:

At the lookout on Mount Penn—you'll have a great view of the city and the valley.

Covered Bridges:

Berks County has five. The best for exploring is Wertz Bridge in Red Bridge Recreation Area, adjacent to the "Road to Nowhere," northwest of Reading.

Tourist Information:

• (800) 443-6610.

Where is it? Southeast, on U.S. 222 and U.S. 422.

Getaway Rating: 2

27

RICKETTS GLEN STATE PARK . . . THE SOUNDS OF SILENCE

(N, R, R&R)

Listen. What is that unusual sound? Why, it's silence. If you haven't heard that sound lately, a visit to Ricketts Glen will renew your memory.

And what's that other sound? Why, it's the sound of a tumbling waterfall. In a part of this park, the sound of waterfalls is constant and beautiful.

If you really want to get away from it all, this is the place. You can enjoy solitude, natural beauty, and tranquility in this large state park. It has both rugged natural areas and tame places where you can enjoy your getaway without having to rough it. If your life revolves around phones, faxes, shopping centers, and fast food restaurants, you'll be able to go through withdrawal up here.

A visit to Ricketts Glen will focus on the natural world, not on modern technology or commerce. Ricketts Glen has a long list of natural attractions, including a lake for swimming, and visitors can stay in cabins equipped with toilets, showers, and kitchens. Ricketts Glen is far from any population center, and noise and congestion quickly become memories to visitors in the park.

waterfall

The most spectacular attraction in the park is the **waterfalls.**
Twenty-two falls, ranging up to 94 feet in height, lie along a
series of hiking trails. The falls are in the **Glens Natural Area,**
a National Natural Landmark. Two branches of **Kitchen Creek**
cut through the deep gorges at **Ganoga Glen** and **Glen Leigh**
and come together at **Waters Meet.** From there they flow
through **Ricketts Glen,** among giant pines, hemlocks, and
oaks.

Many of these trees are big and old, ranging up to 100 feet
tall and 500 years of age. Ring counts on some trees in the park
have revealed ages as high as 900 years. Ricketts Glen lies at the
meeting grounds of southern and northern hardwood forests,
so the variety of trees is extensive.

Hiking is the activity for which the park is most famous, and
seeing the falls requires a good hike. The falls don't challenge

Niagara in height or volume, but they are beautiful. To enjoy the trails fully, you'll have to be in decent physical condition, and sturdy shoes are necessary because the trails are narrow, steep, and wet in places. Hiking is a challenge, so if your physical condition isn't good, stick to the tamer parts of this park.

In addition to the falls, the park has large **Lake Jean,** which has a guarded beach for swimming from Memorial Day until Labor Day. At the beach are a concession stand and picnic facilities. In summer, an environmental instructor offers guided walks and campfire talks.

Boaters may use non-powered and registered electric-powered boats on the lake. Thirty mooring slips and one boat launch are available. During the summer, canoes and rowboats are available for rental.

If you just like to sit and watch the world, the park's cabins provide an excellent view. Ten **modern rental cabins** are available for year-round use. They're furnished and have a living area, kitchen, toilet/shower room, and two or three bedrooms. They're not luxurious, but they are comfortable. Tent and trailer campsites are available all year, and from mid-April to mid-October a campground with hot showers and flush toilets is in operation. In winter, Ricketts Glen turns white and stays that way for a while. It's beautiful, quiet, and far from everything.

Most of the attraction at Ricketts Glen is what the park doesn't have. Don't expect to do any serious shopping or luxurious dining around here. This is a beautiful place to get away from all the technological advances that are a part of modern life. If you haven't heard enough of the sounds of silence lately, pay a visit to Ricketts Glen.

Attractions:
Waterfalls.
Scenery.
Lake Jean.
The sounds of silence.

Dining:

Bring your own supplies. You won't find much around here.

Lodging:

The park has tent areas and ten rental cabins. Reservations are necessary for the cabins. Call (570) 477-5675 for details.

Good's Campground, Rural Route 1, Benton, adjacent to Ricketts Glen, (570) 477-5361.

Cherry Mills Lodge Bed & Breakfast, Route 87, Dushore, (570) 928-8978.

Windward Bed & Breakfast, near Route 87, Dushore, (570) 928-9385.

Shopping:

None.

Annual Events:

None.

The Active Life:

Hiking, swimming, fishing, and boating are favorite activities. Twenty-six miles of hiking trails wind through the park. They vary in difficulty from flat to extremely strenuous. The most scenic of the trails follow the waterfalls. These are also the most strenuous of the trails, dropping about 1,000 feet in less than two miles. The **Falls Trails** are narrow, steep, and occasionally wet. They're not good for the timid or the physically unfit, but they are the highlight of the park, and they're exceptionally beautiful.

Meanwhile, back at the lake, the activities are less strenuous. The large guarded beach is open from Memorial Day weekend until Labor Day. Boaters may use non-powered and electric-powered vessels with proper Pennsylvania registrations. During the summer, rowboats and canoes are available for rental. Horse owners can use nine miles of bridle trails. Trout and panfish are the species most frequently caught in the lakes and creeks of the park.

A Great Place to Relax:

The whole park is good, and the spot along the Falls Trail called **Waters Meet** is excellent.

Covered Bridges:

The park lies in Luzerne, Sullivan, and Columbia Counties, and Columbia County has good collection of covered bridges. The most interesting are the twins—**East and West Paden.**

They're the focal points of the Twin Bridges Park, and the bridges now serve as picnic pavilions. To get to Twin Bridges Park from Ricketts Glen, go south on PA 487 to the village of Forks. Then go east on State Route 1020 to the park.

Sometimes in Winter:

The park is open all year, and in winter it becomes a white wonderland. Cross-country skiing, ice fishing, and hiking through the snow are popular activities, as is sitting in the cabin. The rental cabins are open all year, and hardy types may enjoy camping.

Getting here in winter can be a bit of a challenge. Route 487 from Route 118 is very steep, so climbing it when it's icy can be quite a challenge. Before coming in winter, it's good to call ahead to check on the conditions.

Tourist Information:
- (800) 769-8999

Park Information:
- (570) 477-5675.

Where is it? Northeast, on PA 487, north of PA 118, about 30 miles west of Wilkes-Barre. *(Note:* PA 487 going north is a very steep grade. If you're pulling a heavy load, it's wise to approach from the north.)

Getaway Rating: 5

waterfall

28

ROUTE 209 . . . PENNSYLVANIA'S GREAT RIVER ROAD

(H, PT)

Ferry across the Susquehanna. Learn about the lives of coal miners. Tour America's oldest brewery. Spend the night in a mansion. Go white-water rafting. Dine in outdoor comfort under tall trees.

Route 209 changes its identity many times as it travels across the eastern half of Pennsylvania, and a trip over this mountainous route will show you many of the state's different faces.

If Pennsylvania were to designate a highway as its Great River Road, Route 209 would be a strong contender. In its journey across less than half of the state, Route 209 takes drivers to four major waterways—the **Susquehanna, the Schuylkill, the Lehigh,** and the **Delaware.** Drivers on Route 209 will see farm towns, coal towns, and resort towns. It's never a lonely road, but for most of the journey you can move along without much traffic.

Route 209 begins in **Millersburg,** a very scenic town in northern Dauphin County. Dauphin County is home to Harrisburg and Hershey, but Millersburg seems to be a different world, and in a very real sense it is. **Peters Mountain** separates Millersburg from the southern part of the county, and the pace of life seems a bit slower on Millersburg's side.

Millersburg's top claim to fame is the **Millersburg Ferry,** the only wooden paddlewheeler still operating in the country. The ferry crosses the Susquehanna and takes passengers to Route 15 on the western shore of the river.

Millersburg itself is a little town that evokes memories of a simpler time. The gazebo on the town square is the most visible structure. No big malls have come to the area, and downtown is still a major shopping district. In the farming valley east of town, many Amish families have moved in, and their presence holds down the number of cars on roads other than Route 209.

East of Millersburg, along Route 209, the character of the land changes abruptly near **Lykens.** The farms end and the coal mines begin. Actually, the mining activity isn't especially vigorous in the region, but you'll see evidence of it from Lykens to **Jim Thorpe.** East of Lykens, Route 209 enters **Schuylkill County** and passes through **Minersville, Port Carbon,** and **Coaldale,** places whose names tell the story of the region. Coal once dominated life here, and you can still see a few working mines and the remains of the coal industry. Stop in a restaurant or a bar along the highway and you may meet some miners or retired miners.

Pottsville is the biggest city on Route 209, and it's here where the highway crosses the Schuylkill River. It's not an especially big river at this point, but it gains size as it flows south to **Reading** and **Philadelphia.** Pottsville's biggest claim to fame is that it's the home of America's oldest brewery. **Yuengling** opened in 1829, and it's been at its current site since 1831. Don't look for the brewery along the river, though. It sits high on a hill in the center of the city, and its location seems a curious place. In bad weather the steep hills make life difficult for truck drivers, and horses must have had a real challenge getting up snowy and icy roads to the brewery.

From **Lansford** to **Jim Thorpe,** Route 209 is one long downhill. In **Nesquehoning,** the road runs beside the Nesquehoning Creek and the railroad tracks used by Rail Tours, a tourist line in Jim Thorpe.

Coal mining, Schuylkill County

Jim Thorpe is the busiest tourist town along Route 209. Visitors pour into "The Switzerland of America" to shop in antique shops, ride the railroad, ride mountain bikes, dine in old mansions, and ride rafts down the **Lehigh River.** Jim Thorpe is the midway point on the Pennsylvania section of Route 209 and a fine place to spend a night.

Heading out of Jim Thorpe, you'll drive beside the Lehigh for a few miles and then head into the Pocono Mountains. The next major towns are **Stroudsburg** and **East Stroudsburg,** where Route 209 is one of the main streets. East Stroudsburg is a college town and one of the biggest cities in the Pocono Mountains. If you come on an autumn weekend, you may catch a football game at **East Stroudsburg U,** which plays in the Division II Pennsylvania State Athletic Conference.

In Stroudsburg, you can make a short detour on Route 611 South to the town of **Delaware Water Gap.** There, you can take a ride on the Water Gap Trolley, which runs along the Delaware River and gives a great view of the sights.

In this area, Route 209 enters its most scenic stretch, the **Delaware Water Gap National Recreation Area.** North of East Stroudsburg, Route 209 comes to Bushkill Falls, eight falls on

Yuengling Brewery, Pottsville

Little Bushkill and Pond Run Creeks. Farther north is Dingman's Falls, a 130-foot drop that is the highest in Pennsylvania. While a drop of 130 feet may not sound especially high, it is pretty impressive when you actually see it.

For 30 miles the road hugs the Delaware River, and it winds through a region of vacation homes and vacation businesses. Near the end of Route 209's journey through Pennsylvania, it enters the town of **Milford,** which has become a popular tourist stop. In this region the river is popular with rafters and canoeists. On warm summer days the river looks almost like a highway, and it's shallow enough for people to walk across.

Route 209 leaves Pennsylvania at **Matamoras** and enters **Port Jervis, New York.** On the New York side, Route 97 provides excellent views of the river, and there's no comparable road on the Pennsylvania side.

Route 209 is a highway of water, coal, and mountains. When you're in a meandering mood, it s a good place to drive.

Attractions:

Millersburg Ferry, (717) 692-2442, runs in summer, when the river is deep enough.

Town of Jim Thorpe.
Delaware Water Gap.
Yuengling Brewery, Pottsville, (570) 628-4890, brewery tours Mon.-Fri. at 10 A.M. and 1:30 P.M., and Saturdays in June, July, and August at 11 A.M. and 1 P.M.

Dining:

You can enjoy dining of every description along this route. In Jim Thorpe, for instance, you can choose between a diner and a beautiful inn that are practically beside each other, and in towns all along the route you'll find family restaurants, hamburger places, and ice cream shops. A few of the more famous dining spots are:

Wooden Nickel, 219 Market Street, Millersburg, (717) 692-3003, open 11 A.M.-10 P.M. daily.

Sunrise Diner, 3 Hazard Square, Jim Thorpe, (570) 325-4093, open 5 A.M.-8 P.M. daily.

The Inn at Jim Thorpe, 24 Broadway, (800) 329-2599, lunch and dinner daily.

The Dimmick Inn, Broad and Harford Streets, Milford, (570) 296-4021, lunch and dinner daily.

Lodging:

Motels aren't common on the western half of Route 209, in Dauphin and Schuylkill counties, but from Jim Thorpe to the Delaware River, lodging of all varieties is readily available. You can stay in luxury in Jim Thorpe and in the Poconos. Here are a few of the places along the route:

Victorian Manor Bed & Breakfast, 312 Market Street, Millersburg, (717) 692-3511.

Pottsville Motor Inn, Route 61, (570) 622-4917.

The Harry Packer Mansion Bed & Breakfast, Jim Thorpe's downtown historic district, (570) 325-8566.

Mount Haven Resort, Log Tavern Road, Milford, (570) 296-8502.

Shopping:

Jim Thorpe is best for antiques and crafts. Shops line many streets in the small town. You'll also find an interesting shopping experience in Millersburg, where downtown Market Street is still a major shopping area. Throughout the Poconos, small shops line the road, and Stroudsburg has a downtown outlet center.

Annual Events:

Something is happening every week of the year along Route 209, especially in Jim Thorpe and the Poconos. A few events of the more popular events are:

Spring whitewater season, March and April, Jim Thorpe.

Laurel Blossom Festival, mid-June, Jim Thorpe.

Fall Foliage, early October.

The Active Life:

Whether it's bicycling on the country roads around Millersburg, rafting down the Lehigh or the Delaware, skiing in the Poconos, or hiking through the mountains, the active life is always popular along Route 209. The biggest concentration of activities is available from Jim Thorpe to the Delaware River, so if you want to ride, ski, canoe, hike, or boat, bring your equipment, and you'll find plenty of places to pull off the highway and get a sweat going. Several especially good places are **Mauch Chunk Lake Park** in Jim Thorpe, the **Lehigh Gorge Trail** in Jim Thorpe, and the **Appalachian Trail,** which enters Pennsylvania at **Delaware Water Gap.**

A Great Place to Relax:

This road has plenty of them. The town square in Millersburg is excellent, as are the squares in Jim Thorpe and Milford.

Covered Bridges:

The last one in Dauphin County crosses the Wiconsico Creek northeast of Elizabethville. To reach it, turn north from Route

209 on State Route 1006. Go ⁶⁄₁₀ of a mile. Turn right on Township Route 617, and left on North Road. The bridge no longer carries traffic, and it's a good place to sit and relax.

Tourist Information:
- (800) 995-0969 (Dauphin County).
- (800) 765-7282 (Schuylkill County).
- (888) JIM-THORPE (Jim Thorpe).
- (800) 762-6667 (Poconos).

Where is it? From the Susquehanna River in Millersburg to the Delaware River at Matamoras.

Getaway Rating: 4

Rafters on the Delaware River

29

ROUTE 6 . . .
NORTHERN EXPOSURE
(H, R&R, Meandering)

Fill the tank and put film in the camera. Route 6 is a scenic road where you can actually enjoy the drive. The road passes through small towns and tiny villages. It takes you to many historic attractions, and it offers beautiful scenery as it carries you from Ohio to New York.

Pennsylvania's northern tier is a lightly populated region, and Route 6 is the only highway that crosses it. The mountains in the state run from northeast to southwest, and only four highways—U.S. 30, the Pennsylvania Turnpike, I-80, and U.S. 6—cross the entire state from east to west. For an enjoyable drive, Route 6 is the best of the four. In its 400+ miles, Route 6 skirts only one big city—**Scranton**—and only two other cities of more than 10,000 people—**Meadville** and **Warren.**

For most of its length, Route 6 travels through woods and small towns. Because it's the only major road, it connects many of the towns, but you can drive for miles and miles without encountering a traffic light. Along the route, you'll see many historic sights and attractions, but only around Scranton does Route 6 have a bit of a crowded feeling, and even there it doesn't go through the heart of the city.

Denton Hill, Coudersport

If you like to ride trains, this is an excellent route to follow for a weekend getaway. Five tourist railroads operate on Route 6 or very close to it. Route 6 even crosses the **Continental Divide.**

In **Potter County,** the road crosses the **Eastern Continental Divide,** which reaches a height there of 2,424 feet. On the western side of the divide, rivers flow west toward the Mississippi. On the eastern side, they flow east toward the Susquehanna and Chesapeake Bay.

From Ohio, Route 6 enters Pennsylvania near **Pymatuning Lake,** the largest man-made body of water in the state. At the **Linesville Spillway,** visitors feed fish, and the fish are so numerous that ducks walk on their backs in competition for food. A few miles farther east is **Conneaut Lake,** a small body of water that's a very popular place in warm weather.

Then Route 6 passes through **Meadville,** home of the **Market House,** and **Allegheny College.** The Market House has been working as an open-air market since 1870, and it's the city's social center, with the **Meadville Council of the Arts** housed on the second floor.

The next place of note is **Cambridge Springs,** where people came by the thousands in the 19th century to enjoy the supposed healing properties of the nearby springs, and at one time Cambridge Springs had many large hotels to house the health seekers. The **Riverside Inn** is the only one still standing and operating, and it gives the delightful experience of staying in an old wooden hotel.

East of Cambridge Springs is **Corry,** a small town that's home to the **New York & Lake Erie Railroad,** which operates excursion trains to Cambridge Springs and Meadville.

Continuing east, Route 6 enters **Warren County.** West of the city of Warren, at the junction of Route 6 and Route 62, is the **Blair Outlet,** a favorite shopping destination that offers reduced prices on many types of goods.

East of Warren, Route 6 heads south into the **Allegheny National Forest,** just west of the Kinzua Dam, an impressive structure built to control flooding along the Allegheny River.

Route 6 goes into **Kane,** the little town that calls itself **"The Black Cherry Capital of the World."** The **Holgate Toy Company** makes wooden toys here, and the Knox & Kane Railroad picks up passengers for the ride to the **Kinzua Bridge,** a 301-foot iron structure that's the second highest railroad bridge in the country.

After Kane, the next modest town is **Smethport,** home of the **World's First Christmas Store.** Open all year, it has thousands of Christmas items, and it provides the unusual Christmas experience of shopping in July when the temperature is 90° and the air-conditioning unit is working overtime.

From Smethport it's on to **Coudersport,** the biggest town in a county that calls itself **God's Country** for its natural beauty. Coudersport is a friendly town that on the first Saturday in June is the finishing point of **God's Country Marathon,** a challenging run that goes from **Galeton,** elevation 1,300, to **Coudersport,** elevation 1,740, by way of the Eastern Continental Divide.

As the road goes east from Coudersport, it climbs and climbs up **Denton Hill,** a ski area with the steepest slope in the east. At the bottom of the hill is the **Pennsylvania Lumber Museum,** and at the eastern end of Potter County is Galeton, a small town with a pretty lake in the center of town.

Then the road enters **Tioga County** and soon comes to the **Grand Canyon of Pennsylvania,** officially known as the **Pine Creek Gorge.** The gorge is 1,000 feet deep in some places, and the **Pine Creek Trail** allows walkers and bicyclists to travel along the floor of the canyon.

East of the canyon is the beautiful little town of **Wellsboro,** a popular tourist destination known for the 1869 **Penn Wells Hotel,** the town green, gas-lit streets, and Victorian mansions. Also in Tioga County is **Mansfield,** home of Mansfield University.

East of Tioga County is **Bradford County,** part of a region known as **The Endless Mountains.** At **Towanda,** Route 6 picks up the **Susquehanna River** and runs beside it for about 40 miles. Near **Wysox** is the **French Azilum Historical Site,** which was an original French refugee village and is now open for tours. In **Wyalusing** is the **Wyalusing Hotel,** a well-preserved example of gingerbread architecture that's still operating as a restaurant and a hotel.

East of **Tunkhannock** is the most congested section of Route 6. The road passes north of **Scranton** but it does become a busy road from there to Honesdale. A worthwhile detour in Scranton is **Steamtown,** a railroad museum that remembers the role that steam trains played in the history of the United States. Steamtown is a federally funded project, and the displays are quite good. On weekends from Memorial Day until the beginning of November, Steamtown operates excursion trains.

From the Scranton area to Honesdale, Route 6 is Main Street in towns such as **Carbondale** and Honesdale, a scenic town that holds a vital place in the history of American railroading. In 1829, aboard the **Stourbridge Lion,** Horatio Allen made the first trip by steam locomotive in North America.

Pine Creek Trail, Wellsboro

The **Wayne County Museum** has a reproduction of the original Lion, and the **Stourbridge Line** now operates excursion trains over part of the route that Allen covered. Honesdale is also camp country. In summer, more than 30 camps operate in woods in the area.

East of Honesdale are the small town of **Hawley** and large **Lake Wallenpaupack.** Wallenpaupack is a man-made lake that's popular with boaters, swimmers, and shoppers who come to the stores on Route 6 around the lake.

From Lake Wallenpaupack to **Milford,** Route 6 travels largely through forest areas. Milford is a small town on the Delaware River that's become a tourist destination. Visitors walk its tree-lined streets, dine at outdoor cafés, shop for antiques, and paddle down the Delaware.

North of Milford is Matamoras, where Route 6 crosses the Delaware River and leaves Pennsylvania. At this point, the river is generally shallow and not especially swift, at least in summer, and canoeists can get out of their boats and walk through the water if they choose.

Route 6 is 400 interesting miles, and if you like to go for an interesting and scenic drive, it's probably the best road in Pennsylvania.

Attractions:

Pymatuning Lake, Linesville.

Allegheny Reservoir, near Warren.

Kinzua Bridge, near Kane.

Pennsylvania Lumber Museum, Coudersport, open 9 A.M.-5 P.M. daily, April through November.

Grand Canyon of Pennsylvania, Wellsboro.

Town of Wellsboro.

Wyalusing Hotel, Wyalusing.

Tunkhannock Viaduct, Tunkhannock.

Steamtown National Historic Site, Scranton, open 9 A.M.-5 P.M. daily.

Stourbridge Line railroad, Honesdale, call for schedule.

Dining:

All across the state, Route 6 passes small town restaurants, and you'll even see McDonald's in a few places, but the more interesting eating experiences are waiting in places such as the Wellsboro Diner and the Dimmick Inn in Milford.

Lodging:

Inexpensive motels line the route, and you'll have no trouble finding a room. However, if you enjoy staying in old hotels, this is a good route. Try these places:

Wayne Hotel, 1202 Main Street, Honesdale, (570) 253-3290.

Wyalusing Hotel, 111 Main Street, Wyalusing, (570) 746-1204.

Penn Wells Hotel, 62 Main Street, Wellsboro, (570) 724-2111.

Hotel Crittenden, 133 North Main Street, Coudersport, (814) 274-8320.

Riverside Inn, 1 Fountain Avenue, Cambridge Springs, (814) 398-4645.

You can also stay in some very nice bed & breakfasts and country inns, such as:

Train station, Corry

Oliver's Bed & Breakfast, 1415 North Main Street, Honesdale, (570) 253-4533.

Weeping Willow Inn, 308 North Eaton Road, Tunkhannock, (570) 867-7257.

The Christmas Inn, 911 West Main Street, Smethport, (814) 887-5665.

Day Lily Bed & Breakfast, 49 West Smith Street, Corry, (814) 664-9047.

Shopping:

Route 6 is Main Street in many communities, so you'll pass many stores and many types of stores. You'll find pleasant downtown shopping districts in many towns, such as Honesdale, Towanda, Wellsboro, Coudersport, Smethport, Kane, Warren, and Meadville.

A few of the more popular shopping places along the route are:

Blair Outlet, Route 6 and Route 62, Warren, (814) 726-6271, Mon.-Fri., 9 A.M.-9 P.M., Sat., 9 A.M.-6 P.M., and Sun., noon-5 P.M.

America's First Christmas Store, 101 West Main Street, Smethport, (814) 887-5792, varying seasonal hours, call for schedule.

Black Forest Trading Post, Route 6 and Route 449, West of Galeton. (814) 435-6754, varying seasonal hours, call for schedule.

Annual Events:

County fairs are big business and big social events in the rural counties through which Route 6 passes. The fairs begin in July and last through September:

Potter County Fair, Millport, last week of July, (814) 698-2368.

Troy Fair, Troy, last week of July, (570) 297-2823.

Wayne County Fair, Honesdale, second week of August, (570) 253-1847.

Tioga County Fair, Whitneyville, second week of August, (570) 549-8176.

Warren County Fair, Pittsfield, second week of August, (814) 757-8668.

McKean County Fair, Smethport, third week of August, (814) 643-4452.

Crawford County Fair, Meadville, fourth week in August, (814) 333-7400.

Pike County Agricultural Fair, Matamoras, second week in September, (717) 296-8790.

In addition, many small town festivals and celebrations take place, such as the State Laurel Festival in Wellsboro during the third week of June. Contact local tourist bureaus for full calendars.

The Active Life:

Route 6 spends much of its distance in the woods, so it's a good road to pull over and go for a walk or a strenuous hike. The premiere recreational facility is the **Pine Creek Trail,** which runs 19 miles through **Pennsylvania's Grand Canyon.** You can get on the trail 10 miles west of **Wellsboro.**

A Great Place to Relax:

Pull into a small town, grab a lunch, and find the town green or a park. Some towns with especially nice places to sit and relax are **Milford, Honesdale, Wellsboro, Coudersport,** and **Warren.** In many places along the route, you'll find picnic areas right beside the highway.

Covered Bridges:

They aren't numerous in the northern tier of Pennsylvania. The only one on Route 6 is just west of Coudersport, on private property between the highway and a farm. There's also an unusual one in Honesdale on Route 191. It's unusual because it has a concrete roadway. The covered bridge purists probably wouldn't accept it, but it's a bridge with a cover.

Tourist Information:

• (814) 454-7191.

Where is it? Northern Pennsylvania, from New Jersey to Ohio.

Getaway Rating: 4

Steamtown Museum, Scranton

30

SCRANTON . . . ALL STEAMED UP
(H, R, S)

Look for the plumes of steam and listen for the whistle. Listen for the crack of bat against ball, and do a little shopping. Then prepare for adventure as you go 300 feet underground. In Scranton you'll find steam trains and baseball games, as well as a trip down into a coal mine. In the largest city in northeastern Pennsylvania, you'll have lots of activities to keep you busy, or you can just go up on a mountain and relax.

Scranton produced the things that fueled America's industrial expansion. Coal, iron, and railroads made Scranton a wealthy city, and the history of those industries is a major attraction today. You can go down in a coal mine, ride a steam train, and sleep in a beautiful hotel that was formerly a railroad station. Scranton lies on the Lackawanna River, and the city is a relatively flat place in the river valley. That's why many railroads came right through the city.

To experience the life of a Scranton man of a century ago, head to **McDade Park.** There, the **Lackawanna Coal Mine Tour** will take you 300 feet underground in a real mine. You'll see how men slaved to gather the "black diamonds" that made Scranton the **"Anthracite Capital of the World."** It was a hard and dangerous job, and many miners lost their lives at work.

Radisson Hotel

From a real miner, you'll learn what life was like for miners and their families.

Also in the park is the **Pennsylvania Anthracite Museum,** where you can learn about mining life without actually going into a mine. Artifacts, photographs, and videos explain the mining life and the value of anthracite coal, which is much purer carbon than the more abundant bituminous coal found in other parts of Pennsylvania and the world.

Old King Coal is an important part of Scranton's history, but it isn't the only attraction in McDade Park. The **Pennsylvania Summer Theatre Festival,** featuring the **Scranton Public Theatre,** makes its summer home in McDade Park. The park also has a swimming pool and many recreational facilities, so you can enjoy history, culture, and fun in the same place.

The **Scranton Iron Furnaces** are four massive blast furnaces built between 1848 and 1857 that made metal for the Lackawanna Iron and Steel Company. By the 1880s, the furnaces were the second largest iron producer in the United States. Until 1902, they produced rails for America's railroads. The iron furnaces are the center of a park-like setting that's within walking distance of **Steamtown,** and admission is free.

Steamtown, meanwhile, is an excellent place for family outings. He can spend the day ogling at the old trains while she spends the day shopping at the adjacent **Steamtown Mall.** The mall has over 100 stores on two levels, and a pedestrian bridge across the tracks connects Steamtown with the mall.

Steamtown National Historic Site is a 40-acre plot that was once a rail yard for the Delaware, Lackawanna, & Western Railroad, one of the earliest railroads in northeastern Pennsylvania. The museum has an outstanding collection of steam locomotives, and the most impressive is the **Big Boy,** a massive engine that once pulled trains over the Wasatch Mountains in Utah.

Inside the museum, a film show details the railroad's place in the building of America. You can see steam locomotives, as well as a working roundhouse. There, trains come in facing one direction, and a turntable revolves to point the trains in the opposite direction. For train lovers, Steamtown is definitely worth a visit.

If you're looking for a great escape, pay a visit to the **Houdini Show and Tour,** which celebrates the accomplishments of the great escape artist Harry Houdini. Visitors watch a live magic show and a video presentation, and they can view Houdini memorabilia and photographs.

The **Everhart Museum** in **Nay Aug Park** houses a permanent display of many types of art, including Native American, Oriental, and American Folk. Other display highlight birds, dinosaurs, and Dorflinger glass.

Twenty miles south of Scranton is the city of **Wilkes-Barre,** often joined at the slash with Scranton, as in Scranton/Wilkes-Barre. Outsiders do most of the joining, because the two cities are distinct. They're even in different counties, and in many ways they're rivals.

Wilkes-Barre lies in the Wyoming Valley, and it's this valley that gave the state of Wyoming its name. Like Scranton, Wilkes-Barre was a coal-mining town. Before that, it was the site of the Yankee-Pennamite Wars, a struggle between Pennsylvania and Connecticut that lasted from 1769 until 1785. Many battles occurred on **River Common,** a large park on River Street between North and South Streets. Within the park are the Luzerne County Court House and many historical markers. Pennsylvania eventually won the battle when Congress ruled in its favor, but Connecticut persisted with its claims until 1800.

Wilkes-Barre's appearance changed significantly in 1972 when Hurricane Agnes sent the Susquehanna River out of its banks and over much of the city. A major renovation followed, and the city's industry has been diversifying from its coal base for many decades.

Pocono Downs, one of Pennsylvania's two harness racing tracks, is on Route 315 in Wilkes-Barre, and the **Wilkes-Barre/Scranton Penguins** minor league hockey team began play at a new arena in the 1999 season. Just south of Scranton, the **Scranton/Wilkes-Barre Red Barons,** the Philadelphia Phillies AAA associate, play at **Lackawanna County Stadium.**

In Wilkes-Barre is the **Lion Brewery,** maker of beer and ales. **Stegmaier** beer is a regionally popular brand that Lion produces, and the brewery offers tours of the facilities.

South of Wilkes-Barre, near Freeland, is **Eckley Miners Village,** a coal-mining attraction that depicts the entirety of life in a coal town. Eckley was a "patch" town, which means that the mining company owned everything. The company owned the houses, the store, and even the church. The miners and their families lived in small wooden houses with no creature comforts. The owner lived in a much bigger and more luxurious house, and workers at different levels lived in progressively better homes.

Foremen, for instance, lived in nicer homes than breakers, who were the lowest rung on the mining work chart. Breakers were often boys as young as 9, but adults also held the positions. The job of the breaker was to separate impurities from the coal. It was hard and monotonous work, but at least the breakers were generally safe from the cave-ins and explosions that made the mines so dangerous.

At Eckley, the progression of the homes is clear. The smallest, most basic homes are at one end of the town and the owner's home is at the other end. If you've seen the movie *The Molly Maguires,* Eckley may look familiar, especially the tall breaker, because this is the site where Richard Harris and crew filmed the movie.

Winter often hits this region with deep blankets of snow, and **Montage Mountain** in Scranton is a ski resort with a 1,000 foot vertical drop. Unlike most ski resorts, which are far from population bases, Montage Mountain is practically in the heart of Scranton. It's right beside I-81, no more than five miles from downtown Scranton.

Scranton powered the new nation, and the history of its industries coupled with shopping and outdoor activities makes a getaway with something to interest everyone.

Attractions:

Elk Mountain Ski Resort, Union Dale, (570) 679-2611.

Everhart Museum, Nay Aug Park, Mulberry and Arthur, Scranton, (570) 346-8370, open 10 A.M.-5 P.M. daily.

Hill and Dale Bike Tours, Carbondale, (800) 229-3526.

Historic Scranton Iron Furnaces, Cedar Avenue, Scranton, (570) 963-3208.

Houdini Tour and Show, 1433 North Main Street, Scranton, (570) 342-5555, call for hours.

Lackawanna Coal Mine Tour, 51 McDade Park, Scranton, (570) 963-MINE, open 10 A.M.-4:30 P.M. daily, April through November.

Lion Brewery, 700 North Pennsylvania Avenue, Wilkes-Barre, (888) 295-BEER, tours Saturdays at 1 P.M.

Montage Mountain Ski Resort, 100 Montage Mountain Road, Scranton, (800) GOT-SNOW.

Pennsylvania Anthracite Heritage Museum, McDade Park, Bald Mountain Road, Scranton, (570) 963-4804, open 10 A.M.-5 P.M. daily.

Pocono Downs harness racing, 1280 Route 315, Wilkes-Barre, (570) 825-6681, call for racing schedule.

Steamtown

Steamtown, 150 South Washington Street, Scranton, (570) 340-5200, open 9 A.M.-5 P.M. daily. Excursion trains Saturdays and Sundays, noon and 3 P.M., also Fridays in summer and Fall Foliage season.

S-WB Red Barons baseball, Phillies AAA team, (570) 969-BALL.

Dining:

After 5 Supper Club, 280 Main Street, Dickson City, (570) 383-0321, opens at 5 P.M. Mon.-Sat., Sun., noon-9 P.M.

Amber Indian Restaurant, 4130 Birney Avenue, Moosic, (570) 457-2700, open 11 A.M.-3 P.M. and 5 P.M.-10 P.M. daily.

Amici, 1300 Morgan Highway, Clarks Summit, (570) 586-3000, Tues.-Sat., 5 P.M.-10 P.M., and Sun., 4 P.M.-9 P.M.

Anna Maria's Restaurant, 948 East Drinker Street, Dunmore, (570) 348-0188, open 11 A.M.-11 P.M. daily.

Casa de Mama, 1829 Bundy Street, Scranton, Mon.-Sat., 4 P.M.-till, Sun., 4 P.M.-9 P.M.

Dante's Den, 512 Court Street, Scranton, Tues.-Fri., 5 P.M.-10 P.M., Sat., 4:30 P.M.-11 P.M., and Sun., 4 P.M.-9 P.M.

Gilder Restaurant, 890 Providence Road, Scranton, (570) 343-8036, Mon.-Sat., 24 hours a day.

The Home Plate, 2 Lonesome Road, Old Forge, (570) 457-4944, open 5:30 A.M.-2:30 P.M. daily.

Jim Dandy's, Route 6 and Route 11, Clarks Summit, (570) 586-6000, open 11:30 A.M.-2 A.M. daily.

K Medici, 1140 Route 315, Wilkes-Barre, (570) 822-8688, Tues.-Fri., 11 A.M.-2 P.M., Mon.-Thur., 5 P.M.-9 P.M., Fri. and Sat., 5 P.M.-10 P.M.

Katona, 41 South Main Street, Wilkes-Barre, (570) 825-9080, Mon.-Fri., 11:30 A.M.-2:30 P.M. and again at 5 P.M. daily.

Kelly's Pub, 1802 Cedar Avenue, Scranton, (570) 346-9758, Mon.-Sat., 4 P.M.-noon

Pickett's Charge Restaurant, 64 East Center Hill Road, Dallas, (570) 675-4511, opens at 7 A.M. daily.

Russell's, 1918 Arch Street, Scranton, (570) 961-8949, opens at 4:30 P.M. daily

Saber Room Restaurant, 94 Butler Street, Wilkes-Barre, (570) 829-5743, Mon.-Fri., 11 A.M.-2:30 P.M. and Mon.-Fri., 5 P.M.-11 P.M.

Villa Maria, 1259 Brynmawr Street, Scranton, (570) 344-5355, Mon.-Fri., 11 A.M.-2 P.M., Mon.-Sat., 4 P.M.-11 P.M., and Sun., noon-9 P.M.

Lodging:

Best Western East Mountain Inn, 2400 East End Boulevard, Wilkes-Barre, (570) 822-1011.

Courtyard by Marriott, 16 Glenmaura National Boulevard, Moosic, (570) 969-2100.

Days Inn, 1226 O'Neill Highway, Dunmore, (570) 348-6101.

Days Inn, 4130 Birney Avenue, Moosic, (570) 457-6713.

EconoLodge, 1175 Kane Street, Scranton, (570) 348-1000.

Hampton Inn, Montage Mountain Road, Scranton, (570) 342-7002.

Holiday Inn, 200 Tigue Street, Dunmore, (570) 343-4771.

Orazzi's Blue Ridge Inn, Route 106, Carbondale, (570) 282-7224.

Radisson Lackawanna Station Hotel, 700 Lackawanna Avenue, Scranton, (570) 342-8300.

Ramada Plaza Hotel, 20 Public Square, Wilkes-Barre, (570) 824-7100.

Red Roof Inn, Route 315, Wilkes-Barre, (570) 829-6422.

Victoria Inn, Route 315, Wilkes-Barre, (570) 655-2267.

The Woodlands Inn & Resort, Route 315, Wilkes-Barre, (570) 824-9831.

Heritage Inn Bed & Breakfast, 5 Park Place, Carbondale, (570) 282-7477.

Shopping:

Americana Roads Antiques, Route 29, Springville, (570) 965-2121, Mon.-Sat., 10 A.M.-5 P.M.

Co-Op Farmers' Market, Albright Avenue, Scranton, (570) 961-8251, seasonal.

Curiosity Shop, 640 East Market Street, Scranton, (570) 969-6911, Mon.-Fri., 11 A.M.-6 P.M., Sat., 11 A.M.-4 P.M.

Cynthia Creations, Route 690, Moscow, (570) 842-6060, Tues.-Sat., 10 A.M.-5 P.M.

Giftery, 200 Betty Street, Enyon, (570) 876-4200, Mon.-Sat., 10 A.M.-5:30 P.M.

Heritage House Antiques, 402 North State Street, Clarks Summit, (570) 586-8575, Tues.-Sat., 10 A.M.-5 P.M., Sun., noon-5 P.M.

Liz Z's Wreath & Gift Shop, 706 East Market Street, Scranton, (570) 342-7871, Tues.-Sat., 11 A.M.-6 P.M.

The Mall at Steamtown, Lackawanna Avenue, Scranton, (570) 941-3400, Mon.-Sat., 10 A.M.-6 P.M., Sun., noon-6 P.M.

Susan's Stone Cottage, 701 Shady Lane Road, Clarks summit, (570) 587-0464, Tues.-Sat., 10 A.M.-5 P.M.

Village Pastimes Emporium, Butler Drive, Drums, (570) 788-6613, Thur.-Sat., 10 A.M.-5 P.M., Sun., noon-5 P.M.

The Wicker Gazebo, 710 Capouse Avenue, Scranton, (570) 346-8777, Tues.-Fri., 10 A.M.-6 P.M., Sat. and Sun., 10 A.M.-4 P.M.

Wildflower Antiques, 700 East Market Street, Scranton, (570) 341-0511, Tues.-Sat., 11 A.M.-6 P.M.

Wyoming Valley Mall, 29 Wyoming Valley Mall, Wilkes-Barre, (570) 823-1224, Mon.-Sat., 10 A.M.-9 P.M., Sun., 11 A.M.-6 P.M.

Annual Events:

The premier event in Scranton is the Steamtown Marathon. Held the second Sunday in October, it takes runners from Forest City in Susquehanna County to downtown Scranton. The race features excellent support all along the course, and it's a great experience for runners and spectators.

Ice Carving Championships, February, Lackawanna County Stadium, (570) 969-2255.

Saint Patrick's Day Parade, March, downtown Scranton.

Red Barons baseball, April through September, Lackawanna County Stadium, (570) 969-2255.

Excursion train rides, May through early November, Steamtown, (570) 340-5200.

Luzerne County Fair, September, Dallas, (570) 675-3247.

Steamtown Marathon, October, Scranton, (800) 229-3256.

The Active Life:

Winter is prime time in northeastern Pennsylvania. Snow usually comes in significant amounts, and the hilly terrain provides opportunities for skiing, snowboarding, sledding, and skating. **Elk Mountain** and **Montage Mountain** are major ski areas. In warmer weather, the hills are alive with hikers and bikers.

A Great Place to Relax:

Take a seat on a bench at Steamtown and watch the trains maneuver around the yards.

Covered Bridges:

None nearby.

Tourist Information:

- (800) 229-3526.

Where is it? Northeast, on I-81.

Getaway Rating: 2

Harveys Lake

31

STRASBURG . . .
A RAIL GREAT LITTLE TOWN
(H, R)

Listen for the shrill shriek of the steam whistle. Look out over the verdant farmlands for the smoke from the steam engine. Take in a dazzling Christian stage production. Then spend the night in a real caboose. In Strasburg, you can watch the trains and the story of the Biblical rains.

If you love trains, Strasburg is as good a place as any in the country to spend a weekend. If you don't like trains, you'll still find plenty of interesting things to do.

Strasburg calls itself **Train Town, U.S.A.** because it has many railroad attractions in a small area. In Strasburg you can ride trains, watch trains, learn the history of trains, watch toy trains, buy train memorabilia, and even sleep and eat in railroad cars.

Every year, hundreds of thousands of visitors take a scenic ride on the Strasburg Railroad and visit the **Railroad Museum of Pennsylvania,** which is right across the street, but trains aren't the town's only attractions. In September of 1998, the new **Sight & Sound Theatre** opened, and a long string of sell-out performances followed.

Sight & Sound Theatre is a huge facility that presents live Christian stage productions, such as *Noah,* the story of Noah's building of the ark, and *Miracle of Christmas,* the story of the

Strasburg Railroad passing buggy

first Christmas. The Sight & Sound Theatre that opened in 1998 is a rebuilt, $20 million, 2,069-seat version of the original, which burned in 1997.

The new Theatre has the world's largest fiberglass dome, carpeted aisles, and live animals in the performances. The new theater has a 300-foot wraparound theater, the most modern sound and light systems, and a heavy demand for tickets, so call ahead before you come.

Less modern than the new theater are the engines at the **Strasburg Railroad.** Steam produced by burning coal still moves the cars on this popular tourist ride. As the hulking black engine pulls into the station, the eyes of a child grow wide, whether the child is 6 or 60. The engine hisses, and cameras click.

Eager passengers board the train, with many of them getting in the open cars. The train moves slowly out of Strasburg on its 45-minute ride to **Paradise** and back. The ride takes passengers through farms meticulously tended by Amish families. In summer, the corn is high and everything is green. From mid-July

Strasburg Country Store & Creamery

until early October, the train stops at the **Amazing Maize Maze,** a cornfield grown in a design that presents a challenge to everyone trying to pass through it. Beside the maze is a rainbow of flowers 100 feet long that bends along the side of a hill to create the look of a rainbow on the ground.

The regular ride on the Strasburg is only 45 minutes, so passengers have plenty of time to do other things in the area. The dinner trains that operate Wednesday through Sunday in summer and weekends in spring and autumn have longer rides. The dinner rides last about two hours and come with entertainment such as music and comedy. On the regular ride, passengers can take a lunch, get off at a picnic grove beside the tracks, and catch a later train back to the station.

Pennsylvania has more than 20 tourist railroads, and in many ways Strasburg is the leader. It carries more passengers every year than any other tourist line in the continental United States, and it probably has the best equipment. The company spends large amounts of money to refurbish passenger cars and steam engines before it puts them to work, and Strasburg does work for other railroads. In 1998, for instance, Strasburg refurbished an 1856 locomotive from a museum in Baltimore so that the locomotive could work in the movie *The Wild, Wild West.*

Across the street from the active railroad is the **Railroad Museum of Pennsylvania.** The museum has an impressive collection that recounts the history of railroading in Pennsylvania. Almost every item in the museum has a Pennsylvania connection, and railroad experts have said that the two best state museums are those in Pennsylvania and California, so you can count on an interesting visit. The museum is constantly adding new items, and the collection of railroad cars is large. Inside are comprehensive exhibits of locomotives and rolling stock. The museum has frequent special events, and it provides excellent photo opportunities.

Just down Route 741 from the railroad and the museum is the **National Toy Train Museum,** which is also the national headquarters of the **Train Collectors Association.** Toy trains are almost as old as real trains, and this museum tells the story of the toys. The museum will make every kid's eyes pop with its collection of toy trains made from the 1800s to the present. Hundreds of cars and five operating layouts with push button controls allow visitors to put the trains into motion while a continuous video tells toy train stories.

If the two museums and the Strasburg Railroad aren't enough for you, you can spend the night in a train. The **Red Caboose Motel** uses real cabooses as motel rooms, but these cabooses are much more comfortable than they were when they were working on the railroad. The **Choo Choo Barn** is a 1,700-foot display of Lancaster County. The layout has 14 operating toy trains and over 130 animated figures and vehicles.

Trains have made Strasburg famous, but trains aren't the only attraction in this little town. The village of Strasburg has many historic buildings, and you can see them in a short walk around the town. On the square is **The Creamery,** a general store in a restored 18th-century building that's a favorite gathering place for ice cream and sodas. **Mill Bridge Village** on South Ronks Road details Amish and colonial life on the same site, and Lancaster County's only remaining two-span covered bridge is on the site. The Amish Village on Route 896 shows how daily life unfolds in an Amish home.

For a good look at the Amish world, drive south of Route 741 toward **Quarryville.** A wooded ridge separates Strasburg and Quarryville, and tourists rarely venture over the ridge. It's an area where Amish own most of the farms. On many of them you'll see roadside stands where you can buy fresh produce, and on some farms you'll see sales of quilts, crafts, and furniture. If you come during the school year, you'll see Amish children walking to their one-room schoolhouses.

Strasburg is an excellent place to train, and it has many more attractions. A visit to Strasburg will keep you busy for a day or a long weekend.

Attractions:

Strasburg Railroad, Route 741 East, (717) 687-7522, hours vary by season.

Railroad Museum of Pennsylvania, Route 741 East, (717) 687-8628, Mon.-Sat., 9 A.M.-5 P.M., Sun., noon-5 P.M.

Sight & Sound Auditorium, Route 896 North, (717) 687-7800, call for show times.

National Toy Train Museum, 300 Paradise Lane, (717) 687-8976, open 10 A.M.-5 P.M. daily, May through October 31, open Saturdays and Sundays from 10 A.M.-5 P.M. in April, November, and early December.

Choo Choo Barn, Route 741 East, (717) 687-7911, opens at 10 A.M. daily.

Amazing Maize Maze, July through October, Cherry Crest Farm, (717) 687-6843.

Dining:

Historic Strasburg Inn, Route 896 North, (717) 687-7691, opens at 11:30 A.M. Mon.-Sat., and at 11 A.M. on Sundays.

Iron Horse Inn, 135 East Main Street, (717) 687-6362, lunch and dinner daily.

Street scene

Isaac's, Route 741 East, (717) 687-7699, open 11 A.M.-9 P.M. daily.

Hershey Farm Restaurant, Route 896 North, (717) 687-8635, breakfast, lunch, and dinner daily.

Strasburg Railroad, Route 741 East, (717) 687-7522, lunch served daily from 11 A.M.-3 P.M., evening dinner trains.

Rainbow Dinner Theatre, Route 30, Paradise, (800) 292-4301, Friday and Saturday evenings, Sunday twilights, weekday matinees.

Miller's Smorgasbord, Route 30, Ronks, (717) 687-6621, breakfast, lunch, and dinner daily.

Washington House Restaurant, Route 896, (717) 687-9211, open 7 A.M.-9 P.M. daily.

Willow Valley Smorgasbord, Route 222, Willow Street, (717) 464-2711, breakfast, lunch, and dinner, daily.

Lodging:

Amish Lanterns Motel, Route 896 North, (717) 687-7839.

Beaver Creek Farm Cabins, 2 Little Beaver Road, (717) 687-7745.

Best Western Revere Motor Inn, Route 30, Paradise, (717) 687-7683.

Carriage House Motor Inn, 144 East Main Street, (717) 687-7651.

Cherry Lane Motor Inn, 84 North Ronks Road, Ronks, (717) 687-7646.

Country Side Motel, 134 Hartman Bridge Road, (717) 687-8431.

Dutch Treat Motel, 265 Herr Road, Ronks, (717) 687-7998.

Flory's Cottages & Camping, 99 North Ronks Road, Ronks, (717) 687-6670.

Historic Strasburg Inn, Route 896 North, (717) 687-7691.

Hershey Farm Motor Inn, Route 896 North, (717) 687-8635.

Red Caboose Motel, Paradise Lane, (717) 687-5000.

Soudersburg Motel, Route 30, (717) 687-7607.

Timberline Lodge, 44 Summit Hill Drive, (717) 687-7472.

Willow Valley Resort, Route 222, Willow Street, (717) 464-2711.

Australian Walkabout Inn Bed & Breakfast, 837 Village Road, Lampeter, (717) 464-0707.

The Decoy Bed & Breakfast, 958 Eisenberger Road, (717) 687-8585.

Limestone Inn, 33 East Main Street, (717) 687-8392.

The Manor Bed & Breakfast, 830 Village Road, Lampeter, (717) 464-9564.

Strasburg Village Inn, 1 West Main Street, (717) 687-0900.

Cherry Crest Dairy Farm, 150 Cherry Hill Road, (717) 687-6844.

Maple Lane Farm Bed & Breakfast, 505 Paradise Lane, Paradise, (717) 687-7479.

Rayba Acres Farm, 183 Black Horse Road, (717) 687-6729.

Verdant View Farm, 429 Strasburg Road, (888) 321-8119.

Amish Country View Lodging, 832 May Post Office Road, (717) 687-7179.

Mill Bridge Village Camp Resort, South Ronks Road, (800) 645-2744.

White Oak Campground, White Oak Road, (717) 687-6207.

Shopping:

Amish Country Crafts, Route 896, (717) 687-9935, open daily until 9 P.M. in season.

Country Creations, 321 North Star Road, (717) 687-8743, Mon.-Sat., 10 A.M.-6 P.M.

Eldreth Pottery, 246 North Decatur Street, (717) 687-8445, opens daily at 10 A.M., except Sundays, at 1 P.M.

Lapp's Quilt Shop, 206 North Star Road, Mon.-Sat., 8 A.M.-7 P.M.

J & B Quilts, 157 North Star Road, Mon.-Sat., 8 A.M.-7 P.M.

Mari's Gift Shoppe, Route 896, (717) 687-7691, Mon.-Thur., 10 A.M.-5 P.M., Fri., 10 A.M.-8 P.M., and Sat., 10 A.M.-3 P.M.

National Christmas Center, Route 30, Paradise, (717) 442-7950, open 10 A.M.-8 P.M. daily.

Strasburg Antique Market, Route 741 and Route 896, (717) 687-5624, Wed.-Mon., 10 A.M.-5 P.M.

Strasburg Railroad Gift Shop, Route 741 East, (717) 687-7686, hours vary by season.

Strasburg Country Store & Creamery, 1 West Main Street, (717) 687-0766, hours vary by season.

Wil-Char The Hex Place, Route 30, Paradise, (717) 687-5670, open seven days a week.

The Yuletide, Route 30, Paradise, (717) 687-8711, open 10 A.M.-6 P.M. daily.

Annual Events:

Gordonville Fire Company Sale, second Saturday in March, (717) 768-3869.

Amazing Maize Maze, mid-July through October, (717) 687-6843.

Pennsylvania Dutch Balloon & Craft Festival, early September, Historic Strasburg Inn, (717) 687-7691.

Christmas Spectacular, Village Greens Miniature Golf Course, Route 741 West, (717) 687-6933.

The Active Life:

The farm roads in the area are excellent for bicycling. A 45.9-mile bike tour begins at the **Railroad Museum of Pennsylvania** and takes riders to the Landis Valley Farm museum in Lancaster and to the Ephrata Cloister. Direction sheets are available at all three museums. Golfers can play at the **Host Resort** on Route 30 in Lancaster, (717) 299-5500, and at **Tanglewood** on Scotland Road in Quarryville, (717) 786-2220.

A Great Place to Relax:

Take a picnic with you when you ride the **Strasburg Railroad.** You can get off at Groff's Grove and catch a later train back to the station. At the picnic grove, you'll have a view of some beautiful Lancaster County farmland, and you'll probably see some Amish buggies on the road. It's a peaceful spot with beautiful scenery.

Covered Bridges:

Herr's Mill Bridge at Mill Bridge Village is right beside South Ronks Road, just north of Strasburg. **Neff's Mill Bridge** is on Penn Grant Road, west of Strasburg. From Route 741, turn left at Strasburg Mennonite Church as you're going west.

Tourist Information:

• (800) 872-0201.

Where is it? Southeast, on PA 741 and PA 896.

Getaway Rating: 2

Red Caboose Motel

32

TITUSVILLE . . .
OIL'S WELL
(H, N)

Pedal past the place that changed the world. Relax by the creek with a picnic lunch. Stand in an open rail car and watch the wildlife. Titusville is an excellent place to take a history lesson, to get some easy exercise, and to relax beside a lazy stream.

It's doubtful that **Colonel Drake** had any idea of the impact his success would have on every aspect of modern life. On August 27, 1859, Colonel Edwin Drake struck oil and changed the course of world history. He and others had previously found surface oil in the region, and Drake's was the world's first oil well. The discovery changed the world to an extent that no one could have envisioned. With his backers, Drake drilled on the hope that they could find many uses for the black liquid. They knew that it burned, but in 1859 they had no idea of all the uses that the world would eventually find for their black gold.

Overnight, **Titusville** became the world's first oil boom town. Workers, speculators, and hustlers poured in, and the small town and others nearby simultaneously prospered and suffered. The oil boom brought great wealth to the region. It also scarred the land, fouled the creek, and cost many lives. Drilling oil wells was dangerous work, and it became much

Drake Well Museum

more dangerous with the introduction of nitroglycerine. In 1865, Colonel E. A. L. Roberts received the first patent for an oil well torpedo. Torpedoes were tin canisters filled with gunpowder or nitroglycerine and lowered into the well. They then exploded and loosened oil-bearing rocks.

The trouble was that the nitro was very sensitive, and sometimes it blew up in places other than wells. Thus, it was common for men driving wagons to be blown apart to such an extent that no one could find any traces of them. At the **Otto Cupler Torpedo Company** in nearby Pleasantville, demonstrations show what happened when something went wrong with the nitroglycerin, or when the moonlighter was foolish enough to mix nitro and whiskey.

Fire was also a problem in the oil fields. Drake's original well house burned down two months after the well came in, and no photographs of it survive. After that, fires became common, and they prompted the city of Titusville to purchase the **Colonel Drake Fire Engine** in 1868. It served the city well for many years, and it's now on display at the **Drake Well Museum.**

The museum tells the story of Colonel Drake's efforts, and it houses many artifacts from oil's early days. In addition, a

Drake Well Museum

replica of Drake's derrick and engine house is the most visible structure on the property. The machinery in the well is still running, and the noise is a constant sound around the museum.

From Titusville, exploration for oil spread throughout surrounding counties, and wells paid off in neighboring Venango, Forest, Warren, and McKean Counties. The actual oil deposits in the region turned out to be rather small, and although the boom was a short one, it was the most important one ever. Today, you can still see oil rigs in fields throughout the region, although most of them are rusted and still, and the amount of oil produced is very small.

Downstream from Titusville is the appropriately named **Oil City,** at the confluence of Oil Creek and the Allegheny River. During the boom, Oil City was a major shipping point. In 1865, half the oil shipped in the entire world passed through Oil City.

That was good for business but bad for the waterways. The oil traveled in wooden barrels that broke with some regularity, fouling the creek. The creek has recovered nicely since then, and it's very clean and a popular recreational spot today.

Between Titusville and Oil City is **Oil Creek State Park,** 7,000 acres of deep hollows, ravines, and relics from the oil boom era.

At the southern end of the park is **Petroleum Centre,** which was once an oil boomtown. Today, evidence of oil drilling is gone, but a visitors' center and plaques around the park tell the story of the town. Throughout the park, a few wells are still active, bringing the final gallons of oil out of the ground.

The highlight of the park is the **Oil Creek State Park Bike Trail,** a 9.5-mile paved trail that extends from the Drake Well Museum to Petroleum Centre. The trail is flat, scenic, and shaded. It's excellent for an easy ride or a leisurely walk, and any kind of bike will do nicely. Bike rentals are available at the park at Petroleum Centre.

Operating on the other side of the creek is the **Oil Creek & Titusville Railroad,** which runs excursion trains from June through October. Passengers can board either at **Perry Street Station** in Titusville or at the Drake Well Museum. Perry Street Station has food and souvenirs, and sometimes bands play before the train departs. The ride is slow and relaxed, and the best place to travel during warm weather is in the open car right behind the engine. That car affords the best views and the freshest air. The most spectacular rides take place in October, when the leaves present a brilliant display of orange, red, yellow, and gold.

To extend your railroad experience, spend the night at **Casey's Caboose Stop,** a motel made up of 21 renovated cabooses that now have TV's, air-conditioning, and all the comforts of a traditional hotel or motel.

Near Titusville is **Pithole,** which was America's largest oil boomtown. Explorers found oil in January of 1865, and, by September, Pithole had reached a population of 15,000. The oil ran dry quickly, and by 1867, every resident of the town had left. Today Pithole is a rolling meadow brightened by wildflowers, and a visitor center marks the place where a town stood for two years.

Tyred Wheels Museum in Pleasantville is a transportation museum that covers many modes. The collection includes antique cars, motorcycles, bicycles, and airplanes, as well as miniature tractors, trains, and dollhouses.

In Oil City is the **Venango Museum of Art, Science, and Industry.** Children can take an elementary physics lesson at the exhibit called Scientrific while adults browse through artifacts from the oil industry. The **Oil City Warehouse Mall** is a large warehouse that's home to many vendors of antiques, collectibles, country primitives, and furniture.

Down Route 62 from Oil City is Franklin, home of **DeBence Antique Music World,** a large collection of antique musical instruments from the 1890s to the 1920s. Nickelodeons play old songs, while Swiss and German music boxes play waltzes and polka. On the second floor is the **Wild West Museum,** one of the largest collections of Western memorabilia in the East. The collection includes guns, knives, and personal possessions of Western heroes such as Buffalo Bill and Annie Oakley.

Titusville is small and friendly. Come for a history lesson, a train ride, and a bike ride beside Oil Creek. You'll leave feeling that oil's well.

Attractions:

Debence Antique Music World, Liberty Street, Franklin, (814) 432-5668, Tues.-Sat., 10 A.M.-5 P.M., Sun., 12:30 P.M.-5 P.M.

Drake Well Museum, follow signs from Route 8 in Titusville, (814) 827-2797, Tues.-Sat., 9 A.M.-5 P.M., Sun., noon-5 P.M.

Oil Creek & Titusville Railroad, Perry Street Station, (814) 676-1733, June through October, call for schedule.

Oil Creek State Park & Oil Creek State Park Bicycle Trail, Route 8, Petroleum Centre and Drake Well Museum, (814) 676-5915.

Tyred Wheels Museum, Pleasantville, (814) 676-0756, open 1 P.M.- 5 P.M., Memorial Day weekend through September 1.

Dining:

Flossie's, Route 27 and Route 227, Pleasantville, (814) 589-7457, Mon.-Fri., 5:30 A.M.-9 P.M., Sat. and Sun., 6 A.M.-8 P.M.

Hoss's, 520 North Seneca Street, Oil City, (814) 677-3002, Sun.- Thur., 11:30 A.M.-9:30 P.M., Fri. and Sat., 11:30 A.M.-10:30 P.M.

Oil Creek & Titusville Railroad

Lavender Rose, 305 Duncomb Street, Oil City, (814) 676-8180, opens at 6 A.M. daily.

Molly's Mill, 221 South Monroe Street, (814) 827-6597, opens at 11:30 A.M. daily.

New Ling Chinese Restaurant, 120 Diamond Street, (814) 827-9830, open 11:30 A.M.-9 P.M. daily.

One Way Pizza, 102 South Washington Street, (814) 827-1087, Mon.-Thur., 11 A.M.-11 P.M., Fri. and Sat., 11 A.M.-midnight.

Papa Carone's Inn, 317 South Franklin Street, (814) 827-7555, Mon.-Sat., 11:30 A.M.-11 P.M.

Pasquale's, 423 East Central Avenue, Mon.-Thur., 10 A.M.-11 P.M., Fri. and Sat., 10 A.M.-midnight.

Powder Horn Café, 425 West Spring Street, (814) 827-2438, Mon.-Sat., 11 A.M.-8 P.M.

Perkins, 219 East Central Avenue, (814) 827-7339, open 6 A.M.-10 P.M. daily.

Famoore's Family Restaurant, 18 East First Street, Oil City, (814) 676-4789, open 7 A.M.-9 P.M. daily.

Genova Restaurant, 351 Seneca Street, Oil City, (814) 677-7263, lunch and dinner daily.

Villa Italia, 352 Seneca Street, Oil City, (814) 677-1264, lunch and dinner daily.

Szechuan Chinese Restaurant, 45 Seneca Street, Oil City, (814) 676-1299, lunch and dinner daily.

Yellow Dog Lantern, 218 Elm Street, Oil City, (814) 676-1000, lunch, Mon.-Fri., dinner, Mon.-Sat.

Yesterday's, 220 Sycamore Street, Oil City, (814) 676-8180, lunch and dinner daily.

Yuen's Chinese Restaurant, 11 East First Street, Oil City, (814) 677-0818, lunch and dinner daily.

Lodging:

C'Villa Motel, Route 8 North, (814) 827-1150.

Shadyside Hotel, 117 East Main Street, (814) 827-6923.

Casey's Caboose Stop, 221 South Monroe Street, (814) 827-6597.

Cross Creek Resort, Route 8 North, (814) 827-9611.

Oil Creek Lodge, Route 8, (814) 677-4684.

McMullen House Bed & Breakfast, 430 East Main Street, (814) 827-1592.

Knapp Farm Bed & Breakfast, 43778 Thompson Run Road, (814) 827-1092.

Holiday Inn, 1 Seneca Street, Oil City, (814) 677-1221.

Corbett Inn, 370 Seneca Street, Oil City, (814) 676-0803.

Cuddle Right Inn, 1019 Central Avenue, Oil City, (814) 676-6463.

Shopping:

Country Pedalers, Route 322, Franklin, (814) 432-8055, open daily in season.

Cranberry Mall, Route 322, Cranberry, (814) 676-2353, Mon.-Sat., 10 A.M.-9 P.M., Sun., noon-5 P.M.

Dusty Corner Antiques, Allegheny Avenue, Reno, (814) 676-3171, Tues.-Sat., 10 A.M.-5 P.M.

Grain Loft Treasures, 221 South Monroe Street, (814) 927-0736, Tues.-Sun., 10 A.M.-5 P.M.

The Gift Box, 108 South Washington Street, (814) 827-6332, Mon.-Sat., 10 A.M.-5 P.M.

Wilderness Connection, 601 West Spring Street, (814) 827-6533, Mon.-Sat., 9:30 A.M.-6 P.M.

Hopkins Sporting Goods, 118 Diamond Street, (814) 827-1299, Mon.-Sat., 9:30 A.M.-5 P.M.

Oil Region Book Exchange, 15 Central Avenue, Oil City, (814) 677-4368, Mon.-Sat., 10 A.M.-5:30 P.M.

Oil City Warehouse Mall, 30 Pumphouse Road, (800) 711-9678, open 10 A.M.-6 P.M daily.

Buyer's Fair, 358 North Seneca Street, Oil City, (814) 677-4076.

Annual Events:

Spring Wildflower Walk, early May, Oil Creek State Park, (814) 676-5915.

Nitro Shows, May, September, and October, Drake Well Museum, (814) 827-2797.

Heritage Lecture Series, May, Drake Well Museum, (814) 827-2797.

Oil Field Picnic, July, Drake Well Museum, (814) 827-2797.

Oil Heritage Week, late July, Oil City, (814) 676-8521.

Venango County Fair, mid-August, Franklin, (814) 437-7607.

The Active Life:

The **Oil Creek State Park Bike Trail** is ideal for easy rides and walks. It's 9.5 miles long, flat and shaded, with facilities at both ends and on the trail. The park also has harder hiking trails, cross-country ski areas, and pavilions. When the water is high enough, Oil Creek is popular with canoeists. The **Samuel Justus Recreational Trail** is a 5.8-mile hiking/biking trail between Oil City and Franklin. Bicycle, roller blade, and canoe rentals are available at the Franklin trailhead. Call (814) 676-8812 for trail information.

Golfers can play at Cross Creek Resort, Route 8 in Titusville, (814) 827-9611, at Green Acres on Route 408 in Titusville, (814) 827-3589, and at Titusville Country Club on Hydetown Road, (814) 827-1432.

A Great Place to Relax:

Bring a picnic lunch to the Drake Well Museum. You can sit on picnic benches beside Oil Creek and watch the grass grow as you listen to the birds. The setting is much quieter now than it was in the 1860s.

Covered Bridges:

None nearby.

Tourist Information:

• (800) 332-2338.

Where is it? Northwest, on PA 8.

Getaway Rating: 3

Park in Titusville

33

WARREN . . .
A RIVER RUNS THROUGH IT
(N, R, S)

Spend a night under the stars in the woods. Then head into town for breakfast. Watch the water cascading from the dam. Then spend the afternoon doing some serious outlet shopping. Warren will let you spend a weekend like this.

First settled in the early 1800s, Warren grew slowly at first. Timber was the big industry then, and it's still big today. In 1859, an event occurred in nearby Titusville that changed life in Warren considerably. Colonel Drake struck oil in Titusville, and in the next few years, others found oil in Warren County. Soon the town of Warren was bustling with oil and other industries. At one time Warren claimed more millionaires per capita than any other town in Pennsylvania, and the city's elegant architecture reflects that booming era.

Today Warren is still an oil town. A big refinery operates along the Allegheny River on the east side of town, but the outdoors and shopping are the attractions that bring visitors to this place of 11,000.

If your name has ever been on a mailing list, you've probably received a **Blair** catalogue. Blair's headquarters are in Warren, where the company operates two different stores. The **retail store** at 220 Hickory Street in downtown Warren carries items

Kinzua Dam

from the company's current catalogues. Items at the retail store generally sell for full price.

However, if you stop at the **Blair Outlet** west of the city, you'll find considerably lower prices on fashions, jewelry, home furnishings, and electronics. For dedicated shoppers, a trip to the Blair Outlet is worthwhile, regardless of the distance involved.

As the biggest town in several counties, Warren is a shopping destination, and the downtown district is still the major shopping region, just as downtowns everywhere were before malls. The downtown is compact, however, and you can walk it in just a few minutes. Across the Allegheny River is **Crescent Park,** a pleasant place to sit and watch the river roll lazily by. At the **Struthers Library Theatre,** Warren enjoys the Warren Players during most of the year and a summer playhouse in warm weather.

While downtown Warren is a nice place to shop and dine, most visitors come to spend some time in the great outdoors. The **Allegheny National Forest** covers half a million acres in four counties, and the Allegheny River runs through the forest. Just east of Warren is the **Kinzua Dam,** built to contain the

Allegheny River

sometimes angry river. Before the dam, the Allegheny flooded with regularity, severely damaging the towns in its path. The dam, completed in 1965, has served to control floods and to provide vast recreational opportunities.

East of Warren on Route 59 is the visitors' center for the dam. There, you can see a display that explains how the dam works. It's a fascinating process, and if you walk down to the dam you can see the water spilling out. More impressive is a walk onto the top of the dam. There you can take photographs and watch the large carp that congregate behind the dam.

If you're a novice in the woods, the **Little Boulder Nature Trail** at the dam will give you an easy walk through woods where you can learn just a bit about trees, birds, and animals. The trail is just a quarter-mile long, and the walk is easy. You can follow the trail on your way from the visitors' center to the dam, and if you take the trail you may spot a salamander a squirrel, or even a grouse, Pennsylvania's state bird.

The **Allegheny Reservoir** is 27 miles long with over 90 miles of shoreline, and it's a popular place with vacationers. At the **Kinzua-Wolf Marina** on Route 59, you can rent boats by the hour or the week, from rowboats up to houseboats where you can sleep and ride around the reservoir. Across Route 59 from the marina is a beach for swimming.

Away from the water, the forest is an unspoiled wilderness that puts on its most brilliant displays in October when the leaves change the hillsides to dazzling canopies of reds, yellows, golds, and oranges. The forest is an outdoor paradise, offering hiking, backpacking, camping, picnicking, swimming, boating, canoeing, water skiing, cross-country skiing, mountain biking, and trails for ATV's and snowmobiles. The forest has many camping facilities, and hotels, motels, and cabins are numerous on the highways in the region.

The best way to enjoy the forest is to take a walk through it. More than 600 miles of trails wind through the forest, and you can find trails that are steep and difficult or basically flat and easy. You don't have to go hiking too enjoy the region's beauty. Many spots are excellent for picnicking and sightseeing. **Jake's Rocks** and **Rimrock,** near Route 59 and the dam offer superb views of the river basin.

If you don't care to spend your days wandering through the woods, you'll find interesting places to visit in the cities. The **Warren County Historical Society** tells how settlers carved a city out of a forest. **Gayle's Memories** in Warren sells Christmas items and collectibles such as Hummels and Yankee candles.

Northeast of Warren, in Bradford, is a museum dedicated to two classic American products—the **Zippo** lighter and **Case** knives. Zippo lighters have been around since 1933, and, while their primary function has been to light cigarettes, they've also had some positive accomplishments. During World War II, signal fires set by Zippo lighters saved lives. One pilot brought his damaged plane home reading his instrument panel by the light of a Zippo. Famous figures such as Abraham Lincoln and Elvis Presley have adorned Zippo lighters, and the whole story of Zippo is on display here.

Case knives have been around since 1889, and the company has been a subsidiary of Zippo since 1993. A trip through the visitor's center will take you on a quick journey through Case's long history.

Also in Bradford is the **Penn-Brad Oil Museum** that features a 72-foot tall wooden standard drilling rig used in developing the first billion-dollar oil field. The museum displays artifacts and memories of the town's oil boom days.

Southeast of Warren is Elk County, which is home to two well-know attractions. The first is the **elk herd,** which numbers about 300 large animals. The herd lives throughout the county with a concentration near Benezette.

Some male elk reach weights of 1,000 pounds, with antlers measuring up to 8½ feet. There's no assurance of seeing these animals, but the best viewing times are early morning and at dusk. For information, call the Elk County Visitors' Bureau at (814) 834-3711.

Also in Elk County is **Straub Brewery** in St. Marys. Straub is a small brewer with a reputation for making beer free of preservatives. The company distributes only in Pennsylvania and part of Ohio, so its following is small but loyal. Tours are available Monday through Friday, and the factory store is open Saturdays as well.

The woods are lovely, dark, and deep, and Warren is an excellent base from which to explore the Allegheny National Forest and the Allegheny Reservoir.

Attractions:

Blair Outlet Store, Route 6 and Route 62, (814) 726-6271.

Allegheny National Forest, (814) 723-5150.

Kinzua Dam, (814) 726-0661.

Dining:

Abbanick's, 309 Pennsylvania Avenue E, (814) 726-0800, open 11 A.M.-11 P.M. daily.

Brookside Restaurant, 2750 Pennsylvania Avenue, (814) 723-1087, Mon.-Sat., 11 A.M.-9 P.M.

The Bucket, 14 Main Street, Sugar Grove, (814) 489-500, open 7 A.M.-2 A.M. daily.

Cinelli's Pizza, 340 Pennsylvania Avenue W, (814) 723-0980, Mon.-Sat., 11 A.M.-10 P.M., Sun., 1 P.M.-10 P.M.

Claudine's Pizzeria, 118 Main Street, Tidiouts, (814) 484-0268, Mon.-Sat., 11 A.M.-9 P.M., Sun., 3 P.M.-9 P.M.

Docksiders Café, Route 59, at the marina, (814) 726-9645, open 11:30 A.M.-11 P.M. daily, and 8 A.M.-11 A.M., Sat. and Sun.

Draft House, 707 Pennsylvania Avenue, (814) 723-9818, Mon.-Sat., 11 A.M.-midnight

Forester Restaurant, 2 Lenhart Road, (814) 563-1682, lunch and dinner, Tues.-Sat.

Gilbert's Italian, 1413 Pennsylvania Avenue, (814) 723-4040, open 11:30 A.M.-9 P.M. daily.

Jamie's Place, 219 Liberty Street, (814) 723-3325, lunch and dinner daily.

Penn Laurel Inn, 706 Pennsylvania Avenue W, (814) 723-8300, breakfast, lunch, and dinner daily.

Peppermill Restaurant, 1505 Pennsylvania Avenue, (814) 723-4240, opens at 6 A.M. daily.

Perkins, 115 Ludlow Street, (814) 723-3075, breakfast, lunch, and dinner daily.

Times Square, 220 Pennsylvania Avenue, (814) 723-8320, Sun., 6 A.M.-6 P.M., Mon., 6 A.M.-2 P.M., Tues.-Sat., 6 A.M.-8 P.M.

Lodging:

Budget Lodge, Route 6 East, (814) 723-7350.

Super 8 Motel, 204 Struthers Street, (814) 723-8881.

Wagon Wheel, 1821 Pleasant Road, (814) 723-4238.

Holiday Inn of Warren, 210 Ludlow Street, (814) 726-3000.

Penn Laurel Inn, 706 Pennsylvania Avenue, (814) 723-8300.

Warren Motel, 2240 Pennsylvania Avenue, (814) 723-5550.

Edgewood Motel, Route 6 West, Youngsville, (814) 563-7516.

Mineral Well Motel, Route 6 East, Clarendon, (814) 723-9840.

Horton House Bed & Breakfast, 504 Market Street, (814) 723-7472.

Red Oak Campground, RD# 1, Russell, (814) 757-8507.

Camping in Allegheny National Forest, (800) 280-2267.

Shopping:

Blair Outlet, Route 6 and Route 62, (814) 726-6271, Mon.-Fri., 9 A.M.-9 P.M., Sat., 9 A.M.-6 P.M., and Sun., noon-5 P.M.

Blair Retail Store, 220 Hickory Street, (814) 726-6363, Mon.-Thur. and Sat., 9 A.M.-5 P.M., Fri. 9 A.M.-8 P.M.

Gayle's Memories, Route 6 and Route 62, (800) 242-4825, Mon.-Sat., 10 A.M.-5 P.M.

Just Country Gifts, 168 Main Street, Tidioute, (814) 484-3441, Mon.-Sat., 10 A.M.-5 P.M., Sun., 10 A.M.-4 P.M.

North Village Gallery, 70 North State Street, North Warren, (814) 726-2833, Tues.-Fri., 10 A.M.-5 P.M., Sat., 10 A.M.-2 P.M.

Warren Mall, 1666 Market Street East, (814) 723-7135, Mon.-Sat., 10 A.M.-9 P.M., Sun., noon-6 P.M.

Annual Events:

Autumn. The hills are ablaze with color in early October.

Summer Theatre, Library Theatre, 302 Third Avenue, (800) 720-0450.

Warren County Fair, mid August, Pittsfield, (814) 757-8668.

Warren County Farmers Market, Second Avenue, Saturdays in summer.

The Active Life:

The woods and the waters provide a full range of hiking, boating, and swimming activities. Golfers can swing away at **Jackson Valley Country Club,** (814) 489-7802, **Blueberry Hill Golf Club** in Russell, (814) 757-8620, and at **Cable Hollow Golf Course** in Russell, (814) 757-4765. Mountain bikers, snowmobilers, and cross-country skiers find much to enjoy on the trails through the forests.

A Great Place to Relax:

Crescent Park, in downtown Warren, is beside the bridge across the Allegheny River. It's a good place to watch the river flow. So is the visitors' center at the Kinzua Dam.

Covered Bridges:

None nearby.

Tourist Information:

• (800) 624-7802.

Where is it? Northwest, on U.S. 6 and PA 59.

Getaway Rating: 4

Downtown Warren

34

WELLSBORO . . .
CANYON COUNTRY
(A, R, R&R)

Check into the old hotel and sit for a few minutes in the lobby, admiring the flag made from red, white, and blue light bulbs. Then have dinner in the hotel dining room or head out for a stroll around the town where you can eat in the famous (it says so right on the sign) Wellsboro Diner. In the morning, you can head out to the Grand Canyon to look, hike, or bike.

Wellsboro is a scenic little town that seems as though someone designed it exclusively for weekend getaways. It has plenty of attractions and activities, and it has beautiful places to sit and relax for hours. The town can simultaneously appeal to those seeking a genteel weekend complete with creature comforts and fine dining and to those who love adventures in the great outdoors.

In its February 1998 issue, the magazine *Sports Afield* named Wellsboro **"Pennsylvania's Best Outdoor Sports Town."** The article noted that Wellsboro offers " . . . more fine hiking, biking, paddling, hunting, and fishing than you can jam in a month of weekends." Add in the shopping, dining, train rides, and relaxing, and you'll be planning another visit to Wellsboro before your first one ends.

The attraction that has brought Wellsboro its most fame is the **Pine Creek Gorge,** also called **Pennsylvania's Grand**

Penn Wells Hotel

Canyon. Compared to Arizona's big hole in the ground, Pennsylvania's Grand Canyon is smaller, greener, and much more accessible, thanks to the demise of America's railroads.

For a century, a railroad ran through the canyon, and the public had little access to the canyon floor. That situation changed when the abandoned railroad grade became a rail trail. Now, everyone can walk or bike through the canyon on the **Pine Creek Trail,** which extends 19 miles, from Ansonia to Blackwell. The trail makes a wilderness area easy to reach and enjoy, and only one road crosses the trail in its 19 miles. For bikers, walkers, and cross-country skiers, the trail is a little piece of paradise, filled with beauty and devoid of motor vehicles.

Even if you don't care to travel through the canyon, you can enjoy it from scenic overlooks in state parks on both the east and west rims. In places, the rim of the canyon is a thousand feet above Pine Creek. Birds catch updrafts and float on the wind. Wildlife abounds throughout the region. Deer are common visitors along the trail, and they often come down to the creek. Bears are much less common, but they're around. So are beavers, and you may see a beaver dam on some of the small streams in the area.

Away from the canyon, the Wellsboro area offers many other recreational possibilities. Lakes are numerous, and when the water is high enough, usually in spring, **rafters** rush down Pine Creek. In summer, the water is much lower and much more placid. Public forest lands cover many square miles, so **hiking trails** are numerous.

Back in Wellsboro, life is considerably less rugged. If the idea of a day in the outdoors is your idea of punishment, you'll still enjoy a visit to Wellsboro. You can stroll, shop, dine, and take in a movie without having to move the car. And if your idea of roughing it is a walk around a golf course, Wellsboro has a beautiful course for you.

The most visible sight in Wellsboro is the huge American flag that flies across Main Street. The most famous structure is the **Penn Wells Hotel,** which dates back to 1869, and offers comfortable accommodations and good dining. The Penn Wells isn't a luxurious hotel, but it has charm, character, and history that motels beside the interstate just can't match.

Just down the street from the hotel is the **town green,** an excellent place to do very little. In the center of the green is a **fountain** of Wynken, Blynken, and Nod, and visitors throw coins into the water.

No shopping malls have come to Wellsboro, and downtown is still the shopping district. Stores of many types, restaurants, and a movie theater line Main Street. One store that's a holdover from an earlier era is **Dunham's,** a genuine department store that carries clothes, home furnishings, candy, and much more. It even has a coffee shop, just as department stores everywhere used to have.

Right in the center of everything is the famous **Wellsboro Diner,** where a meal of burgers, fries, and a Coke never goes out of style. The diner opened in 1939, and has operated continuously in the same building on the same site ever since.

Wellsboro has many beautiful old buildings, and a walking tour identifies many of them. For a brochure, stop at the **Chamber of Commerce,** 114 Main Street, or call (570) 724-1926.

Tioga Central Railroad

Trains don't run through the canyon any more, but a tourist line does operate out of Wellsboro. The **Tioga Central Railroad** takes passengers on a 24-mile round-trip to **Tioga-Hammond Lakes** on Saturdays and Sundays, and a few weekdays in October when the leaves put on a colorful show.

The ride is quite scenic, and the tracks run beside Route 287 for most of their length. On Saturday evenings, dinner trains allow riders to enjoy a good meal while they take in the beauty of the hills.

The mountain laurel is Pennsylvania's state flower, and the **Laurel Festival** is a big event in Wellsboro every June. The town takes on a festive atmosphere as bands, amusement rides, craft sellers, and food vendors fill the streets. In late October, **Wellsboro Rail Days** celebrates the town's railroading history, and in December Wellsboro's **Dickens of a Christmas** celebrates the British author of the classic Christmas tale, *A Christmas Carol.*

When winter comes, Wellsboro gets pretty cold, but it's still a good place for a getaway. The Pine Creek Trail is popular with cross-country skiers, and downhill skiers enjoy **Ski Sawmill** in Morris, about 15 miles south of Wellsboro. When Wellsboro is white, it's a pleasant place to relax with a stroll around town or a dip in the indoor pool at the **Penn Wells Lodge.**

Wellsboro has all the ingredients to make a great weekend getaway. Come any time of year and you'll have a good time.

Attractions:

Pennsylvania's Grand Canyon.

Tioga Central Railroad, (570) 724-0990, runs at 11 A.M., 1 A.M., and 3 P.M. on Sat. and Sun.

Penn Wells Hotel, (570) 724-2111.

Blackwell Bikes, Route 414, Blackwell, (570) 353-2612.

Pine Creek Outfitters, Route 6 West, (570) 724-3003.

Ski Sawmill, Route 287, Morris, (570) 353-7521.

Dining:

Penn Wells Hotel, 62 Main Street, (570) 724-2111, Mon.-Sat., 5 P.M.-9 P.M., Sun., 9A.M. to 9 P.M.

Wellsboro Diner, corner of Main Street and East Avenue, (570) 724-3992, Mon.-Sat., 6 A.M-8 p.m., Sun., 7 A.M.-8P.M.

The Native Bagel, 1 Central Avenue, (570) 724-0900, opens at 7 A.M., seven days a week.

Tioga Central Railroad, Route 287 North, (570) 724-0990, dinner, Friday and Saturday evening.

Laurel Café, 2 Tioga Street, (570) 723-2233, opens at 6 A.M., seven days a week.

The Steak House, 29 Main Street, (570) 724-9092, open 11 A.M.-midnight, seven days a week.

Dunkin Donuts, 7 Main Street, open 24 hours a day, seven days a week.

Coach Stop Inn, Route 6, near the Grand Canyon, (570) 724-5361, Mon.-Thur., noon-9 P.M., Fri. and Sat., 11 A.M.-11 P.M., and Sun., 11 A.M.-9 P.M.

Lodging:

Penn Wells Hotel, Main Street, (570) 724-2111.

Penn Wells Lodge, Main Street, (570) 724-3463.

Wellsboro Diner

Canyon Motel, 18 East Avenue, (570) 724-1681.

Sherwood Motel, 2 Main Street, (570) 724-3424.

Colton Point Motel, Route 6 West, (800) 829-4122.

Cedar Run Inn, Route 414, south of Wellsboro, (570) 353-6241.

Stone Haven Bed & Breakfast, 55 Charleston Street, (570) 724-7300.

Coach Stop Inn, Route 6 West, (570) 724-5361.

Grand Canyon Motel, Route 660, (570) 724-4774.

Garden Cottage Motel, 66 West Avenue, (570) 724-3581.

Canyon Country Campground, beside Grand Canyon, (570) 724-3818.

Four Winds Bed & Breakfast, 58 West Avenue, (800) 368-7963.

Shopping:

In downtown Wellsboro, you'll find something that's been disappearing from many downtowns—a genuine department store. **Dunham's** has men's and women's clothing, home furnishings, and a coffee shop. It's even open on Friday evenings, and in warm weather it often has sidewalk sales.

Davis Sporting Goods, 9 Charleston Street, (570) 724-2626, opens at 10 A.M. daily.

Country Ski & Sports, 81 Main Street, (570) 724-3858, opens at 10 A.M. daily.

Armchair Books, 17 Crafton Street, (570) 724-2665, Mon.-Sat., 8:30 A.M.-5:30 P.M.

The Yellow Basket Shop, Route 660 West, (570) 724-6078, call for hours.

Dunham's Department Store, Main Street, (570) 724-2100, open Mon.-Sat., 10 A.M.-5:30 P.M. (Fri. till 8 P.M.), Sun., noon-4 P.M.

Etc. Antique Station, 5 East Avenue, (570) 724-2733, Mon.-Sat., 10 A.M.-5 P.M., Sun., 11 A.M.-4 P.M.

Back Door Antiques, 5 Cone Street, (570) 724-2855, by chance or appointment.

Peggy's Candies & Gifts, 82 Main Street, (570) 724-3317, open 9:30 A.M.-5:30 P.M., seven days a week.

Country Crossroads, 87 Main Street, (570) 724-1210, Mon.-Sat., 9:30 A.M.-5:30 P.M.

Main Street Antiques, 87 Main Street, (570) 724-6910, Mon.-Sat., 9:30 A.M.-5:30 P.M.

The Cellar Door, 17 Main Street, (570) 724-1540, Mon.-Sat., 9:30 A.M.-5:30 P.M.

Annual Events:

Susquehannock Trail PRO Rally, first weekend in June.

Laurel Festival, mid-June.

Rattlesnake Hunt, Morris, second weekend in June.

Wellsboro Railroad Days, last weekend in October.

A Dickens of a Christmas, first weekend in December.

The Active Life:

You can enjoy just about any activity in Wellsboro, with the emphasis on biking and hiking. The **Pine Creek Trail** is the most visible venue, but it's hardly the only good place to ride. East of town is an agricultural valley where the roads carry little traffic. Route 287 north of town travels through a green valley and parallels the tracks of the Tioga Central Railroad. The Chamber of Commerce has created a **bike route.** Maps are available at the office at 120 Main Street, and large signs mark the route.

Hiking trails are on both rims of the canyon, at Hills Creek State Park, and around Tioga-Hammond Lakes. **Packer Park Pool** in downtown Wellsboro is open for public swimming.

A Great Place to Relax:

Wellsboro has a beautiful town green with a fountain of Wynken, Blynken, and Nod. It's an excellent place to sit and enjoy the scenery and the quiet of this small town. The green is just a block from the center of town, so you can stroll for a while and then sit for a while.

Covered Bridges:

None nearby.

Tourist Information:

• (800) 332-6718.

Where is it? North Central, on U.S. 6 and PA 287.

Getaway Rating: 4

Pine Creek Trail

35

YORK . . . HOG HEAVEN
(A, R, R&R)

Marvel at the muscles. Hear the roar of the hogs. Ride the rails. Walk the trail. Purchase the produce. You'll find plenty to do on a weekend getaway in York, and if you're just looking for a little serenity, you'll find it down by the river.

Located between Lancaster County's Amish Country and Gettysburg's battlefield, York isn't as famous as either of those destinations, but it is a place with plenty of history and activities. It's also home to several attractions that have genuine cult followings. If you care about **motorcycles** or **weightlifting,** a visit to York is an absolute must.

In 1777, York was already a busy little place, but getting to it wasn't easy. The mile-wide Susquehanna River separates York County from Lancaster County, so nobody made the trip without a good reason. Because of the river, the **Continental Congress** made the trip to gain a measure of protection from advancing British troops, and from September of 1777 until June of 1778 York was the seat of the Continental Congress and the site of some important historical events.

After learning of an American victory over the British at Saratoga, the Congress declared a national day of Thanksgiving. Not long after that, the Congress approved the **Articles of**

York Barbell Company

Confederation in York in November of 1777, marking the first time that the original 13 colonies joined together as the United States of America.

That act was significant, but it hardly ended the British threat. A plot to overthrow General Washington was unfolding, but the French repulsed it. In February 1778 French General Marquis de Lafayette offered a toast to General Washington at the **Gates House** in downtown York, ending the subversion before it could overthrow Washington.

York's reign as capital was short, and when the politicians left, life returned to normal, which meant growing crops and building a new nation from a wilderness. York became an industrial power, as it still is today. In 1814, York's economy got a big boost with the opening of the longest covered bridge ever built. Stretching more than a mile, it crossed the Susquehanna, and linked Columbia and Wrightsville. The river eventually washed that bridge away, and local citizens built another one to replace it. That one went up in flames in 1863 when Union soldiers burned it to stop advancing Confederate troops from entering Lancaster County. This happened just before the Battle of Gettysburg, and events at the battle might have been entirely different if the Confederates had reached Lancaster.

York has many identities, but the two for which it has gained worldwide fame are motorcycles and weightlifting. **Harley Davidson** has had a plant in York since 1973, when the company wasn't nearly as famous or as prosperous as it is now. The plant is on the east side of York, and visitors can take plant tours Monday through Friday and museum tours Monday through Saturday.

Assembling a Harley takes about 2½ hours, and on the plant tour you can see a motorcycle roll off the line every 2½ minutes. At the museum, exhibits range from the original 1906 Harley-Davidson motorcycle to current models. Several times during the year, Harley enthusiasts gather in York, and the roads nearby, particularly Route 30, host hundreds of Harleys.

If big muscles and physical fitness interest you, you'll want to visit the **United States Weightlifting Federation Hall of Fame.** **York Barbell** and **Bob Hoffman** are famous names in the sport of weightlifting, and this is the city where Hoffman made barbells and popularized the sport. The first national powerlifting contest took place in York in 1964, and pumping iron has been growing in popularity since then.

The Hall of Fame details the history of the sport and the exploits of great lifters. One of the most interesting displays shows old-fashioned strongmen. The museum documents the contests in which those men engaged, and it shows some of the objects they lifted and bent to prove their strength. Another part of the museum deals with the newer sport of bodybuilding and honors the men and women who have pumped hard to advance it.

Fueling those weightlifters requires plenty of food, and York County is an agricultural powerhouse. **Central Market,** located in the heart of downtown, connects farmers and buyers. Vendors sell just about everything that anyone eats, especially fresh produce, meats, and snack foods, which York County produces in large quantities.

Central Market

Utz Quality Foods, located in Hanover, makes regionally popular potato chips, and you can buy them throughout York County. Utz's chips are light and airy, a taste and texture distinctly different from another local brand—**Martin's.** Martin's chips are kettle-cooked, and they're much heavier and crunchier than Utz's. Both varieties are delicious, so don't make a visit to York without sampling them both and making your own judgment on which is better.

You can munch on the chips as you stroll around the historic sites in downtown York. The **Golden Plough Tavern** on West Market Street is York's oldest building, and the **Gates House** is nearby. At 50 North George Street is the **Strand-Capitol Performing Arts Center,** two restored, early-1900s theaters that offer stage productions, music, and films.

At 480 East Market Street is the **Agricultural & Industrial Museum of York County.** Products made in York have touched the lives of most Americans, and you can learn about many of them here. Almost everyone has eaten a **York Peppermint Patty** or been in a building heated or cooled by equipment made by **York Heating & Air Conditioning.** The museum shows many of the products and inventions that have come from York County.

And out in the country, things are happening. In the southern part of the county, the **York County Heritage Rail Trail** beckons people of all ages for a walk in the woods or a hard run. The trail extends 11 miles, from Hanover Junction to the Maryland border, and it has the rare distinction of sharing the corridor with an active train, which can create a few loud moments along the normally peaceful trail. In Maryland, the trail continues for 23 more miles. It passes through woods and farmlands, and it goes through several small towns where travelers can stop for refreshments.

In Glen Rock, the **Glen Rock Mill Inn** is right beside the trail. Trail users can stop and enjoy outdoor dining without ever leaving the trail. In New Freedom, the **Whistle Stop** bike shop and **LaMotte's Restaurant** are right beside the tracks, and **Trail Mix by Peppercorns** is very close. In addition, the **Northern Central Railway** operates there.

The Northern Central is a tourist line that focuses on dinner and entertainment. Most of its excursions take place on weekends, and they all have a meal and a theme, such as a murder mystery, a comedy, or music. Back in 1863, the Northern Central was already operating, and it carried President Lincoln on part of his journey to deliver the **Gettysburg Address.**

Four miles east of New Freedom is **Shrewsbury,** which has become an antiques type of town, with about a dozen shops operating in three blocks of Main Street. The houses are very old, with some dating back to the 18th century, and Main Street is ideal for strolling and shopping. The shops carry an assortment of antiques, crafts, furniture, and collectibles. **Peppercorns Café** offers a cozy setting and casual dining that even vegetarians will enjoy.

If you're approaching Shrewsbury via Route 83 and Route 851, your first impression will be deceptive. Along the interstate, big shopping centers have sprouted, but on Main Street Shrewsbury has many small and quaint shops. So don't be discouraged when you see the big box stores. More intimate shops are just ahead.

Four miles east of I-83 is Stewartstown, home of the **Historic Stewartstown Railroad.** Listed on the National Register of Historic Places, the railroad operates out of a 1914 depot and takes passengers on a leisurely ride through the scenic countryside.

The Susquehanna River forms York County's entire eastern border, and the river provides many recreational opportunities. Long Level, just south of Wrightsville on Route 624, is a good place to sit by the river.

It's less famous than its eastern and western neighbors, but hogs, muscles, trains, and relaxation by the river make York an excellent place for a getaway.

Attractions:

Agricultural & Industrial Museum, 480 East Market Street, (717) 852-7007, Tues., Thur., and Sat., 10 A.M.-4 P.M.

Central Market, 34 West Philadelphia Street, York, (717) 848-2243, opens Tues., Thur., and Sat. at 6 A.M.

Harley Davidson motorcycle plant, off Route 30, (717) 854-3214, plant tours, Mon.-Fri., 10 A.M., 12:30 P.M., and 1:30 P.M., museum tours, Mon.-Fri., 12:30 P.M., and Sat., 10 A.M., 11 A.M., 1 P.M., and 2 P.M.

Historic downtown.

Northern Central Railway, New Freedom, (800) 94-TRAIN, call for schedule.

Shoe House, 1948 Shoe House Road, visible from Route 30 East, call for hours.

Stewartstown Railroad, Route 851, Stewartstown, (717) 993-2936, trains Sundays at 1 P.M. and 3 P.M.

York Barbell Company, 3300 Board Road, York, (800) 358-YORK, Mon.-Sat., 10 A.M.-3 P.M.

York County Heritage Rail Trail, New Freedom.

The York Fair, America's oldest, September, (717) 848-2596.

Dining:

Blue Moon Café, 361 West Market Street, (717) 854-6664, Tues.-Sat., lunch and dinner.

Cobblestone's, 205 South George Street, (717) 848-3866, open 11 A.M.-2 A.M. daily.

El Rodeo, 724 Loucks Road, (717) 845-1341, Mon.-Thur., 11 A.M.-10 P.M., Fri., 11 A.M.-11 P.M., Sat., noon-10 P.M., and Sun., noon-9 P.M.

Embers, 100 Memory Lane, (717) 755-3761, lunch and dinner daily.

Ginmiya, 2524 Eastern Blvd., (717) 755-2577, opens at 11:30 A.M. daily.

Interstate 83 Diner, 5220 Susquehanna Trail North, Mon.-Thur., 6 A.M.-9 P.M., Fri. and Sat., 6 A.M.-10 P.M., and Sun., 8 A.M.-9 P.M.

LaMotte's Restaurant, 7 East Franklin Street, New Freedom, (717) 235-2295, Mon., 12 -9 p.m., Tues.-Thur., 11 A.M.-9 P.M., Fri. and Sat., 11 A.M.-10 P.M., and Sun., noon-9 P.M.

Liberty Limited Dinner Train, 115 North Front Street, New Freedom, (800) 94-TRAIN, call for schedule.

Luddy's Seafood, 360 Cly Road, York Haven, (717) 266-5667, Mon.-Fri., 6 P.M.-10 P.M., Sat., 5 P.M.-10 P.M.

Olive Garden, 1340 Kenneth Road, (717) 845-2264, opens at 11 A.M. daily.

Peppercorn's Café, 42 North Main Street, Shrewsbury, (717) 235-0737, Mon.-Sat., 11 A.M.-8 P.M., Sun., 11 A.M.-6 P.M.

Phil's Restaurant, 960 Hellam Street, Wrightsville, (717) 252-3184, open 7 A.M.-10 P.M. daily.

Pizza Romano, 2350 North George Street, (717) 845-2613, Mon.-Thur., 11 A.M.-11 P.M., Fri. and Sat., 11 A.M.-midnight, and Sun., 4 P.M.-10 P.M.

Round the Clock Diner, 222 Arsenal Road, (717) 848-5344, open 24 hours a day.

San Carlo's, 333 Arsenal Road, (717) 854-2028, dinner and entertainment daily.

TGIFriday's, 1411 Kenneth Road, (717) 767-6878, opens at 11 A.M. daily.

Victor's Italian, 554 South Ogontz Street, (717) 854-7958, open 11 A.M.-2 A.M. daily.

Lodging:

Best Western Westgate Inn, 1415 Kenneth Road, York, (717) 767-6931.

Budget Host Inn, 1162 Haines Road, York, (717) 755-1068.

Comfort Inn, 1401 Leader Heights Road, York, (717) 741-1000.

Days Inn, I-83 and U.S. 30, York, (717) 843-9971.

Glen Rock Mill Inn, 50 Water Street, Glen Rock, (717) 235-5918.

Hampton Inn, 1550 Mount Zion Road, York, (717) 840-1500.

Heritage Hills Golf Center, 2700 Mount Rose Avenue, York, (717) 755-0123.

Holiday Inn, 2660 East Market Street, York, (717) 757-1966.

Holiday Inn, 334 Arsenal Road, York, (717) 845-5671.

Modernaire Motel, 3311 East Market Street, York, (717) 755-9625.

Red Roof Inn, 323 Arsenal Road, York, (717) 843-8181.

Smith's Motel, 4335 West Market Street, York, (717) 792-1310.

Yorktowne Hotel, 48 East Market Street, York, (717) 848-1111.

An Artist's Garden Bed & Breakfast, 440 West Philadelphia Street, York, (717) 854-7688.

Kolter House Bed & Breakfast, 403 North Main Street, Shrewsbury, (717) 235-5528.

Horse Lovers Bed & Breakfast, 405 Thorne Road, Fawn Grove, (717) 382-4171.

White Rose Bed & Breakfast Association, (800) 673-2429.

Indian Rock Campground, 436 Indian Rock Dam Road, York, (717) 741-1764.

Shopping:

Antique Center of York, 190 Arsenal Road, (717) 846-1994, open 10 A.M.-5 P.M. daily.

Antiques on Main Street, 30 North Main Street, Red Lion, (717) 246-8026, open 10 A.M.-5 P.M. daily.

Another Time Vintage Apparel, 36 East Forrest Avenue, Shrewsbury, (717) 235-0664, Wed.-Sat., 11 A.M.-5 P.M., Sun., 1 P.M.-5 P.M.

Christmas Tree Hill, 57 West Market Street, (717) 845-7715, Mon.-Sat., 9:30 A.M.-5 P.M.

Cold Spring Antique Mall, 55 Main Street, Glen Rock, (717) 235-8560, Mon. and Wed.-Sat., 10 A.M.-5 P.M., Sun., noon-5 P.M.

Heart and Hands Gift Shop, 141 West Market Street, York, (717) 771-9610, Mon.-Fri., 10 A.M.-4 P.M.

John Wright Warehouse, North Front Street, Wrightsville, (717) 252-2519, Tues.-Sat., 10 A.M.-5 P.M., Sun., noon-5 P.M.

Junior League of York Thrift Shop, 166 West Market Street, York, (717) 843-7692, Mon.-Sat., 9:30 A.M.-4 P.M.

My Romance Antique Center, 2331 East Market Street, (717) 755-3177, Mon.-Sat., 10 A.M.-5 P.M., Sun., noon-5 P.M.

Snyder's of Hanover Outlet Store, 1350 York Street, Hanover, (717) 632-4477, Mon.-Sat., 9 A.M.-6 P.M., Sun., noon-5 P.M.

The Shops of 104 S. Main, 104 South Main Street, Shrewsbury, (717) 227-9169, Tues.-Sat., 10 A.M.-5 P.M., Sun., noon-5 P.M.

Susquehanna Pfaltzgraff Company, 2900 Whiteford Road, York, (717) 848-5500.

Utz Foods Outlet Store and Tour, 861 Carlisle Street, Hanover, (717) 637-6644, Mon.-Fri., 8 A.M.-6 P.M., Sat., 8 A.M.-5 P.M., and Sun., noon-5 P.M.

Wolfgang Candy, 50 East Fourth Avenue, (717) 843-5536, Mon.-Fri., 8 A.M.-5 P.M., Sat., 9 A.M.-4 P.M.

Whistle Stop bike shop, 2 East Franklin Street, New Freedom, (717) 227-0737.

York Galleria, 1 York Galleria, York, (717) 840-1322, Mon.-Sat., 9:30 A.M.-9 P.M., Sun., noon-5 P.M.

Annual Events:

York County Stamp Show, last weekend in January, York Fairgrounds, (302) 875-5326.

Campers World RV Show, third weekend in March, York Fairgrounds, (610) 767-5026.

Easter Bunny Specials, March or April, Stewartstown Railroad, (717) 993-2936.

Easter Craft Show, March or April, York Fairgrounds, (717) 764-1729.

Cat Show, York Fairgrounds, first weekend in May, (717) 284-2267.

Olde York Street Fair, second Sunday in May, (717) 854-1587.

National Street Rod Association Eastern Meet, first weekend in June, York Fairgrounds, (717) 848-4000.

Invasion of NASCAR, downtown York, fourth Thursday in July, (717) 849-2301.

Riverwalk Arts Festival, last weekend in August, York, (717) 854-1587.

York Fair, 10 days in mid-September, (717) 848-2596.

Bridge Bust, first Saturday in October, Wrightsville, (717) 684-5249.

Greater York Antique Show, second weekend in November, York Fairgrounds, (717) 845-3239.

Christmas Magic, December, Rocky Ridge Park, (717) 840-7440.

First Night York, New Year's Eve, downtown, (717) 854-1587.

The Active Life:

York County is full of golf courses. For a brochure, call **Capital Region Golf** at (800) 942-2444. In winter, try **Ski Roundtop** in Lewisberry—call (717) 432-9631. The Susquehanna

River provides boating, fishing, water skiing, wind surfing, and camping. At the Nature Center at **Richard M. Nixon Park** are more than six miles of nature trails. Call (717) 428-1961 for information.

Codorus State Park near Hanover has **Lake Marburg,** which covers 1,275 acres. Call (717) 637-2816 for information. The **York County Heritage Rail Trail** from York to the Maryland line is ideal for biking and walking. Call (717) 840-7440 or (717) 428-2586 for information and directions.

A Great Place to Relax:

Take a stroll on the York County Heritage Rail Trail. You can sit on benches along the trail and listen to the sounds of silence.

Covered Bridges:

The only one in the county is on the campus of Messiah College in Grantham, on the border with Cumberland County.

Tourist Information:

• (800) 673-2429

Where is it? Southeast, along U.S. 30 between Lancaster and Gettysburg.

Getaway Rating: 2

Northern Central Railway and York County Heritage Rail Trail

APPENDIX

The following agencies provided reference materials used in planning and compiling this book:

Pennsylvania Department of Travel & Tourism
Pennsylvania Dutch Convention and Visitors Bureau
Allegheny Mountain Convention and Visitors Bureau
Allegheny National Forest Vacation Bureau
Bedford County Visitors Bureau
Bucks County Convention and Visitors Bureau
Carbon County Tourist and Promotion Agency
Centre County Convention and Visitors Bureau
Chester County Tourist Bureau
Columbia-Montour Tourist Promotion Agency
Crawford County Convention and Visitors Bureau
Delaware County Convention and Visitors Bureau
Elk County Visitors Bureau
Endless Mountains Visitors Bureau
Erie Area Convention and Visitors Bureau
Forest County Tourism
Fulton County Tourist Promotion Agency
Gettysburg Convention and Visitors Bureau
Greater Johnstown/Cambria County Convention and Visitors
    Bureau
Harrisburg-Hershey-Carlisle Tourism and Convention Bureau
Laurel Highlands Visitors Bureau
Lehigh Valley Convention and Visitors Bureau
Luzerne County Tourist Promotion Agency
Lycoming County Tourist Promotion Agency
Magic Forests Visitors Bureau
Northern Alleghenies Vacation Region
Oil Heritage Region Tourist Promotion Agency
Pennsylvania Rainbow Region Vacation Bureau

Pennsylvania's Northeast Territory Visitors bureau
Pocono Mountains Vacation Bureau
Potter County Visitors Association
Raystown Country Visitors Bureau
Reading and Berks County Visitors Bureau
Schuylkill County Visitors Bureau
Susquehanna Valley Visitors Bureau
Tioga County Visitors Bureau
York County Convention and Visitors Bureau

INDEX